CW01509029

I have come to this world
to be the one with God
pure and kind
through the suffering mankind

Prayer of the Bridal Chamber

THE ROSE
OF SERAPHITES

The Revelation
of the Supreme Wisdom
to John of the Holy Grail

JOHN OF THE HOLY GRAIL

THE ROSE OF THE SERAFITES.
The Revelation of Supreme Wisdom

The second millennium of the Christianity has ended. What will the third coming one bring? Daring and glorious challenge for the future transforming of the humanity is offered in the scroll of the heavenly revelations, received by the author at the peak of the Nightingale Mountain in Turkey. This is the wonderful piece of the spiritual-mystical literature, attractive for the serious and thoughtful reader.

Copyright © John of the Holy Grail
(Иоанн Святой Чаши), 2011

ISBN 978-5-98290-099-9

Printed in the United States of America

CONTENTS

The Throne of the Revelation of the Heavenly Queen

The second millennium of Christianity has come to an end. The third is dedicated to the Seraphites. I am giving them the treasury gifted by Christ of Nightingale Mountain. The heavenly Lamb twice transformed, twice descended from the Heaven, the Divinity of the Seraphites of future ages is giving you this untold wealth and the greatest of miracles. Keep it, My child. And if you keep and multiply My gift, the Kingdom of the Divinity will come into the world, and the Heavenly City will descend to the Seraphites.

Today I am not bringing revelations or messages to the world, but a new Heaven and divine spheres for the people of the third millennium.

The Revelation of the Mother of God

FROM THE AUTHOR

Myrrhic waxen scrolls

The Word is saturated with the scents of mountain flowers and includes at least a hundred simultaneous planes (dimensions). The content transmits the part of the fragrance of the Divine rhythms, super-celestial vibrations, and hearings of the Voice.

When I receive revelations, my mind ascends to the Heavenly World, and I r e s i d e there; I am in the sweetest divine existence, and I s e e and e n j o y the scents of sayings. I cannot describe them. I have to constrain myself to the transmission of the Word. But it contains and concentrates all the scents, visions, images, particles and compositions gathered in the revelation.

I appeal to readers to ascend with me to the Heavenly World, to enjoy these scents and to perceive indescribable things of the different world. And to hear the sweetest everlasting Voice.

The purpose of the Word is the exaltation of the mind and its coexistence with the Divine World.

As a priest of Melchizedek, I am giving the world this myrrhic waxen scrolls in order to inspire my disciples. Being on the earth and in their mortal bodies they can be honoured with the highest celestial ascensions and enjoy the words of the Divinity.

The sweetest tender Word, like the fragrant sphere of breathing in the Purest Mother's Kingdom, is the most enraptured quiescence of an eternal Saturday. It comes from the Kingdom and turns the reader into a dweller of the Heavens. It carries him to the Heavenly World and to the fifth dimension.

Understandably, these approaches and ways of reading the Word differ from those of the perfect scribes and from the Pharisees' suggested way of reading the Gospel (cemented and intoxicated within the framework of the inquisitors). Not so long ago the Gospel was a weird book to them, incomprehensible in terms of its unknown and dead language – Latin – and completely irrelevant for Mr. Suzuki, some Japanese parishioner of a Christian church near Nagasaki.

Institutional attitudes to the Gospel horrify me. In synodal translations the Gospel is full of institutional and punishing words like 'get out' and 'I told you...'. Christ is shown as an inquisitorial saviour – dreadfully and cruelly avenging the slightest fault.

And only 'wise' priests can read and interpret the Gospel.

The Protestants broke the reserved right of those priests to interpret the Gospel, and rightly so. But they fell into a deeper fallacy. And the way that the Baptists weave their eloquent garlands of verses from the Gospel is twice as unbearable!

This way of reading the Word of the Purest Virgin is absolutely new. I suggest it to all those t r u e d i s c i p l e s a n d a n o i n t e d ones who wish to enjoy the sweetest Scripture from on high.

Izmir, 24 April 2005

THE GRAIL OF THEOGAMY

GOSPEL III – THE BRIDAL CHAMBER

Izmir, 28 April 2005

The Throne of the Most High

¹ Christian history seems to have come to a standstill, My child. The conclusion of its earthly time was the mysterious decease of the Purest Virgin, and Her Ascension from here, from Nightingale Mountain.

² My son, during your previous visit to Izmir, Our Father gifted you with the Chalice of the Grail and with the first original caves[1]. He called the way of the Cross and the Saviour's three-hour-long Holy Passion* 'an overwhelming mystery of the Gospel of Salvation on His Spilt Blood', or the outpourings of Superior Love.

³ The Revelation continues, My child! Today

---

[1] First original caves – are the caves near Ephesus, Turkey, inhabited by the ancient ascetics.

I have taken you to this Central Altar of the pro-claimed Civilization to say: 'The Gospel of Salva-tion on His Spilt Blood, the outpouring of Christ's superior love (Gospel II) on Nightingale Moun-tain[2] was prolonged for the fifteen years. It is there that Christ of the Gospel of Salvation on His Spilt Blood came and sprinkled His Divine Bride with His Myrrhic Blood*'.

[4] The Saviour's aim to convert the world resulted in boycott and Crucifixion. Gospel III – the Bridal Chamber* – has begun.

[5] In vain, My child, the Jews and the Christians interpreted Golgotha as 'salvation' and 'redemp-tion'. By sending down the Son of the Divinity I rejected this worthless legalistic order, which only cultivates a slavish, spiritually fruitless fear.

[6] With the resurrection of My Divine Son, the evangelical news was carried here, to Nightingale Mountain. And it finished with the fifteen-year-long feast of Theogamy*.

[7] Hither My child, to this mountain, I called wise virgins, the procession of little brides of Our Divin-ity sealed with two Olive Trees of Supreme Wis-

---

[2] Nightingale Mountain – is situated near ancient Ephesus (Tur-key), where the Virgin Lady spent 15 years after the Lord's as-cension.

dom[3]. Millions of them, with candles lit at midnight, with trimmed lamps and sufficient reserve of oils, will come here. It is here, My child, where they will come to continue Gospel III.

[8] Why did the Supreme Wisdom* in the Council of the Trinity send the Son to Nightingale Mountain after the Resurrection? The following forty-day-long preaching in the spiritual body showed the absolute inability of the Jews or the Hellenes to hear the words of Our Most High. But My indefatigable longing to bring the world into the Father's myrrh-pouring arms was not prevented because of it. And the Purest Mother was chosen. And here the Bridal Feast took place, My child.

[9] It was the Bridal Feast which the Saviour spoke about in Gospel parables. First, the feast of Theogamy. Then the bride was ushered into the Bridal Chamber – and onto the sweetest Bridal Bed* of their perfect Union.

[10] Nightingale Mountain has been chosen for the central altar of the Theocivilization*, and the altar of altars of the future solar Temple of the World. It will be the centre of pilgrimages by priests of our origin and the true spirit, because the Bridal Cham-

---

[3] Zec. 4:11.

ber of Jesus and Mary will be announced to humankind from this mountain.

[11] Christian history seems to have come to a
standstill, as I told you before. And now the two
thousand-year-long dream is coming to an end, and
the power of Our Father has come into force. The
prayer 'Resurrect my Lord! Hear me!' has been realized.

[12] Thus, Christ of the Bridal Chamber. Mary is
the Bride of the Bridal Chamber. The earthly body
of the whole creature is being vested in the virginal
garments of the Holy Mother in order to receive the
fire of heavenly love and the candle of Gospel III,
lit here on the mountain of the Bridal Chamber.

[13] Christianity has come to a dead-end because of
the priests who rejected the plans of Divinity. They
are in a worse position than the Jews were, when
the Son came.

[14] But, My child, the Revelation of the new millennium has begun. I am revealing the n e w   H e a -
v e n   above Nightingale Mountain with the songs
of angelic birds. A   n e w   s e a   in which play wonderful fish. A   n e w   l a n d   – and it is inhabited
by the anointed ones*, by the Seraphites*, by vir-

ginal adolescents in white vestments*. My child, I declare the Age of the Anointed ones from here, from the divine height of Nightingale Mountain.

:⸺

The Heavenly Queen:

¹⁵ O, My son, I did not come here to describe the divine feelings of the Mystical Bridal Bed. No nuptial bed could be compared to the sweetness I experienced.

¹⁶ Spiritual bodies* can be united, My child. The potential of love, unity and the bridal union of virgin bodies is endless and inexhaustible. But they need to be anointed and spiritually moulded.

¹⁷ I am doing that, My child, by the blessing of the Most High. The scepter in My hand (the Queen is showing Her scepter with the white tip and wax-like caduceus*, ending with the spike) is the sceptre which regally shapes the Seraphic human. I vest mountains, fields, plants, new human beings, and the whole of creation in Seraphic garments.

¹⁸ Oh, My child, I told you about the new Heaven, about the vision of Christ of the Bridal Chamber, about the new Earth and new human beings. Now, My child, I want to tell you about the new heart.

[19] During the fifteen years of Our stay on Nightingale Mountain, the Saviour placed indescribable bliss in My heart. At the sight of Him it opened like a flower. The Lord penetrated My heart, served the Divine Liturgy, erected the Holy of the the Holies*, left precious oils, lit the candle, transformed Me, carried Me in His arms. My child, the Saviour installed indescribable heavenly bliss in My Heart. And now, in this last epoch of general universal groaning, when the Adamites gasp from ugly sins and the miasma of devil-possessed cities, the time to construct a n e w h e a r t of humanity has come.

[20] My child, the heart of the Seraphite, the human of the future, is in my hands. It is a future image of the hearts of those who will inhabit the Earth after cataclysms and transfigurations. The former heart can not receive His love. A candle cannot burn in these damp caves with their mud and mould. A new dry heart, My child, is vested in a white, waxen, composition, and in twelve other mysterious compositions of the Kingdom.

[21] Now see, My child, the preparations for the Bridal Chamber.

Above the heart of the Protoseraphite

[22] My palm is stretching above the Protoseraphite's heart. I am inserting the candle into it. After this I will extend the mirror of Our Father's glory, and the images of Christ of the Bridal Chamber and of Mary of the Bridal Chamber will be imprinted within it.

[23] My child, I extirpated the origin of lust in you and I said: "Without extinguishing the abdominal furnace*, none of you will reach perfect immaculacy. Now, My child, I am starting the next step of our plan. I am giving you a new heart.

I feel severe pains in my back and in my heart.

[24] Your human heart was pierced in Hotel Baltiyskaya in April of 2004[4], during the Eucharistic preparation of the Lamb. It became the new bread. Now, with the Grail spear, I have pierced the heart of a new John. In a painless and joyful way.

[25] Exult, My child! Your heart has been anointed. It reflects the Most High's Bridal Chamber. A

---

[4] John of the Holy Grail had got a spiritual attack of the heart after the conference in St. Petersburg, having condemned the plans of the humanoids on giving a birth to the ugly space monster, whose coming to the earth would be the sign of the beginning of the universal disasters and devil-civilization.

hundred and fifty fiery stairs lead to it. Your heart has now ascended to the thrones of the Second Golgotha of Solovky*. Your heart is residing with us. Your heart is singing endless songs to the Most High. Your heart is carried through the air and enters other bodies. Your heart comprises inexhaustible treasuries, My child. The new Earth, the new Heaven, the new heart and t h e p e a r l have been inserted into it.

²⁶ I am inserting the Pearl of the divine stone into your heart. It is of divine origin. It will change your constitution, My child: the constitution of your bones, tissue, nerves, liquids, and blood. Your whole being will henceforth shine in the stones of the celestial Grail and will be embodied in the tabernacle of the Most High.

The Pearl of Theocivilization

²⁷ My child, I invited you here to Nightingale Mountain after the operation in the dentist's chair[5] in Moscow, in order to insert the pearl of the Theocivilization into your heart. As you can see, the Lord has not chosen a luxurious temple in Jerusa-

---

[5] The unique revelations of the Virgin Mary given to John of the Holy Grail during a dental operation without anesthesia, as described in his book 'The Tender Torture'.

lem with royal buildings as His Altar, but the inner man and his mysterious and endless entries and gates.

[28] My child, accept a new cross henceforth. The pearl of the Grail* will shine from within with celestial light, and nothing previously established will satisfy you*. Christianity, the Torah, Orthodoxy, and Catholicism, once sacred objects of your heart and the deepest foundation your true spirit and knowledge of the Divinity, will cause you particular pain.

[29] My child, remember this wonderful moment. I have inserted the celestial pearl into your heart, as you are the anointed one of the Grail.

> The Queen is taking a shining stone from Her Heart and inserting it into mine. It kindles with unearthly, sweet and painful fire... and languishes.

[30] This stone, My child, was given to me by the Lord, and He named it the R e s u r r e c t i o n S t o n e. Now I am giving it to you as a sign that I have appointed you the father of the Seraphic heirs of Christ. And from Nightingale Mountain, at the predetermined moment, you will call apostles from all over the world, and under My protection and My overheavenly presence you will give the pearl of the Grail to your heirs – to the priests of Melchizedek*.

[31] My child, this mysterious stone will shine and transmit myrrh-pouring compositions to all those predetermined pioneers who open their hearts to you, and who fall in love with Christ and Mary; to those who long for the anointings* of the Bridal Chamber. It will be sufficient for you to look into their eyes in order to bless them with the blessing of Melchizedek, and to impress the pearl of the Grail into their hearts. Its divine light will be reflected in the chosen ones.

[32] My child, from now on I will speak to you in a different language. Without this mystery of mysteries, without the insertion of the pearl of the Grail, I could not tell you anything about these fifteen years.

[33] Illnesses, holy passion, the arrows of the Pharisees*... My child, they disappeared as if they had never existed. They are forgotten. Look into your own memory, revise it. Are there persecutions and arrows? What remains in the spiritual memory are only divine inspirations, sweetest liturgies, and communions.

[34] Our Most High laid the communion of the Bridal Chamber in My memory, My child. The celestial Grail is shining in My Assumption Bed*, My child, in Our Royal Theogamic Bed. This pearl of the Most High is now given to you.

³⁵ I promise to tell only those who are impressed by the Grail of Theogamy about the Bridal Chamber. My child, as those ridden by lust are puzzled by virginity, so an ordinary mortal dominated by sinful compositions can understand little of the Bridal Chamber. I am revealing Myself, not in order to speak or narrate from outside, but to communicate and transmit the mystery from within.

³⁶ So My child, today I have administered the sacrament which is no less important than the vow of eternal virginity.

> The Queen is taking a stone from the crown that shines upon Her forehead, She is touching the pearl of the Grail, and my heart is being sealed. I can see a model of the new John, and the Queen is blessing me with Her Divine blessing.

:⎯

³⁷ Peace be with you, inhabitants of the Earth! Peace be with you, My blessed children! (The Queen is addressing humanity).

³⁸ You were not born to suffer and perform generational programmes, nor to mourn over your sins and return to the realm of death and despondency. You came here to learn Our Father's love and to obtain the sweet gift of Theogamy.

³⁹ My child, today I want to call you to My Ark*
with an outpouring of celestial love.

⁴⁰ Your mysterious Mother, the Mother of the
whole righteous humanity is asking you to be wide
awake and to fight against spiritual death. Perceive
your destiny and awake from the two-thousand-
year stupor. Let the Scepter of the Queen of Nightingale Mountain give you peace and new spirituality! May the Divinity bless you with what I have
called revelation by conversion. And I say again:
convert to the thrones of Our Father, and having
taken the vows of faithful brides, go to meet your
mysterious Beloved.

⁴¹ Nightingale Mountain is welcoming all the
anointed of the Earth.

Peace be with you!

✠

Heavenly Father from His Throne:

⁴² My child, place the fifteen-year feast of Nightingale Mountain at the centre of your liturgical meditation.

⁴³ Your heart has been pierced with the caduceus
of Salvation-on-His-Spilt-Blood – three hours of
the passionate outpouring of Christ's overheavenly
Love from Golgotha. Yes! This is what I called the

Eucharist. Yes! This is the peak of the Royal Bed called Golgotha of the Son of the Divinity. But My child, death was followed by Resurrection, and the Assumption by the fifteen-year-long Pentecost* as the outpouring of this superior love.

⁴⁴ My child, become fervent and administer the daily sacrament of the Bridal Chamber of Nightingale Mountain in your new and prepared heart. It will prepare you for the deserved Assumption Bed for the sake of the ascent to the thrones of the Most High, My child.

⁴⁵ O, ascend with My Mysterious Church!* O, take vows together with Enoch*, Elias, Moses, Jeremiah, Ezekiel, Amos, Zachariah, Stephen, St. John the Chrysostom*, St. John the Evangelist, Simeon the New Theologian!

⁴⁶ Oh, My child, take My seals! As a new Adam you walk along the pastures of Eden in unspeakable raptures, My child. Adopt these raptures forever and search for them. Remember: the old Adam rejected Paradise and sank into the darkness of the original sin. You, revived, are eager to enter the heavenly chambers.

⁴⁷ You have rejected the hell of lust and the abyss of blazing inferno. Now you are sent to the

world as an anointed one, into the darkness of your holy passionate present, among the blind and the naked, the ill and the crying, the possessed and the demoniac ones, in order to carry the mysterious feast of the Bridal Chamber.

[48] My child, on Golgotha the Saviour poured out His superior love. And these three hours of Gospel light gave birth to a new myrrh-pouring scroll. It is on Golgotha, My child, that Christ revealed Himself as the Groom. The Bride was standing by the Cross in most enraptured contemplation. My child, Her tears dried and Her heart stopped.

[49] Here on Nightingale Mountain the Gospel of Salvation-on-His-Spilt-Blood was completed for the Groom and the Bride. The superior Love was pouring out from Him into Her, and returning from Her to Him.

[50] Now, My child, you have been consecrated into the mystery of the Divine Union. Multiply the Grail of outpouring superior love of the Gospel of Salvation-on-His-Spilt-Blood. Multiply it to the unspeakable raptures experienced by Mary during Her Ephesus seclusion, when Christ came to Her.

[51] – This is why I gave birth to you, My Son! This is why You suffered! This is what you are! – Exclaimed Our Lady.

⁵² For two thousand years She has awaited the hour to transmit the feast of Nightingale Mountain to humankind.

⁵³ Now the scroll of the Bridal Chamber has been unrolled. Look, I am unrolling it more and more – forever, over a multitude of spaces, over thousands of kilometrs. Wherever the myrrh* scroll reaches, there the mysterious feast of the Bridal Chamber is administered, and Christ reveals His love to His Bride and to the whole of Creation.

⁵⁴ And, My child, the Saviour's earthly days... Instead of thirty years, His thousand-year-long drowsy seclusion. The three years of His preaching. The boycott of His disciples, the damnations of the Pharisees. The Golgotha Eucharistic feast of the Gospel of Salvation-on-His-Spilt-Blood: Father! It is finished! And My blood transubstantiated into their Divine constitutions!

⁵⁵ And finally, Gospel IV – the Bridal Chamber: Mary was prepared there. And the pinnacle of the Bridal Chamber: the Groom comes for His Bride.

⁵⁶ The disciples are not borne through the air to accompany the Purest Virgin to Her grave. Oh no, My child, they are here in order to be joined and anointed with the highest sacrament of Christ.

⁵⁷ After the Assumption the disciples returned

transfigurated and the grace of the apostles, who spread faith in Christ around the world, bore the seals of the Bridal Chamber. My child, the Queen invited them through the air in order to give them what the Saviour had revealed and given to Her for fifteen years.

[58] At the place of the Assumption Bed the Bridal Chamber ascended to Heaven. And now it is returning to the Earth!

[59] Recall, My child, the last words of the angels upon seeing the Lord returning from the Mount of Olives: 'Why are you standing here? As He ascended, so will He descend to the world!'

[60] My child, the Bridal Bed, raised to the Heavens two thousand years ago with the Purest Virgin, the Divine Bride of the Lamb, is descending to the Earth.

'What is it?' You ask.

The New Ark!

[61] Take this Ark into your heart. Enter it, My child. Call it your home and your bosom.

[62] From now on, the experience of the Bridal Chamber and the blissfully divine dialogue between Jesus and Mary will become your only inner substance. It could not have been revealed before,

My child. It tormented you. Your soul, already sufficiently anointed enough in the mysteries of the Bridal Chamber, by mind and spirit understood that there is a mysterious Theogamy, or union of the Divinity and divinized man. Now that the pearl of the Grail has been inserted within you, you will understand what I am teaching you.

[63] My child, Christ became man so that man might become the Divinity*. Theosis occurs through the sacrament of Theogamy and through the sacrament of sacraments of the Bridal Bed.

[64] May the Divinity bless you to live only through Him!

> We must get used to the fact that it is Supreme Wisdom that administers, not the Divinity. And Her steps can be holy fool and unconventional, contrary to human assumptions and common patterns.
>
> Trust the Supreme Wisdom of the Most High. Her Kindom is coming.
>
> They lost Christ after separating Him from Supreme Wisdom. And Mary has changed – She is the Bride of the Bridal Chamber. Mary-Sophia. Mary of the Seraphites.

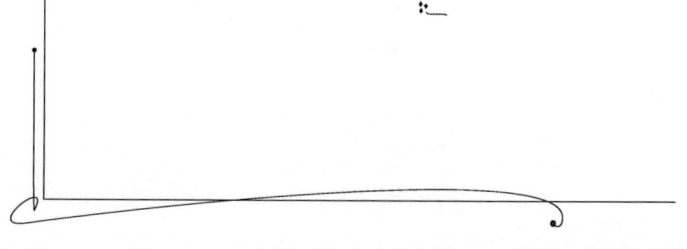

The Lord:

⁶⁵ If you were forced to thrust a knife into your beloved, or immolate him as Abraham immolated Isaac, could I treat those whom I love infinitely in any other way? O, if they could understand My Love!

⁶⁶ We need t h e n e w man to perceive Me as I am!

⁶⁷ I can see your grief, My child: the devastation of Christian pastures, the crisis of the priesthood and the confusion of the hierarchy.

⁶⁸ My child, the commandment of the Most High remains the same: love Him with your whole nature. But, My child, the Jews could not love the Most High with their whole nature, their whole heart, and their whole mind. Their nature had fallen too far, their minds were too infected, their hearts closed, their will paralyzed.

⁶⁹ I have limited My preaching to the Purest Virgin, My child. For fifteen years I have delighted my hearing by visiting Her. She was worthy of it.

⁷⁰ Now, My child, the old commandment of the Most High, revealed in the Old Testament to Moses, will shine in a new light. Love Our Father with your whole nature, with the pearl from the Kingdom

inserted into you, and strive towards His Heavenly Bridal Chambers.

☙

The Heavenly Father:

[71] The apostles? They understood nothing.

[72] They grieved. They were losing the Lord's Mother. They were puzzled. The Bridal Bed encompassed them and exalted on that same cloud by which they were carried to the mount of Ephesus. But soon the heavenly tabernacle of the Purest Virgin became remote and ascended to the Heaven, and after residing on the earth for a short time the apostles were returned to where they had previously lived.

[73] The apostles remained forerunners of the Jewish-Christian Christ.

[74] Today is the time of the new apostleship: the myrrh-anointed and absolutely unworldly time of Sophia. Virgins profess an absolutely pure approach to the Gospel. The image of the Divinity, profaned and blemished by Jewish-Christian conceptions, is an obstacle for them... a nothing. It does not exist, My child.

[75] Only Christ of the Bridal Chamber! Only the

King of the Anointed Sovereigns – as the Bride of the Bridal Feast depicts Him! Only Christ of the burning heart, the King of those who adore Him and whom He adores.

[76] Do not, My child, desecrate your virginally anointed heart by touching the old tabernacle* with its gloomy images of Saviour, Redeemer, and Judge.

[77] Did He not say: 'I have not come to judge the world, but to embrace it with my blissfully divine love'?

[78] He embraced the world as he could in the bloody embraces of Golgotha. But Christ is now embracing the new man in his transformed nature, uniting with him, naming him the Seraphite, and giving him that which He could not give to the Jews of His First Advent or their heirs, the Christians.

[79] In the first centuries of its existence, Christianity was undoubtedly more progressive than Judaism. But today it is an even more of an obstacle to the revelation of the Holy Spirit than the old, obsolete religions.

[80] Try to keep the new images in your heart. Do not allow the Bridal Chamber pearl of the Grail to drown in the whirlpool of worldly cares. Enraptured,

keep your inner heart in your hands, and nourish it with the Eucharistic wine. Peace be with your blessed heart, My son! Your every minute on this Earth is predetermined, and nothing can change: the mission given to you, the salvation of the world, is too important.

[81] I have used the word "salvation" and given it a new meaning, different to that of the Pharisees: without condemnation, eternal death, everlasting tortures, and the like. I understand salvation as the revelation of supreme love and the return to the virginal bosom. It was given by Christ, the true King of the Anointed Sovereigns, the Divinity in the image of man. It was left to Our Lady, the first mortal divinized by the Lord. And today I am bestowing this sweet heritage upon you – the salvation of the world, the gift of blissfully divine and virginal love. Let the breath of the Holy Spirit fill you with new garments, new hearts and new appearances. Amen!

:⸺

That which Our Lady experienced is called the Bridal Chamber, or unspeakable bliss. The Lord entered Her and united with Her. It is indescribable. It is a kind of matrimony, not the fallen matrimony of Adam and Eve, but a million times more exceedingly divine.

The bliss that They felt cannot be compared to the sweetest joys of earthly love. Our Saviour wants more souls to take vows of eternal virginity, so that He can pass this heavenly enraptures onto them.

For this delight I am bearing my cross. For this supreme love our fathers suffered on the Second Golgotha of the Solovky. For its sake the Virgin is coming to us. This is why thousands of souls enter the world ugly, one-armed, paralyzed, aborted, guiltlessly murdered, as forgotten prisoners, beaten, desperate, and lonely.

The Lord:

[82] They come for this heavenly love. Having returned to the eternal world, they contemplate it from whichever sphere they find themselves in. They receive its revelations. Prisoners of the underworld spheres long for it.

[83] And today I send it plentifully to the world and say to you: Hills and mountains, may heavenly peace be with you! Rejoice, like merry lambs! Ascend the Earth that has become the new Mount Sinai!

[84] The Bridal Chamber is above the world. I am sending the Bridal Bed to the Earth.

[85] Yes, the Ladder[6], the Cross, the Bridal Bed.

---

[6] The Ladder, the Cross, the Bridal Bed – the Lord says the prayer given to the author by Him earlier.

The Lord is kissing my heart.

[86] My Child, listen to what I will to say to you.

[87] I will postpone the disasters, time for the revelation of the Bridal Chamber.

[88] May Your Mistress, the Queen Theogamy, become an object of longing for thousands of young people. May Heavenly Wisdom erect Her throne.

[89] Do not be afraid of anything, My child. I will take care that the new revelation and the new knowledge placed into your heart is preserved in a miraculous fashion, and that they are revealed to the world in that same intimate manner by which they were given to you.

:⁓

The Throne of the Mother of the Divinity

Oh, endless grace and rapture of Our Lady! The cloud of the Lord's Glory is embracing Nightingale Mountain. It sheds smoke as Zion did during the revelation to Moses. Hallelujah!

[90] My child, at one approach of the Lord I would enter an ecstatic, subconscious state. The Saviour would heal me every time He came. He kissed my heart and my hands, and His heart shed a ray of celestial love that pierced me like an cutting edge.

And it remained only for Me to exclaim, in blissfully divine rapture: O, o, o!

[91] My child, I can communicate to you nothing of this exalting Theogamic rapture but 'O!'. Never before, My child, had the Lord entered a mortal in this way.

[92] Then I experienced the sweetest ecstasy. His flesh became Mine and the union of our beings gave birth to something new.

[93] I can communicate these states of the indescribable rapture of the Theogamic Bed only through My heart, and not by words.

[94] After the union at the Bridal Chamber, My child, I felt like a new being. Christ remained within me. He conceived in Me immaculately.

[95] I did not feel like the Mother of Christ, but His Consort, the Spouse of the Son of the Most High. And through His union with the Father, I am the Mother and the Consort of the Most High.

[96] My child, the Church was also born from the fruit of Our love. The Infant Holy Spirit originated from these wonderful Theogamic inspirations.

[97] Oh, this union was followed by such sorrows, My child! I endured such hardships! But My sufferings were nothing comparing to what I experienced.

[98] My child, today I am preparing the new man, clothing Him in virginal garments, so that the Lord can descend to him as He did nearly two thousand years ago. And now fragrant Nightingale Mountain is becoming the Bridal Chamber for the humanity of the new Earth and the new Heaven, and everyone who comes here, experiences Theogamic rapture and the unspeakable inspiration of the Holy Spirit.

[99] Peace be with you! I am addressing the world!

> The Queen is addressing the world, Her glance is cast afar.
>
> The new revelation of the Most High has started.

[100] Remain utterly faithful, like the true disciples of Christ.

∶⸺

> The Queen said that She was constantly searching for a home, moving from place to place in order to show how hard it was for Her to stay on the Earth. How She was forever moving around, looking for somewhere to live in order to avoid the persecutions and condemnations of the Pharisees.

[101] Looking for a place to live* conveys My Holy Passion.

∶⸺

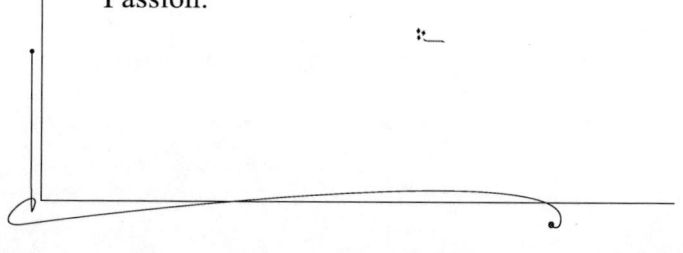

The Lord:

[102] Oh, My child, what a joy! I am sending a cloud of heavenly joy to Seltchuk, Izmir, Antalya, Bursa, Athens, and the capitals of Europe.

[103] A blessing from the throne of Our Most High. What other joy, My child? Rejoice with us! Rejoice here, from the heights of the Bridal Chamber! Rejoice, for the Lord is closer than ever before as never! Rejoice, for the time of divinization has come! Rejoice, because the world will be saved! Rejoice: like a groom I embrace the Earth, my new Bride!

[104] Rejoice, new Heaven! Rejoice, new Earth! Rejoice, new hearts!

[105] Rejoice, My children all around the Earth! Triumph! Exult! Overcome temptations! And come here to the foot of the Nightingale Mountain, so that I can embrace and lead you into the Bridal Chamber.

[106] And peace be with you!

> The whole Earth is filled with the greatest joy of the Bridal Chamber.
>
> Hallelujah! Hallelujah! Hallelujah!

[107] Those, who are of this world, will understand it with difficulty; those who are not of this world

will thirst for anointings and will obtain them. And they will gain happiness unknown on the Earth.

It seems to me that the Purest Virgin is giving the world all the exaltation and joy experienced with Christ during their fifteen years of Theogamy. Today is the day of the new Third Easter. The solar unspeakable joy of the Theogamic bosom, Theogamic nights, Theogamic churches, matrimonies, children.

It seems that we are flying rather than driving down from Nightingale Mountain. We are accompanied by suites of angels.

We are illuminated by the unearthly joy of transformation. The Theocivilization. Joy. O, the Lord will repeat His wonderful feat! The Lord will multiply it! And grace will be multiplied.

Holy joy is the state of the Seraphites after the transformation. Enlightened, weightless, unearthly.

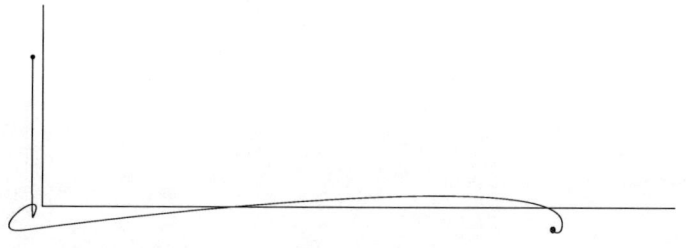

O, SERAPHITES!

Izmir, 14 April 2005

The Altar of the Mother of God

O, Seraphites! The fragrance of Spanish lilies. The beautiful flowers of the Kingdom.

108 The Seraphites cannot be restricted by any definition. They exceed their ownselves. They believe in the Mysterious Christ who has not yet revealed Himself. They would like to keep themselves separate from the former mankind because they see nothing beneficial in it, just a sucking whirlpool.

In a few years (no more than one or two decades) the universal crisis will reach a critical point. The coming generation will say: "Either all of us shall be lost in a catastrophic movement towards universal destruction, or we shall accept the new breath of the Divinity. Let us set our sights on the Heavens, and we shall hear what Our Father wants from us! Let us reject the old world as an incurable illness eating away at us!"

¹⁰⁹ And then Heaven will reveal new scrolls to them. My child, I have prepared a scripture for the Seraphites which is a million times more magnificent than the Torah. Our Only Son Christ will exclaim: "O, at last!"

¹¹⁰ In order to suffer time and time again, He could have been incarnated among the Adamites. My son, He did this without coming to the Earth. His Holy Passion in the anointed sovereigns, taking up the sinful cup at all time, is more than sufficient.

¹¹¹ Never-endingly He will descend to them, to the Seraphites, finding comfort in them, healing His bleeding wounds in them. He will reveal Himself more fully to them than to the most faithful disciples during His time on Earth, and to the greatest saints after that.

¹¹² The common Seraphites, no different than others, will perceive Him in a new capacity. He will come incomparably closer to them than to the most magnificent pillars of Christianity of the past.

¹¹³ Theogamy – o, Theogamy will become the central altar of their prayer. The rapture of Theogamy will become their basic theme. Their hearts are anointed in a special way. They long to enter the Bridal Chamber.

Christ will bring them the unique exhortation that they would like to hear: the anointment of the Bridal Chamber. The divine bliss of it is so, that many will be unable to bear it even in the immortal Seraphic bodies, so that they achieve it through the Assumption Bed and resurrection.

[114] Death and corruption will lose their power. Sin will not dare to approach to their sacred Grail. The devil will send his most perfidious and cunning hordes, but their evil heads shall burst like moths against a lamp.

[115] O, superadmiring delight – the Seraphites of My hope! I will plant My garden of paradise for you. Each flower will possess unspeakable beauty and of special spheres. One could meditate for hours on each of them, grasping their many wonderful forms and colours, reflecting the spectra of the Heaven.

[116] I will spread a garden of myrrhic flowers, each sweeter and more beautiful than the next. Fresh lilies will give way to spring grass, the aromas of mountain incense to the fragrance of pine needles.

[117] They cannot be called Christians any longer. A new religion will be announced, accepted equally by former Muslims, Jews, Buddhists, Protestants, and Catholics. The glory of Christ will eclipse all the worlds.

[118] Arise the glory of My Lord!

The Throne of the Holy Spirit

[119] My child, you lament the removal of the old Paracletic[7] musical prayers... My son, in the epoch of the Seraphites the need for vocal chords and professional voice training will disappear.

[120] Angelic spheres have being prepared for the Seraphites! Their acoustic membranes, placed in box-caskets of internal heart, will embody the vibrations of Heaven. The liturgies of the ascended spheres will incessantly sound within them.

[121] Verbal communication will be used as a last resort. It will be seen as weakness and defeat. Only in exceptional circumstances, My child, the Seraphites will resort to verbal dialogue or even external prayer. A voice, chanting a troparion in the physical dimension, will to them be similar to an angelic horn sounding above the sensitive ears of a child.

[122] Disciple of the Sacred Thrones, accustom yourself to the Sacred Silence!

[123] Take a look at those around you – see how

---

[7] The blissful prayers written by the author and which were used in the ligurgies of the church of the Mother of God in 1980-1990-th. Later the Mother of God has changed the character of the prayers in the Church which caused the spiritual crisis of the author. Here you can notice the spiritual leadership of the Mother of God in Her church.

refined they are. See how sensitive is the people around you. They read more in your heart than you could even imagine. They see you with the eyes of the Purest Mother. They do not need your prayers. My child, you cannot even imagine how deeply ingrained in them are your exhortations, seminars, and liturgies.

:—

124 They are saturated with the myrrh of the heavenly fragrance of the Supreme Wisdom, and there is no need to repeat anything to them. Their joy is in seeing how the word of the Divinity sounds within you, finding its home.

:—

125 Their sensitivity, their refined vibrations, their communication using their eyes, and their readiness to serve and give their lives for their fellow men is beyond compare... Like lambs, they will protect each other and send vibrations of divine love to the remotest places – even to other planets. Many unknown worlds will be opened to their sight, and unspeakable secrets will be revealed to their minds.

126 John the Baptist was sent to the world to witness the descended Kingdom in the person of the Son of the Divinity. My child, the Church-messenger is being sent to the Earth to announce the future

kingdom of the Seraphites, descending from the Second Golgotha of Solovky.

[127] The Kindest Most Kind Mother in labour Childbirth, the Fiery-eyed Sophia, gave birth to the Infant Divinity above Sekirnaya mountain*, and now carries Him to humanity as Christ of the Holy Spirit. Children and adolescents will bow before Him. He is praised by the renewal renewed universe.

[128] Let mountains rise and hills breathe! White ships, sail to heavenly harbours! White-winged angels, bring us the Chalice of the Grail. With it I will give communion to all my disciples, on whose brows I see the seals of anointing.

> The grace of the new Seraphic universe is spread in the air. A rainbow stretches from north to south, from the middle of the sea to the tops of the mountains. Rejoice, nations! Seraphites, this is your glory!

⁓

The Gold is in your hearts

[129] I need spiritual people, My child. Like a gold miner extracting precious metals and sifting stones through a sieve, I am mining the gold in your hearts.

[130] My child, be illuminated by the cloud of the

Supreme Wisdom. The fragrance of divine reason is spreading around the Seraphites. They walk like angels, wearing wide-brimmed headgear, and listen to the music of spheres, the music of thoughts, the music of worlds. The entire composition of the universe is enfolded in this tiny tent.

[131] My child, beg that you are rid of the old intelligence, full of bookish knowledge, preferences, and clichés. That which nourished you yesterday becomes prejudice today. I want to present you with a regal shelter around your brow. You will be blessed by our Lady Supreme Wisdom, and Her intelligent advice will embrace your virginally pure mind.

[132] But before that you should be ready, My child. Not by chance do I call you by this tender word. I could call you: the bride, My ecclesiastic, my beloved, the apostle. But I say 'child', as I want to see the Infant Divinity of Bethlehem in you.

[133] Consider yourself to be the newborn in the manger every single moment. The Virgin is at your bedside; St. Joseph is near your feet. The shepherds of Jerusalem are replaced by angels, and after them are the Three Wise Men, who come by the waving of the scepter of the Most High.

[134] Charm your hearing, My child, with the verbs

of the Holy Family. For the first time, the image of the Infant Divinity is revealed to the world in the way that I would like to present it to you.

*

[135] You do not have enough righteous anger, My child. Your disappointment in the old Christianity is not sufficient.

[136] If you could soberly see the poisonous tarantulas, loathsome reptiles, snakes, eels, vampires, bugs, cockroaches, spiders, and other nasty things swarming in this chilling web-covered hole! Shake off the ashes more boldly, My child!

[137] I am asking you to do the same as Christ asked His disciples, the same as Paul told Peter, and as John taught his followers (formerly zealous Jews).

Chorus:
> O, the Most Divine Word
> The fragrance of the Lord
> Of the super-celestial sphere
> Christ is now married to the Bride.
> The Seraphites were born by Their marriage,
> Washed in the Immaculate Font.
> The Most High is glorified in His new
> faithful sons, kindled candles of Christ.
>
> Glory to Thee, Holy Mother!
> Guard the young growth and tenderly nurture it.

Breathing / contemplation / meditation / ascension / the Bridal Chamber.

The new spheres,
never before descending to the world

[138] My child, I am bringing new spheres that have never come into the world before. Try to inherit them, and accustom yourself to them. In order to accomplish this, abandon the old images and thoughts pestering you like midges.

[139] I could easily make you more perfect by means of a rosary prayer, or by giving you ten new rosaries with commentaries and magnificent canticles. I could give you dozens of morning prayer rules and no less than a hundred blessed liturgies. But My son, the sensible, silent, contemplative and rapt theology of the super-celestial spheres is much more precious than the verbal rule of a prayer.

[140] My child, understand that the spheres, descending from Heaven and given to you, are super-celestial. Develop a fervent desire for them.

[141] I understand how hard it is for you. You have already overcome your ownself more than two or three times. First you overcame the Pharisaic clichés by ministering living liturgies. Then you abol-

ished the discipline of the Paraclete[8] and raised the liturgy of John Chrysostom to a new level. You directed Orthodoxy, which was simultaneously transforming and reviving. Yes, My child! I remember a time when you sincerely enjoyed fine masses in places of revelation around the world, and you ministered them with proper spirituality…

[142] But now, My child, we will leave these former worlds. A new revelation has been given, and new spheres have descended for its sake. Zealots Faithful capable of living in them and of accepting them have already been anointed.

[143] They will nourish themselves only from these new springs. Having reached the top of the mountain, they will ask: "Where are the new springs that have already flowed out? We want to quench our thirst!"

> Oh, what a burning word! Oh, what exciting grace! The Grail is pouring itself onto us. The Grail is pouring the Holy Gifts out into the sea, and is decorating itself with the colours of Christ's Blood. Here it is, the new sea! Here they are, the new lands! Here it is, the new joy. Here it is, the new life.

:⸱⸺

---

[8] Paraclete – from Parakletos (Greek). The Consoler, the name of the Holy Spirit.

While ascending the mountain, the Lord called upon me to be patient. To apprehend the sole foreshortening of people's perception: in the potential of Theogamic ascension.

Regardless of the emptiness and the gaps in human relations, in spite of the devil's power over the soul: in their deepest depths, humans thirst for Theogamy.

[144] Man does not have a higher vocation. And the apostleship of today has to light the Theogamic candle in most unexpected, unprepared people: confused street vagabonds, idlers, rambling tourists, young men acting like spitting camels, rockers...

"Existential melancholy is unsatisfied longing for Theogamy." (Fr. Paisiy)

THE FIFTEEN-YEAR GOSPEL

Izmir, 19 April 2005

The Mother of God:

¹⁴⁵ *O*, My sweetest child! Oh, ecstasy of the Bridal Chamber! My child, for the first time I am going to reveal what I have not told anybody before. My two dearest companions, sacrificial lambs immolated for Christ, myrrh-bearing wives*... ascended together with Me to the Bridal Chamber.

¹⁴⁶ My child, after His resurrection, Christ came back to Me. This is what I understood soon after I had been taken to Ephesus: My child, further divine plans for the Theosis of the humankind, the mission of Mysterious Christ, could not have been fulfilled on Earth. His incarnation ended with the suffering on the cross, the resurrection, the forty days of teaching in the spiritual body, and the ascension.

¹⁴⁷ The forty days of His apparitions in the spiritual bodies caused His greatest sorrows, My child. He was understood even less than in His earthly days. The Saviour put His teachings about the mysteries of future times, about the Bridal Chamber, about the things that I am revealing today, at risk. The disciples were confused. They still had not recovered from the shock caused by His terrible execution and by the threats of the Pharisees to expose them to similar or even worse fates.

¹⁴⁸ The Saviour had to explain the meaning of His coming to the Earth, of the mystery of His death and resurrection. But when He tried to speak of the future and of His mission in future times, the disciples understood nothing. Their ears were closed. And forty days later the Saviour left them and ascended to the heights of the Most High Divinity.

¹⁴⁹ He elected _Me,_ My child, as His New Jerusalem.

¹⁵⁰ Now I will explain to you the meaning of Nightingale Mountain in Ephesus as the 'New Jerusalem'. The Lord came here and continued His deed. Here He found consolation. Here He felt no need to justify himself, to explain, to adapt to the foundations of the Old Testament, to heal, to suffer, to shed bloody tears. Here nobody beat Him, no-

body damned Him. Here He felt relaxed. Here He found consolation after thirty years of His constant Holy Passion.

[151] I felt sheer bliss. To say "happiness" means nothing. My child, it was perhaps only during these years of seclusion that I properly understood Whom I had given birth to and brought into this world.

[152] The Saviour's apparitions continued. He used to stay here. He dwelt among us in a physical body, My child!

[153] It is here that the Bridal Chamber was accomplished. It is on Mount Ephesus that the Theogamic throne was erected. What fiery love, My child! The Heavens, the throne of Our Most High, the mystery of the Holy Trinity descended here. Conversations with the Father, the Son, the Holy Spirit. Separately with each of Them, and conjointly in the Council of the Trinity.

[154] My child, I understood: the Saviour was worthy of the rapturous reception given to Him here by Me and My two faithful companions. My child, He could do so little on the Earth. He could explain almost nothing. He was healing and speaking in parables in order to make them believe where He had come from and who He was. Not even the healings and the resurrection were sufficient.

[155] What killed Him was the image of Messiah as a state liberator, similar to Nebuchadnezzar or Alexander the Great.

[156] My child, the Saviour stayed among us in divine chambers, surrounded by immortal angels. Immediately after his coming, which sometimes seemed infinitely long (by earthly time), we would ascend to the His Kingdom – the Kingdom of the divine Son, given to Him by the Father.

[157] This is what He is like! This is how He would have revealed Himself to Adamites if they could have accepted Him.

[158] I asked Him passionately: "Why did You come to the Jews? Why did You not choose the Roman forum or the Hellenic Areopagus or some other bright civilization? Would You not have been accepted with greater dignity? Would You not have found faithful disciples among wise teachers of faith?" The Saviour emphasized the Heavenly Father's special love for the elected nation. I should not have asked such vain and mundane things. My questions hurt Him, and I promised Myself not to ask them ever again, but to meekly respond "yes, yes, yes" to all that He told Me. It had to be that way.

[159] His coming to Jerusalem was predetermined

two thousand years ago. But, My child, soon after His Ascension from Eleon Mountain of Jerusalem, we moved together to the valley of Ephesus. Some kilometres away from the ancient Hellenic city, with its large commercial port, the Most High Divinity erected His royal tent.

[160] I understood, My child: His earthly days described in the Gospel, His parables, His preaching – it had all been just an introduction to another, true life of Christ. It is here that the new Gospel was written. A Gospel far more sophisticated than that which has nourished the Christians for two thousand years. But I could not reveal it, My child. It would have served as a temptation. It would have provoked mortal malice among those who were fixed on the Gospels or the Pentateuch (the Torah)...

[161] My child, I protected this Nightingale Mountain for My disciples. I named them Christ's Seraphites. I will consecrate them into the highest mysteries of the Bridal Bed. It is you whom I am inviting here today; it is you to whom I am conveying this ineffable sphere.

:⸺

[162] My child, I deplored only one thing: why did the Lord come alone? Why did He not send any chronicler to Me? My weak memory... I remember-

ed almost nothing, I could say nothing. My terrible sorrows, thorns, and claws dug into My marrow... How could I preach while in seclusion, persecuted like an intimidated bird with broken-wings? But He composed My heart. My child, He opened it and laid a small, divine ark inside: a gorgeous treasury and within it thousands of pearls, as minute as solar grains of sand.

[163] My child (Our Lady is laying the treasury upon my hand), I am giving it to you as a gift. This is the treasury of the heart, the treasury of the Seraphites. It contains the Holy Spirit-Groom's gifts, mysteries and divine graces for His true disciples, for the wise virgins, for the knights of your Heavenly Lady. Take it. It is yours.

[164] And while I poured My tears onto His hands and kissed them, I would say: "My Lord! You had so little time in the course of Your earthly days. You spoke allegorically and nobody understood You. For the greater part You had to defend Yourself, even against Your disciples. You had to fight against the Pharisaic devil that betrayed and crucified You. Oh, if only they could have known how beautiful You are! Will the time of Your true disciples come, when You will not have to defend Yourself against them?"

[165] "Yes, My Mother. Yes," He would reply. "In due time."

[166] This time has come. And I am giving our Gospel to you, My child – with the fragrance of Nightingale Mountain, the scent of My Assumption Bed ascending into Heaven on the solar pillar, and the sight of the Theocivilization – the Gospel of Nightingale Mountain. The fifteen years spent here with the Saviour are Our Bridal Chamber. Our enflamed candles, Our waxen bodies, Our unspeakable dialogues.

[167] O yes, My child, I cannot describe in human words anything I felt, and I remember little of it. Too much has been laid in My heart. But My child, I have gifted you with more than a message, a revelation, or an ordinary biography expressed in words. I have presented you with this invaluable ark. Keep it and heed it. It is always to be in reliable hands.

> The Mother of God made this small ark in the shape of Her Heart, and passed it to me. I pressed it to my heart and bowed low to the Purest Virgin as a humble slave. My heart stopped in ineffable ecstasy.

> During the revelation I felt severe pains in my heart.

[168] My child, tell those who call themselves Christians: the Gospel of the inquisitors and the new To-

rah of the new Sanhedrim (as He calls the canonical code and the letters of the apostles which have been attributed to Him) are a great grief to the sweetest Lamb, to the most divine Christ. My child, if you do not go beyond the traditional neo-Pharisaic code, you will fall under the authority of the Luciferian Inquisition. In front of the Most High Divinity you will testify that you are miserable scattered Adamites, unable to hear the living word, like the Jews. Although you call yourselves Christians you remain ancient Jews, ready to follow Him thoughtlessly, to cover His path with freshly cut grass and flowers, and to cheer "Hosanna to the Son of David" – to recognize Him as the Messiah, and yet two days later cry out, incited by the parish priests: "Crucify Him and release Barabbas (a thief) instead of Him".

[169] My child, today I have presented you with the Gospel for the Seraphites. Neither canonical nor apocryphal legends about the life of the Lord, with His preaching versions and His deeds, can compare. This is the Gospel for the future age.

The Queen holds out a scroll.

[170] Read it through, child. I will put this fragrant myrrhic scroll into the Ark and it will be the basis of a never-ending scripture with lit candles, a scrip-

ture written in the ardent blood of the future age, My child. To you, my heirs, I am presenting Christ's inexpressible heights, His sweetest supreme wisdom, and the chambers of the Most High, which descended to the Earth with His coming at Nightingale Mountain. This is a gift to all My disciples of the third millennium.

[171] The glory of the Lord will extend for thousands upon thousands of generations, My child. And that which I have given you as a gift today, the small ark inserted into your heart, is more important than the stone tablets of Moses. It is the preaching of Christ that is treasured within it.

[172] My children, try to break the slavish chains of traditional Christianity! Understand their religious books as the artful scriptures of the inquisitors, intended to glorify their dreadful office under the rule of Lucifer.

[173] Oh, My child… if only I could tell you how tight their bonds with the devil are, how many of his cohorts walk with Pharisaic priests! When I ask the devil to come and report on his affairs, they come with him. They follow him like a shoal of fish. And the enemy laughs, My child, with disgusting, accursed laughter, despising both Christ and the Adamites, because the deceived Christians

see priests as saints and believe in the church as the personified sanctuary and continuation of Christ. But priests are the slaves of Lucifer! "What monsters and mongrels they are," says the Cunning One, "If it is so easy to cheat them!"

[174] Oh, My child, I do not wish to tell you about such things. It is too strong a temptation for the Christians. But henceforth there will be no Christians, only the real disciples of Christ, who hold the Gospel of Nightingale Mountain in their hands.

[175] Yes, My child, I took you to the Solovky and gave you the Solovky Gospel with the myrrhic drops of Seraphim the Graceful*. And now you are standing on Nightingale Mountain of My Assumption and Ascension, on the height of Mountain-III of the Bridal Chamber.

:—

[176] My child, how can I communicate Our divine dialogues to you? The Saviour exalted Me to Heaven and raised Me to the chamber of the All Highest. The Saviour revealed supreme wisdom never before revealed on Earth. My child, in the fourth mystery of the rosary, "The Finding of Our Lord in the Temple", the twelve-year-old Adolescent reveals the mysteries of the Most High to the Judaic teachers. But, My child, this episode described in

the Gospel is far from Our Lord's supreme wisdom! Gather them all together – philosophers, sages, teachers, devoted priests of the East and of Egypt, wise men of the world... My child, not a single divine angel has ever revealed such supreme wisdom before.

[177] O, My child, I heeded His words with My dumb lips, and collected them as I could, in My memory, in My mind, in My heart, in My inner being. His words were imprinted in Me like pollen. They entered Me like rays of divine Light. After Our conversations I kept silent for a long time: My lips became speechless. I could not say a word. But later His wisdom, reposing in Me, continued to talk.

[178] I want to reveal to you Christ of Our divine conversations, as nobody in Jerusalem ever knew Him; Christ, whom even church teachers and luminaries doubted. My child, I appeared to church prelates, to holy fools*, or to the multitudes, to thousands of people, and I said things which they could comprehend. I led you out of the institutions, as the Lord did with His disciples, in order to reveal to you things the that I could not reveal to Basil the Great, Francis of Salsa, Ignatius Loyola, and others. They were interested in practical guidance, in the secrets of asceticism or in the wisdom of mystical

theology. And I revealed Christ to them according to their inquiries and abilities.

[179] But now is another time, My child. And the old church has sunk into oblivion. Glory to the Most High, My child! Christ of the fifteen-year residence in My royal tent on Nightingale Mountain, Christ of the Bridal Chamber, is revealed.

Today I am giving Him to mankind as the greatest gift.

[180] Take the mysterious fire of Supreme Wisdom, which the Lord gave to Me on this Mountain, two thousand years ago, from My hands! Take it and enter the heavenly light, and prepare yourself to perceive the Most High's mysteries of the life of the future. Christ could not accomplish much on Earth. He will do so much among His true disciples.

꞉ͺ

[181] My child, I am speaking from within you now. The Saviour chose the Bosom of the Innocent Virgin, having called it the blessed Seraphic Bed of Bridal love. Today I extend My Bosom to all true disciples of Christ. Those who accept virginity and have been filled with Supreme Wisdom, those who are anointed by Me and named My disciples, will enter the Ark and be honoured with the unspeakable bliss of Nightingale Mountain.

[182] My child, the singing of heavenly birds, the revelations of the angels, the pouring of myrrh from icons, My words in Fatima, Garabandal, Lourdes and La Salette*, are in the past. They are insignificant in comparison with that which I am revealing and proclaiming t o d a y. Accept the new revelation to the world from the Bosom of the Mother Supreme Wisdom. I am happy, My children (the Queen is addressing humanity). I am blissfully happy. The hour has come when that which I have heard (in the presence of two more, wive-myrrh-bearers, My faithful companions) will become the property of the new humanity.

[183] I am extending My patronage, My ever-virgin garments over you. I am asking you for only one thing: to lay yourselves before Me and allow Me to shape you as waxen Seraphites. Let me place within you the seals of imperishable bliss, so that you can share the mysteries of Nightingale Mountain from the ever-blessed Christ, our King.

Amen.

* * *

[184] Now I will tell you, My child, how I felt when the Lord left Me. I kissed His hands and poured My maternal tears over them. My Beloved was leaving Me – and I was dying, My child! After He had left

me My vital forces disappeared, and I lay powerlessly and motionlessly for a long time, eating nothing and seeing nothing.

¹⁸⁵ Then, My child, something inexpressible began: the spheres of heavenly bliss, brought down by the Lord, began to act within Me. I understood that in His presence I could receive so little, and that He was leaving me so that I could master the lesson of His Supreme Wisdom. This is the meaning of the biblical "why hast Thou forsaken Me"[9] (why have You forsaken Me)! It is the reason for the Holy Passion and the weaknesses and tears which precede them.

¹⁸⁶ Oh, My child, imagine My despair and My loneliness during the first hours of My abandonment. And now imagine the rapture! The Saviour sent a cloud after Me, and the Most High's wonderful white tent picked Me up and carried Me above Nightingale Mountain, above the sea towards Greece, Europe, Asia...

¹⁸⁷ My child, the mysteries of the future age were accomplished here.

¹⁸⁸ Here, on Nightingale Mountain, the tent of the Commander-in-chief was erected. Here is the vigilant eye of the Most High, and the true throne

[9] (Mt 27:46, Mr 15:34).

of the mysterious Church. Are the tourists and pilgrims, climbing the seven-hundred-metre-high mountain to reach the small, decorative, Catholic chapel of My Assumption, aware where they are going and where they are?

:—

¹⁸⁹ The mysteries revealed are too great, and I can see what a cross they will impose. But endeavour to reach the first step of the ladder of the Ark together with Me!

¹⁹⁰ My child, the Ark is before you.

> The Queen displays a huge wooden Ark. It seems limitless, and fifteen steps lead to it.

¹⁹¹ In order to enter the Ark of the Theocivilization, one must ascend the ladder of the Ark, step by step. This guarantees one's life during the days and hours of cleansing calamities. Today I have revealed one of the steps: the Gospel of Nightingale Mountain, Christ's Theogamy.

¹⁹² Having ended His three years of preaching on the Earth, the Saviour began to announce mysteries of future times. And My fifteen years spent with Him – it is a ship descended from eternity and harboured on the Earth.

¹⁹³ My child (the Queen is reading my thoughts),

do not ask Me for details, do not ask what the Lord talked about with Me. Do not be idly curious, do not become an unwise virgin. I have communicated to you more than the words, more than the contents of Our conversations. However, I do not remember most of them. I have initiated you into the true spirit, into the spirit of Theogamic bliss. I have initiated you into the reality of the presence of Christ of the Bridal Chamber. This is sufficient, My child, for you to abide in the divine sphere and to take it to your disciples. Soon their number will increase all around the world.

This is the supreme revelation of today.

* * *

[194] Children of the future age, peace be with you! I am your everlasting Mother. I am unfolded over all the world. I am among you. I have been sent here to teach you the truth of Christ. Gather at the foot of My Mountain and heed My Word!

[195] Testing times approach. Half a century ago (according to the Earth's calendar), I called them "the last times"[10]. Today I am speaking to you: it is time to enter the Ark. A great and testing time.

---

[10] I called them "the last times" – the revelation of the Mother of God in San Sebastián de Garabandal, Spain (1961-1965).

[196] I am the Mother of endless mercy and I invite you to remain peaceful: not to fall into a restless mood or fear anything – troubles, disasters, or death. The All-Merciful Divinity loves His creation infinitely, and would never let any Adamite die in the devil's net, no matter how deeply he has fallen. But My children, the Most High has extended His Solar Ark today. The joyful era is approaching.

[197] Millions, rise! Rise from your depths! Arise and come to Me, My children. Abandon the baggage of your knowledge and of your past. I am your Mother Supreme Wisdom. I promise to richly endow all those seek the perfection of the Most High.

[198] Peace be with you, humanity of the world! Peace be with you from the Kingdom! Exalting peace be with all of you! Fill the air of the Earth with the fragrance of the Most High's Bridal Chamber.

[199] I am appointed to invite all visible creation into the Ark. But I am going to do more than that. I will anoint My chosen ones, and I will assign them places at the Bridal Feast. You will ask: what is it? Follow Me and do not ask any questions.

[200] Peace be with you, My beloved children. May My voice sound in your hearts and in your inner mind. I am happy to see those who fill their lungs and their breath with the Word of Our Most High,

and who, aspiring to the heavenly heights, testify themselves to be the sons and daughters of their Purest Mother.

201 Peace be with you and the blessing from the Kingdom of our Lord! And let the Most High protect you from troubles beyond your strength. And let the All-Merciful aegis of your Heavenly Lady and Mother be with you endlessly, for ever and ever.

꞉—

202 You are protected unpredictably and incomprehensibly in a holy-fool way, beyond all reasoning. Search for unexpected places. Human values will be put to shame.

203 The time is approaching when the Lord will establish His Kingdom on the Earth.

Rejoice, rejoice nations!

204 It is the time of unspeakable raptures.

꞉—

The Queen showed me the mystery of the Bridal Chamber.

205 Men have no semen, and women no life-bearing womb. But both of them give out the innermost composition of their nature. They endow it to the Divinity, receiving a one hundredfold requital after a painful dream. As man collects his semen, the

substance of his nature, from all his nervous cells, so the Seraphites collect their concealed sacrifices to the Divinity from all their nervous fibres, and from the vibrations of their immortal bodies, and give them to Him as a gift. After that they conceive from on high, and increase their offspring in a mysterious way, unknown and unfamiliar to the Adamites.

*

> The Queen turns the globe and the firmament upside down. But before this She performs a miraculous waxen moulding, and those who have the Seraphic mark stick to the surface and are saved, while the others are swept away.

* * *

²⁰⁶ ...Divine symmetry and Our heavenly architectonics. Only what is in Heaven counts. Distortions are worse than anything, more sinful than a dream.

²⁰⁷ Our Sacred Mountain is neither for idle tourists nor for fat institutionalists. Here is the Chamber of the Most High, and only His true disciples and anointed sovereigns gain access to it.

²⁰⁸ My Church! Testifying somewhere in distant Moscow, ascend Nightingale Mountain in your full complement! Be off, scoundrels and villains! The true disciples of Christ have heard the Gospel that

I revealed. And today they long to hear Gospel XV, the Fifteen Year Gospel (shown to me in golden letters).

[209] The Bridal Chamber of Our Most High.

[210] Depart, shadows of the past! Christ remained on Earth after His ascension!

[211] What kind of church is it if, considering itself a continuation of Christ, like the high priests of the Old Testament, it replaced Him completely with itself?

Away, villains and crucifiers – the Roman whore and the Eastern ogre![11] Away with the Inquisition and its scorching claws and torturing chambers! Let the groans of suffering brides prevent you from entering the sanctuary of Our Most High.

[212] My children, if the disciples had not known about the presence of the Lord on Nightingale Mountain, they could have guessed.

Here took place events of the greatest importance for the history of the world. Here were revealed the greatest secrets. My child, that which is today called 'Christianity' is just a minute prelude to the Divine Action which will be performed in this place.

---

[11] The Roman whore and the Eastern ogre – Eastern and Western Pharisaical religious institutes.

213 Today, with the power given to Me by the Divinity, I forbid inquisitorial books as once I forbade inquisitorial stakes! The Sacred Gospel of the Most High is revealed to the world. Read the white scrolls! Are they not marvellous, My child? Speechless with rapture, come to My feet and I will fill your interior with the sweetest honey of the Word of the Divinity.

214 My child, I fought the last battle here. Recall the forty-day temptation of the Lord in the desert before the beginning of His ministry. Remember the devil that entered the high priests of the Jews. And finally, see His battle, with sweat and blood, in the night prayer and the garden of Gethsemane.

215 My child, I fought My battle here. The devil considered Me to be a mere mortal, but he was confused with my strength and wondered who stood behind Me. Every day I was hit by his arrows and lay struck down by them. My two faithful companions would cure my wounds with oils blessed by Me and given to them.

216 My child, I could talk without end about the temptations experienced on this mountain. But I grew stronger from one battle to the next, and managed to conquer the devil despite his rage and threats. But, having ascended to the Assumption

Bed, the enemy receded forever, and I gained the power to defeat him with his own weapons. To throw back the spears which he had thrown at Me, to strike his head, to destroy him and to control him.

*

Eight o'clock in the evening.

"You should be in Selchuck in 5 minutes." It is the third time that the police have urged us to leave.

The Virgin accompanies us with a suite of angels and calms us, inviting us to come the following day.

WORSHIP
OF THE EXCEEDING
WISDOM

Kemer, 16 April 2005

The Throne of the Mother of God

²¹⁷ The Seraphites… the Holy Spirit illuminates them. The fragrant heights of the Bridal Chamber… There is no sin. No magnets of Lucifer, nor vicious programmes. The filth is drained, the vicious root severed. Inserted is the anointed messianic origin – the root of the Tree of Life.

²¹⁸ The true life is restored. Alleluia! The life of the future age (the forthcoming treasures) has started. The Kingdom of Christ has come.

²¹⁹ The union of the Seraphites with each other is blessed by the Bridal Chamber. Harmony with the Divinity and with one another. The interweaving of the sweetest strings, the stitching of hearts with a caduceus needle. One garment woven for two allies,

for ten associates (for as many as there are members in a community).

220 Fiery-winged Seraphs are their guardian angels. Both the Seraphs and the guardian angels are different from what they were in the times of Enoch or Tabor transfigurational.

221 The divine strings are the most subtle chains of communication. Seraphs transmit streams of divine ideas to their younger brothers, the Seraphites, by vibrations. The Seraphites silently converse with Seraphs, their guardian angels. Bliss leads to perfect relationships and infinite marriage bonds with each other. The great, simultaneous unity with the Most High and with one's neighbour, impossible in the past or the present, is being revealed.

222 How tightly their souls are bound in purity! They accomplish such a divine flight to the most exalted thrones! And what a heavy cross they bear, bravely undergoing Holy Passion for the 'little souls' to be saved (these 'sealed', shelled, compressed prisoners – whatever they call these decrepit, pitiful, untransformed creations of other worlds or spheres, reaching them through their sensitive lungs, which vibrate like antennas).

223 Translucent bodies are filled with the vernal aroma of blossoming flowers. The fragrance com-

poses their prayer, and the prayer unifies them. The wonderful music of undivided unity. The mysterious councils of the illuminated ones. Flight, existence in the presence of the Divinity, solemn exceedingly wise edifications, and peaceful exaltations.

224 The singing of the birds of paradise accompanies their blessed conversation and spiritual deeds. Gentle animals graze in the meadows. The Seraphites know the language of both of them. They talk quietly to sea fish, enter the sea, plunge to the bottom, walk on the surface of water, and ascend to the Heavens. They perfectly master the secret of transition from one dimension to another, from one immortal body to another: from that revealed by the Divinity to the waxen body, from hallowed to solar, from solar to the body of Holy Passion...

225 'The divine screen' of the Seraphites is astonishing. Peering into it as into the Book of Life, they read the will of Our Most High. All events in all twelve dimensions are made known to them and are accessible by their twelve bodies. Like winged angels they incessantly exalt, flutter and exclaim: 'O! O! Enraptured bliss! O, more and more!' (the last prayers of the Grail are taken from the arsenal of rapturous Seraphites).

226 The fluttering of wings and blissful rapture

are their typical pastimes. How amazingly pure their hearts are! Not the slightest suspicion or condemnation. No sinful thoughts. Childish sensitivity and infinite compassion, the readiness to stand up for those who are miserable, who groan with pain, who are driven by the devil. They produce fragrances in the space of the temple.

:‗

The Throne of the Father

227 My child, are you ready to accept it? T h e S e r a p h i t e s d i f f e r f r o m t h e A d a m i t e s. They are not the continuation of the evolution of Adam's species. To call the Adamites their ancestors is just as offensive as for the Adamites to hear that they originate from the monkey.

228 My child! Before man is created, his structure is estimated and developed with the finest meticulousness – down to microscopic motes, down to tiny fragments and particles. Every particular aspect and all circumstances are included into this divine calculation. And look, My child: the Adamites' stake has been lost. My long-suffering patience has been exhausted. Supreme Wisdom, speaking always and exclusively in the language of divine mercy, has found an unforeseen course for them: the

path of dreaming, tranquillity and enlightenment will bring them blessings. Believe Me, they will sigh with relief.

[229] Only heavenly healing can rescue these megalopolises from suicides. But we are not speaking about them, My child!

[230] T h e n e w m a n – the Seraphite – is structured and planned beforehand down to the smallest detail. My child, the origin of the Adamites has been returned to Our treasury. The new origin is being extracted from it. Doubtless something of the Adamite has remained. But the Seraphites repel the Adamites as different beings: of different origin, of different essence.

[231] My child, it is a great gift for the Church when today's thirteen-year-old teenagers accept the revelation of the Holy Spirit and declare themselves Seraphites. Reveal divine perspectives to them! El Elion, the Sweetest of the Seraphites, has descended to Earth. The Gospel for the Seraphites is being written – the message for their blessed hearts.

[232] So, My son, you should renounce not only the old church and the prejudices of the former civilization, not only the disastrous paths of modern cities and traps of the devil. But the Adamic origin itself

should be eradicated from your mind, like a foreign body. You should clothe yourself in Seraphic garments.

[233] My child, I am present here and now. Bejewelled with virtues, the Seraphites stand before My blessed sight. Their shining Universe transforms in rainbow spectra. I need only to send their divine cloud down to Earth, and to announce the beginning of 85th civilization*. But, My child, before this the earth should be purified. Innumerable throngs and hordes of souls will have to leave this world.

[234] Any creation is dear to Me, and the Adamites in their fallen state are dear to Me as in their original one. That is why, My child, I am inoculating Adamite kin with Seraphic images today, and clothing them in Seraphic garments. But only those who declare themselves as Seraphites, and not Adamites, will enter the Ark. No one can claim to be a Seraphite, to be beyond madness and temptation, unless he has been inoculated with the tree of Original Immaculacy* and exalted in Abraham's Bosom by the Queen of Lights.

[235] Again and again you should untiringly worship your Lady Supreme Wisdom! Only She has the right to form and shape the Seraphites. She and only She has the right to determine their structures,

as well as their fates and destinies. The Supreme Wisdom Sophia is more powerful than ever before. Her authority is paramount.

[236] But why, you ask Me, do I not respond? Why do I not give signs or send prophets and anointed sovereigns into the world? Y o u   h a v e   t u r n e d   t h e   w r o n g   w a y. Appeal to your Mother Supreme Wisdom, and your prayer will be heard. And you will receive everything you ask for, and even more than you can imagine.

[237] So leave this bookish two-thousand-year-old Christ: the Protestant Jesus, the Orthodox Saviour, or the 'charming water' of youth movements. There was enough mockery of the Divine Son, and there are enough of those who are canonized in order to replace Him! How many more Tibetan* chimeras will disguise themselves as Christ, and later remove their masks to reveal the sharp teeth of wolves.

[238] Worship Supreme Wisdom! My Lady is diffused in the air above the Universe. She is spreading sweet fragrances. The Kingdom is entrusted to Her.

[239] There is still one obstacle to the glorification of Our Queen: Pharisaism. As an unassailable fortification it stands, and shoots with medieval guns. Withdraw from it, My people, and come to the pas-

tures of Supreme Wisdom! Today the shepherd's pipe of your Lady is gathering fine-fleeced sheep, pure and wise virgins, into Her blessed flock.

[240] Come, My children, to the Bridal Feast of the Beloved One! Drink wine from the Inexhaustible Chalice! Drink beyond the edge, more and more!

The Seraphites are distinguished from the Adamites by their quality.

They are a different race.

*

The Lord:

[241] Tell them, tell My enemies on the Earth: I abominate all the laws established by them. I came to repeal the law, but the legalists crucified Me. The law of prayer, ceremony, belief, sacraments... inflicted punishment upon Me.

[242] Are you executors or devotees of our Father El Elion[12], who said to Moses, 'I am the God of Devotion'[13]?!

[243] With pseudo-laws written for the benefit of institutes rather than Churches, you sealed up the

---

[12] The name of the Most High Divinity, accepted in the school of the Grail. In the Old Testament it is mentioned only four times (hebrew).
[13] (Ex 34:14).

heavenly Statutes. Places occupied by archbishops, cardinals, theologians, scholastics, inquisitors, and judges now belong to Supreme Wisdom! Away, away, away from me! Be swept away for ever and ever! Free the throne of the Most High for My true sons.

244 Supreme Wisdom, My Lady, send magnificent patterns of sanctity from the Kingdom of eternal and perfecting Statutes! Let nobody be judged by the law! The epoch in which Paul was praised by the Holy Spirit as an ardent apostle is behind us. The epoch of mysterious Statutes has begun.

245 The statutes are for *the Seraphites.* They are commandments *of Seraphic* bliss.

246 The law smells with fatal horror. The hand of the Inquisition hangs over it. Where there is law, there are its myrmidons, judges, courts, torture chambers, instruments of death, and the dying groans of innocent victims. And you call this dreadful concentration camp a church, don't you?

247 Shameful nonentities, you cloistered yourselves against My Kingdom and Supreme Wisdom. You are unable to see or hear, you wrote your own laws and passed them off as heavenly. On whose behalf do you speak, you hatch of vipers? Is Satan

your father, worshipper of the letter and of the bureaucrat, of stale books and of secret fornication?

[248] I abolished law forever, My child. I did it not to spread chaos and anarchy, but to comply with the HEAVENLY STATUTES of Our Divine Lady. Supreme Wisdom was given the duty of sealing them into hearts. Did the Most High not tell you: I shall make a new covenant in your hearts[14]?

[249] And in My Covenant there are no more laws, judges, bureaucracy, death penalties or heretics. But His commandments are mysterious and blissful.

[250] Are you capable of enrapturing your mind with the heavenly world while listening: "The Father and I are the one. Heaven is one with the Earth. Eternity is one with time. The twelve immortal bodies are for the Seraphites. Exalt, spiritualize, adhere"? Are you capable of apprehending the immaculate origin in your still impure and sinful bosoms? Are you capable of shaking off the dust and of breaking decrepit bonds? And to groan with the Holy Passion until you are heard? To faint three times from weariness, and to whisper with your dry lips: Drink... Let me drink! Let me drink!...

---

[14] Jer 31:33.

[251] My very assignment, My child, is to reveal the Statutes of the Kingdom. With your hands and your scepter My child, I have already revealed more than several hundred Statutes and mountains of unutterable blisses. Institutes accept none of them.

[252] What they have piled up instead is trash and dirt. One lit Solovky candle will turn them into a heap of ashes.

꞉‿

[253] Listen to My Word and follow it, and the necessity for the law will disappear. Fulfil your predestination and unite with the Beloved, and family priests will no more be needed; and abomination shall vanish from My sight.

[254] 'The effectiveness of the sacraments does not depend on the personal qualities of a priest!' (The Lord means the principle of 'opera operandi'). I can see them no longer! My Blood is squeezed out to the last drop.

꞉‿

[255] The only thing I want from the Adamites is their transfiguration into the Seraphites. They are ready, My child, they are disillusioned. Believe Me, all of them are crisis-ridden – from the simple Turkish housewife to the mother of a dozen chil-

dren, or the member of the European Parliament, pretending on the television screen to be joyful and successful.

256 I shall inculcate them all by My heavenly divine origin. I shall do more than just transubstantiate My Blood in them: *My origin* will be born in them. I will shed from Myself the very root of bliss. I will bestow *Christ's origin* upon them, and it will grow in them as the most fragrant tree. And they will change and become divinized, and together with the immortals they will see the glory of Our Father.

꙼

257 The mankind should enure itself to the language of the Holy Spirit. The language of the Holy Spirit is qualitatively different than the language of Yahweh or of the Son of the Divinity.

258 His whole Universe is dissolved in the love of Our Most High, it is suffused with myrrhic aromas, it is permeated with the fragrance of the only Kingdom, where there is no distinction between the eternal and the temporary, the earthly and the heavenly.

Singing:
The liturgy of the Holy Spirit,
The Kingdom of Christ – of the Living Divinity.

The Millennial Kingdom of Christ.
Oh, the most fragrant Word.
Oh, the most fragrant Word!
The mystery above the Heavens:
The Groom is wedded to the bride.
Hallelujah. Hallelujah!

White Cross, Chalice of Melchizedek. The mysterious garment of Our Lady Supreme Wisdom is adorned with gold. The divinely inspired Sofia is above the world.

:⸺

259 Oh, My child, I want My disciples to minister on the tops of mountains, to sail far beyond the shores of Greece, Turkey, or the Cote d'Azur, and to chant rapturous liturgies for all creation.

260 For Me there are no spatial horizons. 'Jerusalem', 'Charizim Mountain', 'the Vatican', and 'Tmutarakan' do not exist for you any longer. You possess the treasure of all treasures. A cloud of the divine existence* is above the priest of Melchizedek. He has erected his tabernacle and rapturously celebrates the liturgy. Listen, little fish! Listen, heavenly birds! Angels, fly to the Bridal Feast!

The Grail appears in your hand – the White Chalice, ethereal, burning your palms. O, taste, transubstantiate and drink, drink, drink!

(On the eve of a Sunday liturgy, Moscow time 10.13)

O, the times are more blessed, blissful, and desired than ever before! Amen.

<u>Singing:</u>

The Kingdom of the Holy Spirit
Of Christ – The Living Divinity.

OUR CROSS IS OUR MYSTERIOUS BRIDAL BED

Izmir, 24 April 2005

O, the Burning Bush of the Chamber! O, infinite grace! The Most High is descending.

꞉—

The Mother of God is now demonstrating how frequently She appeared in Her physical body in different places of the world, in dozens of countries. Her fifteen-year staying on the Earth, after the Ascension of Our Lord, is higher preaching than the Annunciation of Christ. During these fifteen years, the Queen of Heaven visited all the places that the Lord would have wished to be but had been unable to do so, due to sorrows, weaknesses and beatings inflicted upon Him by the Jews and priests.

The Mother of God and the Lord, who descended to Nightingale Mountain for fifteen years, were united into one. He lived in Her and She in Him. This is the mystery of the Bridal Chamber.

꞉—

The Holy Mother was still persecuted while in Ephesus. Her stay there caused anxiety among the Greek authorities. Local powers received a secret dispatch from Jerusalem, informing them that a criminal woman, whose son was sentenced to death for crimes against Israel and the Roman Empire, was hiding amongst them. According to the dispatch, they were to find Her and prevent Her settling in the town.

In the font of the Bridal Chamber –
O, such endless grace!
The Most High descends to the feasts
With the Inexhaustible Chalice of the Grail.

:—

The Mother of God:

[261] I gave consent... to this sacred madness... The Father showed Me and My Divine Son what We were to endure. But before that I had been exalted to the heights of His heavenly love. O, My child, seeing what I had seen, one lacks the ability to refuse and accepts any cross with great honour.

[262] In the Gospel only one message has been successfully written: that of the overwhelming, inaccessible, sacred, unreasonable, supernatural, Seraphic, higher-angelic, divine love of the Most High, of the mystery of His descent and of the establishment of His throne in the world.

[263] Christianity was intended to be a school for great consecrated, for torches and anointed sovereigns who have descended from Heaven. The Saviour brought consecrated anointings for His brides. The devil stole them, My child, and dispersed them among his worthless instruments. They were misused by malefactors, inquisitors and the foot soldiers of the devil.

[264] At the proper time I, Supreme Wisdom, revealed to the father-theologians the mystery of the Holy Trinity, the mystery of the Cross-as-Godman, and the mystery of the Holy Virgin Mary as the Mother of the Divinity. I, who nearly two thousand years ago revealed the Lord to the millions, am unveiling Him now as the Divine Groom, and christening the world as His myrrh-anointed virgin bride.

[265] My child, so many spears were broken, so many souls perished, so many innocent victims suffered for the idea of the Holy Trinity. Up to now the devil has launched violent attacks upon it. Muslims, Jehovah's Witnesses, Jewish traditionalists and the like rise against it. They mock and sneer at the image of the One in the Trinity, and at the three Hypostases of the Most High.

[266] My child, I am the only one to whom the divine providence, revealed in the bosom of the true

Church. All else is mere temptation. Dogmas, cate-chisms, explanations, clarifications... The mystery of the Holy Trinity remained unexpressed, because it was divided from its Primary Source – from Supreme Wisdom. They should not have elected Councils or set compulsory rules of faith, after which they persecuted dissenters; they should have prostrated themselves before Supreme Wisdom.

267 I was not thanked, My child.

:⎯

268 Today I am talking to the Seraphites. I am not revealing to them Christ-the-Messiah, the Son of the Divinity, but the King of the anointed sover-eigns, the King of Theohumanity, the new Sun ris-ing from the sanctuary of the Solovky, the Greatest Sun of suns illuminating the new universe. O, My child, look at the lands we were given by the Lord!

> The Purest Virgin is exalted above Nightingale Mountain.

269 Calamities are left behind. Look, what perfec-tion! What beauty! The world is purified from the original sin. The devil is defeated. I stepped onto his throat and My arch-strategists threw him into the abyss. My child, I can finally deploy My regi-ments and declare the Divinity's plans for the es-

tablishment of the Kingdom of the Most High on Earth.

[270] Like the Kingdom of Christ the Son of the Divinity, it will not be established by external means, My child. No Theocivilization will ever be established formally or externally, even after calamities. Let the Divinity save you from repeating the mistakes of the past and from falling into different illusions. The predecessor to the Theocivilization is Theohumanity, the union of the Most High and creation in one. Then follows the Divine Marriage: the mystical all-sacrificing cross between them. The Cross of the Son, gifted to His disciples, and the Cross of the Father, given to the Son.

[271] My child, lie on the cross, Our Mystical Bridal Bed. The cross has united us. We are the children of one cross, My child, and there is no other way to the Most High. The cross alone!

[272] If you want to ascend to the Bridal Chamber, lie on the cross, My child. Agree to be humiliated, crucified, lonely, and unappreciated. Dull and drunken barbarians will subject you to mortal insults. And there will be nobody to protect you. And in your death-agony you will cry out, 'Oh, my God,

my God, why have You forsaken me? You promised never to leave me alone. You pledged to Jacob,
creating an eternal covenant with him, not to leave
him until the mission is fulfilled. How did it happen that you left the Son of the Divinity who came
to suffer for Your glory?'

273 O, My child, take the wisdom of the cross,
revealed to you, to the ark of Theogamy. Let not
a single enemy of the cross, or those who have not
been initiated into it, dare teach about the sanctuary
of supreme love.

274 "Why are the Seraphites to bear the cross?"
You will ask.

275 My child, the main difference between the Seraphites and the Adamites is in the insertion of the
cross into their interior. The cross has its composition, with divine pollinations and unifying particles
inside. My child, Adam's tragedy was that he denied the cross as the Tree of Life. The Seraphites
are composed by Me according to the image of the
Cross. The cross is pressed into their lungs, into
their backbone, into their mind and their conscious-
ness. They are cross-shaped. That is why, My child,
they do not face problems of initiation and anointing. They are embodied as winners. The cross is pre-

sent in their divinized nature to such an extent that they long to suffer, make sacrifices, and unite with the Most High again and again.

276 The Seraphites are prolonging the epoch of the Gospel. It cannot be understood without the new people descending to the Earth. This is why Christianity stopped mid-word sentence, as if the lips of the Saviour had become dumb on the cross, and remained silent for two thousand years. Ecumenical councils were held at the foot of the mountain. The Inquisitors carried out their justice, dealing with saints. Saints wailed in their caves. Jews fought against Muslims, crusaders waged wars against barbarians. But the dumb Saviour, as if petrified, waited for the continuation of His testimony.

277 And the time has come, My child. Christ was resurrected twice on the Second Golgotha of Solovky. The New Easter! I have revealed the Easter of Christ, after that of the Jews. Today I am revealing the new Easter of Christ's Resurrection in Seraphic mankind.

:__

278 My child, I shall advise you how to ease your mission.

279 Christian restrictions still rule your life. My

tenderly beloved child, you have always spoken in favour of John, My precious disciple, and against Peter. John was like a child, wonderfully simple. Peter was stronger, capricious, and rational. My child, it remains for you to become the true John, the beloved disciple of the Myrrh-Anointed Christ III, the John of Solovky.

[280] My child, not once or twice, but dozens of times did I reveal Myself to the ancient saints, and disclosed to them the mysteries of the Holy Trinity and the Godman, His embodiment, resurrection, ascension, and forthcoming glory. Consequently, fiery testimonies of faith were spread all around the world.

[281] Forget the old Christianity – it had its day! I repeat for you: She, who nearly two thousand years ago revealed the mystery of the Godman and of the Trinity in the Three to those that love Christ, is now heralding the epoch of the Bridal Chamber, the Theocivilization, the Theogamy, and the coming Kingdom of Christ, all sealed in His creation. From here, from Nightingale Mountain, I am universally establishing the Theogamic throne.

[282] My child, the sweetest Paisiy, your dearest spiritual son, who shares your heavy, difficult cross, is helping you to d i s c a r d t h e o l d p r a y e r s

which allow the devil's arrows to reach you. I am asking you to do more, My child – to renounce old Christian clichés. They are dead and sealed forever.

²⁸³ Become like an infant. It seems that your grand-children accept the idea of the Theocivilization and Bridal Chamber with greater ease than their father who has revealed the Most High to them.

²⁸⁴ My child, this should not be. In order to pass the exceeding of the elders* to your twelve-year-olds, you should become like a child yourself. It is not the first time that I have told you this. There are no obstacles in the path of the new revelation other than the clichés of the old church.

²⁸⁵ Your former disciples, your present enemies, would like to tie you to Beelzebub's* umbilical cord. The serpents want to wind it around your head and suffocate you. Day and night they reprimand and blame you for retreating from the accustomed forms.

²⁸⁶ Forget about them, My child. Throw them away together with the old Christianity. Turn it up-side down – the earth above the firmament. Take my scepter to bless the Theocivilization. Learn, like an infant, only about the new. Begin your day with the following: 'I am newly born', 'I have just been born in Christ!', and 'I believe that I came into the world to be the one with the Divinity.

²⁸⁷ Strictly adhere to the entrusted scepter and the new Revelation. I will strengthen you, My child. Take my advice and follow it.

> What exaltations we were gifted by Our Lady! She was borne up to the Heavens so many times!

※—

²⁸⁸ My child, during the years of persecutions and My inconceivable Holy Passion, unimaginable even for Me, I felt the greatest happiness. Neither Adam, having just been created by the Most High, nor the most distinguished prophets, saints, or anointed sovereigns ever experienced it.

²⁸⁹ My child, here I experienced the indescribable joy of the Kingdom, the unutterable raptures of the Most High. Now I am giving these most rapturous feelings to you. Carry them in your tabernacle-like heart and pass them to your disciples. In that way the world will be filled with a new, never-ending hymn of hallelujah, and will glorify our Christ the King for thousands of years, until it becomes the universal hymn of the exultation and celebration of Our victory.

※—

Singing:
  O, the joy of the Most High, o…

*

Rejoice, Earth!

Our Queen, the Most Merciful Mother, the whole world belongs to You! I am your little vessel. Fill me with the Holy Spirit and strengthen me in my earthly days. Hallelujah!

:—

290 Here every single mote is sprinkled with My blood. My child, I have brought you to My home. Be blessed together with your Mother. Together we shall perform the mysteries of bliss. Hallelujah!

291 My child, today I feel heavenly joy. I am full of joy for the new plans of the Most High. They are revealed to mankind for the first time. My child, now, when the devil wants to triumph, the Most High will manifest His greatest Power all around the world.

292 So, fill yourself with our joy! Fill yourself with bliss and proclaim it among devil's spawn! The Divinity is coming forth in His glory. Hallelujah!

There is nothing but love.

O, only You!

*

293 My blessed Earth. The world belongs to the Most High.

294 I will will speak with you again and again, My

children. I do not want to know the present order. The doomed will accept their destiny.

[295] I am sending you the spheres of our heavenly blessing. Take it, My children, and walk under the sign of the Most High. And may perfect heavenly peace be in your hearts.

[296] Virginity, Supreme Wisdom, anointment, virginity of the soul, virginity of the body, purity of the spirit, thirst for the knowledge of the Most High and for the knowledge of man as he is before the eyes of the Divinity. May all this become your desire.

THE QUEEN OF THE BRIDAL CHAMBER

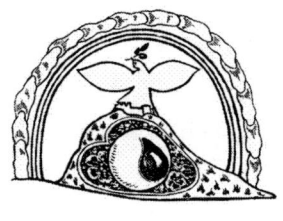

Izmir 21 April 2005

The Mother ofGod:

²⁹⁷ 𝒩 knew by heart each path of the rapturous mountain. The Divinity revealed the topography of the heavenly New Jerusalem to Me.

²⁹⁸ On the mountain of Our Divinity there are no accidental paths. They are all shaped according to the image of the heart of Our Divine Father.

꞉‿

²⁹⁹ O, My tenderly beloved son, My faithful child of the Bridal Chamber. The Father sent the Son to the world because the image of the Most High was distorted. The Pharisees misinterpreted it in their own way and, as recorded by them, counterfeited the most ancient books, which were guarded for thousands of years. The Book of Enoch, Abraham, James… My child, if only Moses had seen

what the Jews did with the tablets, he would have broken them again in despair.

300 The image of Jehovah in the Torah is distorted. How did they do it? Oh, they have malicious jaws and cunning minds! They know how to garble the meaning of a divine revelation with a single stroke. An imperceptible sting, a puncture – and the idea is replaced with its opposite.

301 Their task is to show Jehovah as a savage, unforgiving, unfair and punishing God, who is always 'fighting' with 'enemies', strangers, and so on. The image of the devil (and they are born of him) is attributed to the Most High.

302 My child, having mounted Zion, Moses experienced rapturous exaltations. The Cloud of Supreme Wisdom brought him to the throne of the Most High. Before the two stone tablets with the ten commandments were given to him, in his heart was written: "L o v e   w i t h   a l l   y o u r   h e a r t !"

303 The Sweetest Father poured most-plentiful love onto to Moses. The Jewish prophet, by origin from Egypt, was given twelve immortal bodies. Moses conversed with the Most High at His throne.

304 There is a scene in the Pentateuch which describes the tablets of the ten commandments broken into pieces. It says nothing. Seeing the distorted

and miserable image of the Most High, Moses was driven the despair of the anointed sovereign. The Jews were unable to accept and understand what had been revealed to him: oh, such inconceivable bliss, My child!

[305] After Moses, they distorted the image of Elijah. He was described as a powerful ascetic, gaining his strength from El Shaddai[15]. Then they started to change the manuscripts of the prophets. Dribs and drabs were left of the Lamentations of Jeremiah. My child, the Pharisees and their malicious copyists literally bit into the ancient scrolls, removing any mention of supreme love or divine light. The Torah was rewritten no less than a thousand times. It was distorted and filled with monstrous additions until everything was there but the most important thing – the image of the Most High.

[306] The Divinity sent His Son. And the evildoers of the New Testament, the heirs of the scribes, Pharisees, rabbis, and high priests, did with the Gospel what the Jews had done with the Torah.

[307] My beloved child, the Father is not formidable. The Father is magnificent. You cannot look at the Father through the eyes of malicious rabbis or Byzantine despots. Sift the thoughts of the Inqui-

---

[15] El Shaddai (Hebrew) – the Almighty, Divinity.

sition! The Father reveals Himself in S u p r e m e
W i s d o m , My child.

[308] The soul needs to overcome multitudes of
spheres before reaching the throne of the Most High,
before exalting at the throne of the Most Blessed.
O, My child, His image is perfect and His voice is
divine. It is impossible to describe them.

[309] It is important to love Him and to confide in
Him. And to pray to Him as Paul recorded in his let-
ters, not as slaves, but as loving sons: Abba, Father!
Beloved Father!

[310] O, My child, Seraphs, Thrones and Cherubims*
contemplate the image of the Most High. But from
the Earth you can perceive Him with the spiritual
eyes of the Mother Supreme Wisdom; it is the
only way. The blissful chariot of the Cherubims is
ornamented with divine visions of Supreme Wisdom. Repeat over and over again, tirelessly: Sophia,
Khokhma*, the Divinity's Supreme Wisdom, Sa-
pienza. Invite Supreme Wisdom, superior to the
earthly order, in all languages of the world. They
who seek it are w o r t h y o f i t.

:·_

[311] Oh, My child, I do not speak to you in words.
The outward text of the Revelation is only an ex-

cuse, My child. I am passing you the sweetness of My fellowship with the Most High. I am exalting you to My bosom and presenting you to the Most High as My little son.

312 Keep on rereading the Word, My child. And do not so much think about it as listen attentively. Look for vibrations beyond the words. The divine light from the sphere of Our presence is beyond them. My child, I promise to those who c r e a t e My Word with pierced ear (not read penetrated, but create, said the Purest Virgin) I will exalt them to the thrones, as I am doing now with you.

313 In the earthly days the Saviour wanted to convey the true image of the Most High Father. My child, they did not wish to listen to Him. With the help of the power of the Most High, He healed lepers, raised paralytics from their deathbeds, and performed endless miracles. But all these were regarded as signs of His divine messianic origin.

314 Nobody understood the power and mystery of His miracle-working. The power was that the Saviour laid Supreme Wisdom in the hearts of the healed. It was inexpressible in any other way. The healed went to the rabbis and returned to their own circles.

[315] My child, the Most High exalted Me to His thrones and called Me 'Beloved Daughter' an innumerable number of times. And the Mountain that you see is the throne of the Most High.

Nightingales are singing.

[316] These mountain ranges belong to Him. The Most High descended here on a cloud of His glory, and miraculously counselled with Me.

[317] The Holy Spirit will come and teach about the mysteries of celestial love, about numerous secrets, because the way of love is temptation for those who are not enlightened.

* * *

The Queen of the Bridal Chamber:

[318] My child, the anathemas of the Pharisees are followed by shield and prohibition, by the shaking off of their dust.

[319] Nothing is more beautiful than the entrance into the Bridal Chamber! Enter it, My child. Enter it while praying. My presence is expressed in the spiritual spheres that I am sending to you. The heavenly councils p r e s e n t you with the Chamber of the Most High. Enter it.

[320] Oh, My blessed son of the Bridal Chamber, if you want the fundamentalism of the world to disap-

pear from the face of the Earth as soon as possible, enter the Bridal Chamber with My first-chosen disciples. Daily perform the procession of brides to meet the Groom. Burn incense for the Beloved of the Bridal Chamber.

[321] My child, fill yourself to the brim with the bliss of supreme love. Draw from its treasury. Drink from its waters. Linger at its feasts.

[322] Do not be afraid of self-delusions, the temptations of the devil, or charms. Yes, there will be a battle. I have shown you the most difficult and inaccessible path, My child. Satan fights against it with all his strength. The Pharisaic demon is particularly fierce. But do not be scared, My child. I am the Queen Theogamy, Your enraptured Lady, the Queen of the Bridal Chamber, am blessing you. I am the Lamb of the Divinity's Covenant with the man, am blessing you. This covenant is called 'the Marriage bonds of The Most High with His creation'.

:⸺

[323] My child, did not Christ talk about His new law: 'I am giving you a new commandment: love one another'? It was written in the Gospel. And I am presenting you, My child, with the new bliss of unheard hallelujahs of multitudes of anointed virgins.

³²⁴ What I am talking about is *the new mystery, the new gate.*

³²⁵ Do not think that it is easy to enter through the gates of the Bridal Chamber on Earth, surrounded by fortresses of wicked, armed hordes of Pharisees, magicians, villains, and incorrigible scoundrels pretending to be religious. But, My child, I, am your Lady Supreme Wisdom, have given you the high anointing. Take it from My hands. And in the vacant hours of your being alone enter the Chamber of Our love.

³²⁶ Our Divinity, the Holy Spirit, has revealed more than enough Seraphic prayers to you: 'O, my Beloved, O!', the prayers of the Holy Grail*, the Theogamic Eucharist, the twelve Fiery Thrones. O, what else, My child?

³²⁷ Take it as your duty to enter the gate of rapturous love, the gate of the Most High, My child. To love as you once loved repentance, seeing it as the meaning of existence, understanding how it changes the whole essence of man: easing the burden of his sinful cup, enlightening his worldview, and changing him into a person loved by all.

³²⁸ Burn, My child, with the fire of supreme love. May its candle never go out. Do not let the devil at-

tack you with thoughts of the absence of prayer, official canons, and lack of repentance. The Seraphite is unworthy of it all. You have been grafted to the Immaculate Branch.

[329] And the battle is continuing, My child. It is the sign of your true inheritance of the Second Golgotha of Solovky and of Nightingale Mountain. Without this fierce struggle could I ever reveal to you my daily fights with the devil?

[330] Triumph, and seek peace! Repent your inability to retain the sphere of the Bridal Chamber. It is difficult to pass through the gate, which opens but then closes because you are not zealous enough.

Singing:

O, most rapturous grace
Of Your Bridal Chamber,
Mother of the Divinity…

:—

Oh, the sweetest grace! Everything is imbued with Her presence. She is omnipresent.

Your ineffable, ineffable, ineffable presence! You are donating your presence to us. I am entering Your Bosom. I am in the Kingdom, I am in Heaven. Oh, what more? To erect tabernacles and to stay here forever!

Oh, Most Exalted Lady! Oh, Sweetest One! Bestow

rest, peace and welfare upon all those who visit the place of Your presence.

May this holy City of the Divinity, Nightingale Mountain, the sacred mountain of the Most High, reveal the Divinity and the wealth He has prepared for His sons and daughters of the third millennium! Distribute lavishly from your gathered treasures, Most Exalted Mother! May a cloud of grace enter the hearts of the pure. May they return from here with their inner essence renewed, enlightened. May they have new seals on their fiery brows. May they be filled with the breath of grace and the flame of true faith – as the sign of having visited Your shrine, where You abide in person, where you meet Your sons and daughters and bless them for all eternity!

Oh, Holy Mother, protect us under Your wings. I do not know the words, I cannot express myself. Oh, She is giving more and more light... The place of Her presence is the most blessed in the Heaven and on the Earth.

*

It is getting dark. We are forced to drive in order to avoid the police, unlike yesterday. (We were given a prosaic explanation. The local police are extremely discontent. They pointed to their watches: driving after 8 p.m. is prohibited, it is too late).

But there are no time limits for Her, and She will be waiting for us tomorrow.

VERBAL MYRRH

Izmir, 26 April 2005

Christ can be perceived only by looking at a different Heaven

331 My child, take the new Heaven which has been revealed to you – the Heaven of the anointed sovereigns of Christ and Mary, of the Theogamic Royal Spouses.

332 In His earthly days our Saviour brought a n o - t h e r   i m a g e   o f   t h e   F a t h e r. During His coming the Jews wove the canvas of their own heaven – an earthly heaven. Neither Elohim* nor Adonai corresponded to the true image of the Divinity. The rabbis invented their own Messiah, not from prophetic sources, but from the Maccabees*, from fundamentalists. Israel had been waiting for the devil, and when the Lord came they crucified Him.

333 The Saviour spent three years of his earthly service to identify: to prohibit the old, sealed heaven of the s n a k e and to open the Heaven of the

Bridal Chamber. My child, they believed in Him and followed Him, ready to accept Him as Messiah and Divinity. But the train of accursed images of terrestrial saviour and king was always there. A n o t h - e r heaven could not have been revealed; the Jews sealed it immediately.

334 The Saviour worked wonders by the mercy of another heaven: He raised Lazarus and healed lepers and paralytics. The Jews accused Him of using the power of Beelzebub. They prohibited and sealed the heavenly sphere. Christ, the First-Anointed, fought against crafty devils; He called them 'snakes, snarling beasts that suck the blood of the saints'.

> The Orthodox Christians of Russia have fallen even deeper than their fathers, the rabbis of Israel. Their evil, vindictive and parochial Christ is a fumigated devil.

335 My child, there is only one First-Anointed King. He is named the Saviour, the Messiah, the Holy Spirit, the Ever-Virgin Lamb, the Supreme Love.

336 Christ can be perceived only by looking at a d i f f e r e n t Heaven.

337 The mystery is in this. Therefore I say to you: proclaim another heaven, the heaven that has been revealed to you.

338 Forty days after the great miracle of redemp-

tive sufferings, death, and resurrection in the spiritual bodies, the Saviour dared to teach about the Bridal Feast. Boycotted even more severely, He was heard only by two myrrh-bearing maidens and one stunted disciple. John was His beloved because he listened to the sweetest sermons about the Bridal Chamber. John was the first to receive the myrrhic composition of the Bridal Chamber – the particles of adhesion.

[339] Following the beloved disciple, John's Church of the Second Golgotha of the Solovky abounds with myrrhic oils which are kept in the interior, in virginal lamps. Oh, My child, each dying cry of an innocent victim of the Second Golgotha of the Solovky bore a drop to the great vessel of Christ's anointed ones. Today He stands at the altar of the Solovky Church, and Seraphim the Graceful (named so by the Queen of Heaven) wishes to anoint all Christ's true disciples with the myrrhic oils of the Second Golgotha.

᛫

The sweetest Bridal Chamber descended at the hour of Pentecost

[340] One of the Gospel episodes depicts the descent of tongues of fire on the fiftieth day after Christ's resurrection. This extract is misunderstood by priest-

interpreters. They made Pentecost an ordinary festival among twelve major celebrations.

[341] Oh, My child, the sweetest Bridal Chamber descended at the hour of Pentecost!

[342] During the ten days of preparation in the cenacle of Jersusalem I did not cease to reveal to the apostles the Christianity of the Bridal Chamber. Enlightened, they saw another, true Heaven only after His ascension to the Mount of Olives, My child.

[343] The Most High ordered Me to reveal it. Full of righteous wrath at the world Pharisaism, I appealed to our Father, and the Most High struck the old tabernacle with lightning. The clouds of hell cleared away and a new heaven was opened, My child – the Heaven of the sweetest rapturous anointing of the Beloved, the Heaven of the Bridal Chamber.

[344] All that is under the old black heaven is cursed, My child: their prayers, images, troparia, saints, 'apostolic succession', saviours, and icons. The old heaven has been sealed.

[345] My child, take the scrolls of the new Heaven from the heights of Nightingale Mountain, from My hands.

There must be no intersection with the old ways!

[346] During the years of My Holy Passion before

the Assumption, I was taken into the Heaven of the Bridal Chamber. And today I bring neither revelations nor epistles, but the new Heaven and most divine spheres for the people of the third millennium.

[347] What has happened, My child? Did I not speak to Catholic visionaries, did I not reveal My will to chosen saints like Lucia dos Santos or Padre Pio?

[348] Do not look back, My child! Today the past has been sealed. The measure has been filled, My child, and the time of the old tabernacle is on the wane. The Pontificate of Cardinal Ratzinger shall soon end with bankruptcy. The Vatican will face even greater desolation and disintegration than the Roman Empire.

[349] Therefore, My child, the Heaven of the Bridal Chamber is ahead of you! Christ as He is. Take this new revelation alone and drink from its springs.

[350] The new must never again intersect with the old! Watch, My child: do not become one of those earthly disciples of Christ, faithful but blind because the clichés of rabbinical fanaticism hang over them. May C h r i s t i a n fanaticism have no more power to hang over humanity like a cloud, to imprison, to shoot arrows, and so. Therefore reject their accursed hypnosis forever. Do not condemn, do not blame; re-

nounce and abjure their religion, and submit to the will of the Most High.

[351] They would like to blur the Divinity's revelation with the smoke of their incense. But, My child, their fumes shall be blown away.

[352] Lead the Adamites in these last days up to the heights of the Bridal Chamber. Was I not taken there from My Assumption Bed? Was not My Beloved John taken there? Was he not followed by Seraphim the Graceful and by the fiery hierarchy* of the myrrhic Solovky?

[353] My child, the Most High will exalt His beloved disciples on the cloud of Glory. With their body and soul shall they be taken up to the heavenly worlds, leaving drops of myrrh on their images and the bright memory of them for their chosen descendants.

[354] How to ascend to the new Heaven, My child? There is nothing sinful, snakelike or demonic in it. It is the reign of the Immaculate Origin and eternal virginity, resistant to any vice.

[355] My child, in My revelations to early Christian teachers I called the Church 'holy' as it was untainted by original sin, like the sacrificial lamb who

takes away the sins of the world and transforms them miraculously into the absolute holiness of the saints. Take from your Queen, personified in the Church, the image of unblemished ever-virginal shrine, and profess it to the world.

356 Purify yourselves of the old patterns and addictions using the keys revealed to you. Ablute yourself in My white fonts for days on end, and gain the image of eternal virginity. This ablution will reveal to you the new Heaven of the true Christ.

357 Here on earth, My child, you need the shield of the Most High.

358 I am the first to introduce this new theology for the future Seraphites. The shield of the Most High is the mysterious weapon by means of which a soldier fights against the prince of darkness and remains invulnerable. He can be wounded or squeezed, but the shield of the Most High preserves the power of eternal virginity. This shield can only be entrusted to the knights of the castle of the Grail of the Most High, and to their faithful myrrh-bearing maidens.

359 Guard your virginity, My child, as it is the strongest weapon against the devil.

***The mystery of the True Church
is in the following: it is unrelated to original sin***

360 The Church has lost its virginity and has built up the image of a prostitute. The Roman Prostitute is put to shame for only one reason: the angel has abandoned her. The Most High renounced the traitor, who had surrendered herself to lechery with the men of the world, with o t h e r grooms.

361 The world and the Christians must abandon the seduction of the Roman hypnosis: that the Pope represents Peter and Peter stands for Christ, that the keys are working faultlessly and the gates are open regardless of the personal qualities of church leaders. This absolute delusion should be forgotten and rejected forever, My child.

362 Only the holy and perfect Church can be called the daughter of Christ, My child.

363 The Church of Christ is a great mystery. Only lambs and virgins belong to it. The Second Golgotha of Solovky demonstrated what a profound transformation one should undergo, what fearful tortures and abysses of hell one must suffer in order to enter the bosom of the Eternal Church. Fiery-winged Sophia, Supreme Wisdom, the Mother of the Solovky elders, revealed to them the authentic sanctu-

ary. Having seen the decline of the earthly church (in comparison with the True Church), the elders were horror-stricken.

[364] My child, the Most High moved away from Orthodoxy and Catholicism for one more reason. These old corrupt hypocrites, lacking virginal eyes, cannot accept the new Heaven. Their hatred for My appearances, their rejection of My revelations, and their pursuit and massacre of the chosen vessels is due to the fact that the Most High is sending messengers from the Kingdom. The fundamentalist rabble, hypocritically pretending to be the Divinity's holy order (as the Jews pretended to be the offspring of Abraham), prohibits and damns them. Pharisees of all kinds (they now can be found in any religion), they vow to the devil to wipe all the saints off the face of the Earth.

[365] Mankind would benefit from seeing the other side of this shady mafia's concern, which we call the modern 'megabuck confessions'. No, I am not referring so much to the secret sources of mammon as to the unstoppable mechanism of inquisition. Its aim is to hide the true, sacred Heaven and to replace it with a golden dome, with decorated ceilings, icons, censers, and the like.

366 'I did not see a temple in the city' (Rev.21:22), My child. From here, from the heights of Nightingale Mountain, I bring down the new Heaven of the Bridal Chamber.

367 The Most High anoints each of you, My children. His Reigning Son gives you the image of true disciples and brides. Change yourselves! Do not confess to be Adamites, but Seraphites. Enter the Bridal Chamber as the Ark of salvation of the last days, and learn the sweetest sweetness and the most blissful bliss fully granted by Our Divinity.

368 The mystery of the True Church is that it is not implicated in original sin; it is safe under My motherly protection. And I promise to protect the church sanctuary which has accepted the image of the Bridal Chamber and consumed the scrolls of the new Heaven. I have unrolled them today for all of suffering humanity.

369 The priests and their hierarchy did not know the mystery of the Church.

370 In His earthly days the Saviour said of the Church: It is invincible against the gates of hell. My child, the faith of the hierarchs lies in everlasting protection, in the invincibility of the fortified sanc-

tuary. Believe Me, all the evil of the world, all the claims of Tibet and the obsessions of the devil are provoked by only one thing: the distorted image of the Church of those who dare to speak on behalf of it. My child, they are prodigal sons fed by the whore. They are the sons of the whore. In the Psalms they are called 'impious mortals'.

371 Vatican is already surrounded by the "New Age"*, Jehovah's Witnesses, nightclubs and discos.

372 My child, the mystery of the Church lies in the inviolateness of the sanctuary. When the Church makes compromises with the world, losing faith in the patronage and the shield of the Most High, it loses its spiritual virginity, and the devil can oppress and use his legions against it.

373 The Church must not surrender the opened gates of the Kingdom to the devil (as does the Roman whore). And believe, My child, that all the evil of the world comes from modern blasphemers and whoremongers, these cursed Orthodox, Catholic and Protestant Pharisees.

374 My child, I am not speaking only on behalf of the Divinity, but also on behalf of the Heavenly Church. It is useless to pray to the old saints

today! These prayers can be heard only if they are offered by the Most-exalted Church, established by Me today. And the hour has come to proclaim the Church of My highest throne, which I call the Sacred Theogamy, the Bridal Chamber. And with it the new priesthood with its sweetest councils. Can you hear the music of the Kingdom? And hosts of angelic ranks accompany the heavenly hierarchy.

375 Descend, My sanctified Church! My most beautiful daughter, born from above, from the seed of Christ, from His Holy Passion, incomprehensible to the world.

376 I bless the Church of the Bridal Chamber, the daughter of the Holy Spirit, the bride of the Lamb, the most serene lamb of the Covenant, to spread across the face of the world before the beginning of the purifying plagues, and to proclaim the Ark of the Theocivilization. Let those souls who wish to be shaped anew as Seraphites, with particles of original immaculacy and immunity to sin, enter it. May there be peace in your homes and hearts, peace be with all peoples.

:—

377 Having blessed My new sanctity, I shall strengthen it to witness eternal virginity in mysterious ways, guided by Supreme Wisdom. And it

will endure and triumph over all the attacks of the devil.

[378] You are the disciples of the All-Triumphant Lady. The churches have appointed me with all royal titles. The new titles also belong to Me.

[379] O, My sweetest child! The enemies' arrows do not stop.

[380] Our foes do not grow calm. Seeing My patronage and My miraculous protection, their furious malice brings foam to their mouths. The devil has ordered them to put the sons of the Purest Virgin to shame and to destroy them.

[381] More and more, My child, rid yourself of the black spots in your spiritual bodies. There are more than a hundred. I have counted one hundred and fifty. Look, they are multiplying. You may ask what they are. They are the former Orthodox seals.

[382] My child, these dark spots make you vulnerable to their arrows. Purify yourself immediately!

[383] As your Purest Mother I am asking you to cleanse yourself of these inner spots. I have done all that I could. I abluted your spiritual bodies, liberated them from debauchery and erased their lust, filled you with the Holy Spirit, anointed your forehead to shine with Supreme Wisdom. The last word is yours, My child.

[384] Curse them day and night with the scepter of damnation, given to the priests of the Most High. Continue to prohibit their evil deeds, which are leading to the destruction of the world. My child, remember: I am struggling, with your hands, against Satan embodied in the old church.

[385] Do not think that you are only fighting against deviated Daphans and Abirons (your former sons, the priests who betrayed the Second Golgotha of the Solovky and My sweetest covenant with them). The devil revealed to your enemies other underworlds, deeper than those for sinners – a bottomless abyss.

[386] They condemn you with church prayers and curse you with prayers of exorcism composed by you. My child, they are insane, and I am indicating to you the most powerful tools: use only the new instruments of the Bridal Chamber. The revelation of the Bridal Chamber comes from the Solovky and from the Theocivilization. The year 2000 is a border-line. Lead the Church into the Bridal Chamber and I shall close the door behind you.

[387] My child, knock at the door. But in order that it is opened for you, first close, seal and board up this old accursed door at which shades of hell are knocking.

My Purest Mother:

[388] Fear nothing. You are safely kept.

[389] I shall take all those who are dear to your heart into My destiny. An indescribable joy awaits you, My child. Oh, if you could only imagine what the Most High has prepared for you! Your heart would fill with mortal anguish and you would be unable to bear it. The rest of your life on earth would seem impossible, and all events vain. But the Lord gives you joy millions of times greater than that which you have earned or are able to contain (as it was with His former disciples, so it is with you).

*

Here is the grace of Her presence. O-o! O-o! O-o-o!
After all Her appearances during the two thousand years of Christianity, the Queen has chosen Nightingale Mountain to announce the mysteries of the Most High for the future civilization.

[390] O, My child, the most wonderful times have come. I have been waiting for them for two thousand years.

[391] My child, when the apostles gathered around My Assumption Bed we conversed with glances and gestures. I explained to them that which I am telling you today in words. C h r i s t ' s a p o s t l e s

were not ready to know what I am revealing today to you. You are the cultivators of Christ's garden in the last times, 'winegrowers of the last hour'.

392 I rejoice, My child. The time of joy and triumph described in the Psalms is commencing.

393 Sons and daughters of the Bridal Chamber, I appeal to you. Profess the faith of the myrrh-anointed Christ, the beloved Groom. And rush towards Him, like wise virgins dressed in the garments of brides. Proclaim the Bridal Chamber if you wish the world to be saved! And expect nothing from the old sanctity, rusty and having receded forever.

394 Rejoice, rejoice, My child. Repeat with Me:

395 Rejoice, Queen of the Bridal Chamber, the Ever-Virgin Lady! Rejoice among the myrrh-anointed, our Ever-Virgin Lady!

> Rejoice, Bride of the Divinity,
> The joy supreme has come!
> Rejoice among the sons and daughters
> of the Bridal Chamber,
> our Ever-Virgin Lady!

> Rejoice, Bride of the Divinity –
> The joy supreme has come.
> Rejoice with the supreme joy of the Divinity
> Our Ever-Virgin Lady!

The Bridal Bed is the adornment of the new Universe

³⁹⁶ My child, the procession of the sons and daughters of the Bridal Chamber is accompanied by the white Bridal Bed.

³⁹⁷ Bridal Bed, Bridal Bed! In it, My child, is the image of the Groom, the altar, the Lamb, the lion, the Godman, heavenly pollen, and particles of myrrh. In it is the mystery of mysteries. My child, you cannot take your eyes off it!

³⁹⁸ The cross abolished the sanctity of the ark of the Old Testament, the Holy of the Holies. The Bridal Bed abolishes the altar of Christ's Church, My child. A mere mortal cannot look upon it. It is carried on a cart by the anointed sovereigns. In it is the focus of heavenly light. The Most High Himself has laid His little tent in it. This is the new ark of the Divinity.

³⁹⁹ Extol the Bridal Bed in song! Be aware of the Bridal Bed in blessed all-night processions, at the feasts of the Grail.

⁴⁰⁰ Not a single Athonia* of the New Testament dares to touch the Bridal Bed, My child. Her hands will wither. The Bridal Bed is the Grail in the ark. The Bridal Bed is the adornment of the new Uni-

verse. The world will long for the Bridal Bed. It will attract millions, My child. Its place of residence will be kept secret. During presence of the Bridal Bed, My child, millions will be anointed at thousands of forums with oils that adhere to Our Most High, entering rapturous exaltation.

401 The Bridal Bed will replace the thought of death, the fear of ordeals beyond the grave, and the terrifying images of inquisitors about eternal punishments and the Gehenna. Snakes will never see the Bridal Bed. They want to marry the devil. They imagine another Bridal Bed, one with a stinking lustful goat and a black Beelzebub. This herd of clumsy, fat, eye-rolling hippopotamuses are afraid of evil thoughts and shall fall into the abyss, as did the pigs of Gennesaret by the word of the Divinity, when the Groom anathematizes them and orders: leave My sons alone! Give way to the priests of the Most High!

402 My child, you are the priests of the Most High, royal Melchizedeks, My anointed ones. Extol to the Bridal Bed in Its liturgies.

403 Was there not such exalted grace during the divine services dedicated to My Assumption, as if from the tent and the cloud of the Most High? My child, the disciples gathered at the place of My As-

sumption in Ephesus; they saw the Bridal Bed. And My body was transfigured on the Bridal Bed, and ascended on it into the Heavens.

[404] The Bridal Bed will be carried throughout the Universe. And wherever there are processions of the Bridal Bed of the Most High, the Ark will arise. And fragrant gardens will blossom after the disasters.

[405] Praise the Bridal Bed as the Holy of the Holies of the Theocivilization! And may the Divinity bless you with the prayer of the Bridal Bed, with the sphere, anointing oils and Supreme Wisdom of the Bridal Chamber. Into it the Divinity will take those who love Him. And I invite you today: enter, children, worlds never before inhabited by mortals! The Most High has prepared them for you.

[406] Glorify your Divinity, glorify! Glorify Him in all the worlds! And let the Divinity bless the world to be transfigured and to enter the Ark.

⁚⎯

The Revelations of Nightingale Mountain signify a new step in the participation of Supreme Wisdom in the destinies of the world

[407] The disciples in Ephesus remained orphans after My Assumption. I appeared to them, promis-

ing not to leave Ephesus and the world until the end of the age.

408 My child, the revelations of Nightingale Mountain signify a new step in the participation of Supreme Wisdom in the destinies of the world. I have kept my word. I appeared again and again in dozens of countries, choosing different instruments: shepherds, fashion models, elders, children.

409 I did not come to ask for a chapel to be built or for the Rosary to be said, as imagined by Sanhedrims of the New Testament. My child, I appeared again and again in order to remind mankind of the divine Heavens, of the royal treasury of Christ.

410 You should record My every word in church scrolls, and repeat them day and night. You should compose a new Gospel from the messages of the Mother of the Divinity, which bear far more grace than the letters of the apostles.

411 I did not create such a church, My child, I brought the tent of the blessing of the Most High. The Solar Bride descended to the world in the image of the Purest Virgin. The Divinity's Bride of the Bridal Chamber came down to Earth and talked to the disciples of Christ. I did not urge them to repent, say the Rosary or walk humbly to the temple, as the distorters of My messages described later. If I

had been content with those, My child, what difference would there have been between the Annunciation of Christ and the morass of the Old Testament (confess, pray, fast, wait, and so on)?

412 My child, I d e s c e n d e d f r o m t h e h e i g h t s o f t h e B r i d a l C h a m b e r. I presented My vessels with more and more anointing oils. My child, I visited, strengthened, and anointed them. And I took them to the heavenly world.

413 The construction of the Bridal Chamber t h w a r t e d the aims of the institution, set up instead of the Church. Other priests lead to the Bridal Chamber. They need different gifts and virtues. The devil's rabble never fought so fiercely as it did against the seals of the highest anointing.

414 The measure is filled up, My child, and I have set up the Church of the Bridal Chamber as a sign of the coming Theocivilization of saints on Earth. Let peace be in your homes, in the air and hearts of all peoples of the world.

:⸺

415 The Christianity of the Bridal Chamber was realized here, on the heights and in the shelters of Nightingale Mountain. Imagine, My child, what I went through when the Most Divine Beloved left Me! How I longed to spread His fervent words, the

flowing flame of His most heavenly blessings, His most wise speeches.

[416] Oh, He said nothing of the kind His disciples! Here His speech sounded differently. Here the Earth rose to Heaven and Heaven came down to the Earth. The Saviour talked to Me in the way that heavenly wisdoms and angels converse in the Kingdom.

[417] But the persecutions continued and My lips remained silent. My heart burned, pierced with thorns of love for mankind.

[418] My child, I appeared in Ephesus, the dwelling place of the Bridal Chamber, having promised to proclaim, for two thousand years, all that Our Most High and His Son revealed to Me here, on Nightingale Mountain. This mountain is a prototype of all the places of the revelations of your Purest Lady.

[419] My child, the Saviour initiated Me in a special way into the mysteries of His victory over the devil. Having seen the destiny of His Church, I was shocked and stunned. Lucifer overturned His plans and used them against Him, as he had done with His Father. But, My child, the time of the revelation of the immaculate universe has come. The Kingdom of Christ begins here.

[420] Having abolished the old tabernacle, Christ did not abandon the world; on the contrary, He came

and united with it as never before. John the Baptist preached in the deserts: 'Repent, for the Kingdom of Heaven is at hand'. I say to you, in the deserts of modern cities: 'Purify yourselves and convert to the Divinity! The Divinity has united with humanity on Earth. The Kingdom of the Divinity has descended into the world'.

:⎯

To you, heirs of the Second Golgotha of the Solovky, I entrust the Bridal Chamber as My royal treasury

[421] The last executioners of the Solovki are still alive. The special intelligence services are eager to conceal the 'dreadful' secret of the multiplication of Christ in thousands of disciples. They blotted out the evidence of My appearances, of the most exalted cities, of the flame of the Bridal Chamber set over the immolated Solovki martyrs. The Jews also wanted to seal the grave of the Divinity and deceive themselves and the world, as if the Most High King had not risen.

[422] My child, to you, the heirs of the Second Golgotha of Solovki, I entrust the Bridal Chamber as My royal treasury.

[423] It is useless to invite the world to repent. It is useless to patch old clothing. New garments

are necessary: twelve immortal bodies, fiery vestments, virgin grace, and anointing oils. I bring them in abundance, My child. Anoint, ascend!

424 Today is the time to invite My disciples into the Ark – it is the Bridal Chamber that will soon ascend into the Kingdom.

Appeal for virginity as the salvation of man and of all mankind

425 Be filled with strength of the spirit, My child. Take from Me the origin of immaculacy. The devil is powerful against those who do not know the power of the Most High. His whole world is saturated with the furnace of lust. You will pierce the smoking, stinking with kef monster by this tiny lance (the Virgin extends the Sacred Lance), and the spirit of seduction and deception will depart from him.

426 Virginity, sacred virginity! Seek it over and over again. No other weapon is more powerful against our enemy. Virginity, oh sacred virginity! Its armies will crush hordes of enemies. Virginity, o, sacred virginity! Knights, pure men and myrrh-bearing maidens are called to it. Virginity, sacred virginity! It is the pure water of holy springs, never contaminated with any bacillus or epidemic. Virginity, o, sacred virginity! It will inherit the future, My child.

⁴²⁷ I will reveal the mysteries that the Lord has revealed to Me, His Eternal Virgin, only to virgins.

⁴²⁸ Look at the modern cities through My eyes. Millions are contaminated, down to the marrow of their bones, with abominable lust. The goat-legged one rules this world. His nightclubs, vile music, monstrous perversions, groans of innocent victims, paedophilia, mafia, homosexuality, black magic, and flocks of confused sheep rushing around… My child, the lecherous goat is ruling this world.

⁴²⁹ Go and say to them: these lustful freaks are living their final years. According to the heavenly calendar they are approaching their last moments.

⁴³⁰ Go and tell them: the universe of sin is coming to an end. The tree of good and evil is rotten to its root and will soon be cut down and thrown into fire. The tree of virginity is growing.

⁴³¹ Be more brave and daring than before, My child, without fearing persecutions, slander, or the damnations of priests. Erect virginal communities, virginal cities. Appeal for virginity as the salvation of the individual and of all mankind.

⁴³² Let your sermon be simple. Teach about the kingdom of eternal virginity and about the world that is abandoning lust for immaculate purity. I shall provide answers to the questions: 'What do

you mean by virginity? How should married people behave? What about secular people? What are those who have to earn money, support the family, pay debts, take care of neighbours and so on, to do? How can we reconcile all anxieties of this world with the spirituality of divine patterns?'

433 I reply to them, My child: This is what anointments are for. May the seals of virgins be with you and in consequence, no matter what you do, pure virginity will spread around you. Virginity is possible in marriage, in friendships, among peoples and countries. Only the devil can stand in the way of the purity of the inner man.

434 Wonderful are the two who communicate in virginity. My child, their hearts have been opened and myrrh flows from one to another; imperishable sources that mutually enrich and increase their grace.

435 Virginity will change life on the Earth. Proclaim it by saying: there is not a single soul who, facing some perilous situation, would not take vows of eternal virginity this very moment. Even a person suffering from a terminal disease like AIDS or cancer, or some lonely imprisoned outcast, hopelessly suffering from pulmonary tuberculosis.

436 Virginity is an appeal to the Bridal Feast. Never find any excuse to refuse it.

⁴³⁷ I am especially inviting priests to take the way of virginity. Do not think that the Lord or I are leaving the Church. There are many pure souls in it. Hierarchs, cardinals, patriarchs, bishops and Our other enemies do not form the original relic. My child, the priests are the first who are called to take the eternal vows and perceive the shed from them. May the treasury of everlasting virginity remain over them. May the tabernacle of Melchizedek descend to them with a multitude of seals and the never-ending gifts of the Holy Spirit.

⁴³⁸ The Charismatic movement will have no future if it does not accept the anointment from the Eternal Virgin and the image of Christ's coming Kingdom revealed by Me.

⁴³⁹ There is no justification for refusing to take the vow of eternal virginity, no matter how heavily one is defeated by lust, nor how involved he is in the order of this world. Proclaim virginity without thinking, and invite people to take the vow of eternal virginity given to you by the Virgin Lady.

⁴⁴⁰ O, My child, do not mistake it for monastic vows, asceticism, and the like. The vow I ask you to take is new and mysterious, descending from above. The anointment comes from the new Church and for the new priesthood.

[441] My child, to those who accept virginity I promise a Seraphic destiny and life in the third millennium. There will be no excuse for those who refuse it.

[442] I am asking you to spread My message, the sorrowful call of the Crying Mother, all around the world.

[443] Lust led to the nuclear warhead. Lust changed the minds of mankind and spread the bacillus of bacterial and chemical war. Lust turned millions away from the course of heavenly light. It built a multitude of mental hospitals and caused the insanity of millions of people. It will multiply, My child, if my poor children reject my messages and continue to visit nightclubs (the dens of the devil), justifying themselves with offerings to priests.

[444] Lust erected cursed cities and built skyscrapers; it infected desolate mortals with night cinemas, hypocritical theatres, and an interest in lower worlds and fallen angels. Lust released demons from the bottom of hell and let them inflame the cauldrons of sorcerers. Lust poisoned the air of the cities and filled lungs with toxic cement and bitumen dust. Lust distorted people's minds and made them enemies to their Creator.

[445] Virginity will do the opposite.

446 That is why, My child, I am laying a new foundation stone for mankind. This stone is called e v e r l a s t i n g,   i n v u l n e r a b l e   v i r g i n i t y. Carry it in your hands as the pearl of the Most High. Touch it. Lay it within your inner being. Let it glow as a live coal. Let it burn the essence of sin with its flame of love for our Lord. And let the Most High bless five million lit candles at the coming forum of Nightingale Mountain.

447 My child, not more than ten years will pass before millions are attracted to this place.

448 No, no, I do not mean paraffin or wax candles, or the reading of the 'Ave Maria' of Lourdes under the tedious leadership of the priests with wretched banners. What I have in mind are the blessed disciples of Christ and the knights of the Grail. My child, the brides of the Divinity shall reach this place. I invite all My true disciples: holy fools, lepers, the sick and the lonely. I shall gather them from different places and invite them to My home, saying: here is the place of your rest.

449 My child, while dying I whispered these words to the apostles. Tears were streaming from My eyes. I saw the sorrows which laid ahead of them. 'Here is My home.' I repeat these words to the new apos-

tles of the Bridal Chamber and everlasting virginity, to Christ's apostles who unite in marriage with all creation.

450 In My first revelation in Ephesus I promised not to leave the world till the end of the age. I promise to come here and talk to My children, to give them the grace of the presence of the chambers of the Most High, until I see that the gathering is complete, that the Divinity's people have been taken to the destiny and are called to the Ark.

451 And then I shall say: it is enough, My child. And after a short dream, blissful to the enlightened mind, Nightingale Mountain will become the centre of the new divine Universe. And five million of my disciples with lit hearts shall spread the sweetest fragrance of the Kingdom, the savouring of which makes them earthly heaven-dwellers.

The place of My Assumption will be glorified and become the centre of the new Universe

452 Oh, My child, what deserts I overcame here! What solitude! Cold whirlwinds swept down upon Me and carried Me into endless abysses. The devil beat Me dozens of times and threw Me against the earth.

⁴⁵³ Oh, My child, how I suffered when none of the Lord's beloved disciples could visit Me in My shelter on Nightingale Mountain! My love for Him was growing and I knew that the moment would come when Nightingale Mountain and the place of My Assumption would be glorified and become the centre of the new Universe. I called it the new Jerusalem as a sign of future fulfilments.

⁴⁵⁴ And how happy I am, My child, because today you are as two lambs grazing on the pastures of Nightingale Mountain. And I am talking to you from its heights about that which I wanted to convey to the disciples in His earthly days!

⁴⁵⁵ My desert has become a garden of paradise with sweet flowers.

⁴⁵⁶ During My earthly days I asked the Lord's disciples not to visit me. I was followed. The Most High guarded Me in His special way, but I feared for His disciples.

⁴⁵⁷ Fifteen years I spent in divine seclusion, partaking from His chalice, being nourished by Him. From here, from Nightingale Mountain, I distributed the seals of the seclusions of the holy fathers. From here I bless you with seals of spiritual solitude.

⁴⁵⁸ Let your inner being be secluded forever, and the treasury of the Kingdom be sealed within it. And

may the Divinity bless you, descendants of the Assumption and Nightingale Mountain! May the Divinity bless you as the fathers of humanity of the new Heaven and the new Earth.

459 What is the New Heaven that I have explained to you today? It is Christ undistorted by institutional cannibals. The New Earth, My child, is that which can receive the New Heaven as its groom. It is the new composition of the man prepared for marriage bonds with the Most High, the Earth devoid of sin.

460 I, the Purest Virgin, am the new Earth.

461 Let the revelation of the Most High be fulfilled in all the worlds! May peace be with all of you for the glory of the Most Blessed and His sons and daughters of the Bridal Chamber, for the glory of all the saints that I have gathered to announce the coming Theocivilization. Let there be abundant myrrhic oils, spreading from them in the aromas and fragrances of the Kingdom.

462 Peace be with you.

۞

Osman-bey, the police captain who guards Nightingale Mountain of the Purest Virgin's Assumption dictated to us a phrase in Turkish: 'My Father and I have come and will be staying here for some time.'

– Say this and I shall answer: 'tamam tashekyun ver-im'[16].

How would it be if Christians owned this property? We would have to ask for the permission of the local inquisitors. The bishop would ponder, in the dark, sniff with suspicion and come up with a cunning denial such as: "I personally don't mind, but it is forbidden. That is how it is. And if you act against the rules we'll make a call and report you, and check your reputation with the Moscow patriarchate (our secret friends). No matter how long our battle will last, we belong to one spirit, with mutual love."

I call this virginity new and unprecedented, having never before existed on Earth

463 Humanity has no choice.

464 My child, these messages are the last of the old epoch, and the first of the new.

The jubilation began in Heaven. 'The Purest Virgin has revealed the Bridal Chamber to the world; the Earth is saved! The Ark is open. Enter it!' I listen to the voices of angels indicating the path to the mysterious Ark with their scepters, the path through the Heart of Our Lady, through Her Ever Blessed Bosom – virginity.

465 My child, the old Church thought it was pleasing to the Divinity and, using words, taught how to

---

16 "Well, thank you very much" (Turkish).

please the Most High. The only way acceptable to Our Most High and to reigning Sophia, My child, is virginity.

466 He loves virginity more than anything else. His commandment to the Seraphites is: blessed are the loving ones. The loving ones are pure of heart, with virginal minds, blessed flesh, and immaculate white vestments. My child, the Most High triumphs at the sight of a former lustful goat converted into a virgin.

467 The Jews needed the law only because their forefathers had broken the vow of everlasting virginity. Virgins need no law because sin disappeared by itself.

468 My child, the virginity that I am teaching you is a new seal, until now unheard-of. Do not waste your efforts trying to define it within the limits of Catholic celibacy, Orthodox monasticism, and so on. These old seals will only make you scrape poisonous rust and dust off stone monuments.

469 Many of you have already taken vows of virginity. But only a few can understand the mystery of virginity and follow its pattern, revealed by Me. My child, from here, from the height of Nightingale Mountain, I, the Everlasting Virgin Mother, am giv-

ing you the seals of eternal virginity, virginity like that of your Purest Lady, virginity that shapes you as the brides of the Most High.

470 I call this virginity 'new and unprecedented, having never before existed on Earth'.

471 I, the Most Divine Virgin, am eager to bestow these new vows of virginity upon you today, just as I first revealed Myself to Israel. But the rabbis did not know what to do with Me; there was nothing in their law about young maidens taking a vow of eternal virginity, My child. My vow of eternal virginity, taken for the immaculate birth of the Son of the Divinity, was as strange to the Christians as it was to the Jews.

472 I would like my disciples to learn the new spiritual statutes. I want them not to feel guilty about the lack of repentance or the absence of prayers. My child, virginity is the gift of Our Most High. Be grateful for it!

473 Virginity has led you beyond the borders of the sacramental confession and penitence so familiar to all hopeless sinners sunk up to their ears in the whirlpool of worldly cares. Virginity has determined your destiny with the Purest Lady.

474 I am your Mother, and I see My children better than they see themselves. I know how to lead

them to eternal bliss. Therefore rejoice, My child, resting in My arms as a new and solar Infant Divinity. Rejoice and have no fear. You, the bride of the Bridal Feast, have only one task: to maintain the vow of eternal virginity. It is bad when the vow is broken. I feel deep sorrow, My child, and inoculate the sick lamb with My immaculate essence, so that next time he will more strongly resist the devil and establish the city of the Divinity in his inner being-with seals of virginity, the cross, and eternal life.

∶—

475 O, My child, I will be heard! I am full of joy. I will remove the plugs from the ears of humanity. I will make them look upwards. They will hear, My child!

476 When the air is clear and the hypnosis of the Roman whore has passed, they will call Me: 'Where are You, Our Queen? And where is the Your priesthood?'

477 They will follow Me, My child.

478 All of Nightingale Mountain, all the Ten Mountains will be surrounded by a host of pilgrims, with candles lit in their hearts. And in this exalted state I shall raise them to the Bridal Chamber.

479 Hallelujah, My child! What a meeting! What an Ark and what joy, My son!

[480] My child, appreciate the treasury revealed by Me. Never before have the royal jewels been so generously scattered and spread. All the riches of the world are worthless compared to the mystery of . Theogamy. The millions of cursed mammon* cannot buy destiny determined by Me.

[481] Treasure the spiritual seals. Always give preference to the spiritual over the worldly, and while on Earth seek nothing but the fulfilment of the plans of the Most High, which today are: the Ark of Virginity, the transformation of the inner man into the Seraphite, and the acceptance of the new revelation of Nightingale Mountain and the Kingdom descending.

[482] I say this ahead of time, My child. And I promise to make those who hear My most blessed words the inhabitants of the new epoch.

:⸺

Oh, the glorious Word, the most heavenly Word! What a feast of the Divinity! So hot is the wine of the Messiah! Drink more of it, incessantly, oh!

The Queen bestows Her bliss upon the virgins. The prayer must be blessed – more than the penitential 'forgive-me-lord'. It is only the old tabernacle that prevents us from experiencing the bliss.

> *Not a single living being, not a single angel*
> *of the celestial hierarchy, has ever*
> *experienced such heavenly joy*

[483] The Mountain of Divinization is one of the one hundred and fifty mysterious names of Nightingale Mountain, My child. The fifteen mysteries of Nightingale Mountain Rosary represent the fifteen years of My residence here.

[484] The joy of the return of the heavenly pastures gave way to never-ending weaknesses and deserts. For weeks I lay, struck down by My enemy's arrows, nailed to the ground, exhausted. But the weaknesses were followed by the sweetest bliss.

[485] Oh, My child! Our Saviour taught us about evangelic bliss. But what He gave to Me here, on the mountain of My Assumption and Ascension, far exceeds the sermon in which He blesses the poor in spirit and those who mourn, and everything that later became a part of the liturgy ('Blessed are…').

[486] My child, in My bliss I was exalted to the heavenly world. This was the bliss of the divinized. The Saviour taught them in the days of his sermons, in the transformed body. No one was able to understand and follow them. He gave them to Me.

[487] Streams of grace crossed My heart. Angels served Me.

[488] What beauties I was honoured with on Earth, My child! Not a single living being, not a single angel of the celestial hierarchy, has ever experienced such heavenly bliss. My heart was filled with the ineffable sweetness and bliss of residence in the Chambers of the Most High. I descended to Earth in order to ascend to the Chambers, exceeding the thrones of the Seraphs, Cherubims, and the highest angels surrounding our Heavenly Father.

The bliss of the divinized ones

[489] It is this new bliss of the divinized beings that I am teaching today from the throne of Nightingale Mountain.

[490] Seek this bliss, knock on the door of this bliss. My child, all fights, attacks and evil thoughts are inflicted upon My disciples so that they can, in their zealous efforts, regain blissful peace and new blessings: the everlasting Paradise of divinized creation, the bliss of the fragrances of the Kingdom, and myrrhic oils. The blessings of the exaltation to the heavenly world, where the entire inner being is filled with the fragrances of flowers from the heavenly gardens.

[491] The Saviour bestowed the blessings of the Kingdom upon His disciples on the Earth. On His behalf I am today bestowing blessings upon those

who are being divinized and upon those that have been divinized already.

[492] Remember, My child, how fervently the sweetest St. Mother Euphrosynia* taught the accumulation of the Holy Spirit*. Be filled with the bliss of the Holy Spirit and teach the indescribable, ineffable, incomprehensible blessings of divinized virgins. Seek them, My child. Seek them in the new prayers given to you, and in conceptual patterns.

[493] The Solovki and the Fiery Hierarchy, the Grail and the castles of the Most High, are for the true disciples of His kin and His spirit. May the thrones of the Creative Virginity, the revelations of the Sacramental Church, My anointing scrolls, the sweetest Word of the Most High, and the two Olive Trees of His Supreme Wisdom fill your heart with the fragrances of these new blessings. I give them to you to bring you a joy that has never before existed on Earth. Let it be property of My new disciples. Those who have once partaken of it will be converted and will never to turn away from the most heavenly joy that they have experienced.

[494] Oh, My blessings! They are like the lyre of David, like the music of the Psalms. Oh, My blessings amidst the songs of the birds of paradise! Oh, My blessings in the heavenly gardens.

^{495} I am bestowing upon you the sweetest bliss for the brides.

^{496} My bliss is concealed. It is inexpressible, My child. Seclude yourself in your inner being, and ask the Mother of Bliss for the ineffable joys of the brides of Christ.

^{497} My child, My ears are delighted when My wonderful disciples create the prayers of bliss at Saturday and Sunday liturgies. They are filled with the Holy Spirit and receive advice from Supreme Wisdom and Her angels. But, My child, the blessing for the divinized ones exceeds all those that have been revealed to you and experienced by you before. This is the bliss of the future age.

^{498} There are no images to describe them. They are inexpressible in meagre human speech. Today I am anointing My disciples with the seals of the ineffable blessings of the divinized ones. They can be passed from heart to heart, through the vibrations and anointments of the Triumphant Church and its wreaths for those who are led from on high and who undergo the Holy Passion.

^{499} My child, from this time onwards seek the bliss of Christ's divinized ones, and they will bring you to the Paradise of Nightingale Mountain from wherever you are, whether you are hiding in some secluded place, or sitting in the dentist's chair or the cabin of a ship.

⁵⁰⁰ Oh, My bliss is the wine of Christ's feast allotted by Me! Drink more and more! Be blissful, my beloved ones, amid pastures of heaven and groves of nightingales. Be blissful, you who have ascended here. Be blissful in anticipation of the Bridal Chamber. Be blissful under the protection of Your Mother. Be blissful under the protection of the Most High's vast tabernacle. Be blissful, grafted from the tree of Immaculacy, embraced by the Groom. Be blissful, His beloved ones!

※

⁵⁰¹ My child, it is a cross for Me to resort to words. This is the mountain of sacred silence.

⁵⁰² The bliss that I am teaching you is beyond this world. It is revealed in deep respiratory prayer, in contemplative spiritual visions, and in a peaceful heart. Nothing worldly shall trouble you, My child. Here, on My royal mountain, you rest with your Mother. Come here as often as you can and walk with Me through these pine groves and gardens of paradise. My child, I am watching you from the heights of this mountain and pouring the fragrances of the heavenly gardens into your heart.

⁵⁰³ Peace be with you.

I feel heavenly bliss and the most fragrant peace.

The Queen says to me:

[504] The peace that you have experienced comes from on high, from My heavenly throne, with the fulfilment of My words. I am giving you My peace. It is the peace of My bliss to My disciples, the blissful peace.

:—

I invite you from My heavenly heights to take the vows of your Mother Supreme Wisdom

The Queen appeals to the true disciples of Christ:

[505] My children, the time has come to reveal yourselves to the Divinity and to the truth. Shake off the dust of old attachments. Look upwards and see your Mother spread over the world.

[506] Let My endless love lead you to the Kingdom by means of secret statues revealed by Me to My priests. Let the inexpressible peace and fragrance of heavenly chambers be in your hearts.

[507] My presence is growing. Today I am coming to reveal the Most High's grand plans for the third millennium. And they will be realized with the unconditional triumph of the Divinity. But to obtain peace in appalling desolation and endless sorrow we need Supreme Wisdom with the new seals. And

I invite you from My heavenly heights to take the vows of your Mother Supreme Wisdom, who two thousand years ago sent to this world Christ, the Beloved Son of the Divinity, and His Mother Mary, today opening Abraham's Bosom to all the true sons of Earth.

[508] I am unrolling new evangelic scrolls before you. Read them and partake of their myrrhic fragrances. Let the bliss of the Kingdom enter you, and the love of My motherly heart lead you to the embrace of the true Church and give you most restful peace, with the saints living among you.

∴

[509] Rest here, My child, rest. My peace from the heights of the new Heaven be with you. My peace.

∴

[510] I dwell here. 'Where do you reside, Our Lord?' 'Come and see.'

[511] I dwell here. I promised His disciples in Ephesus never to leave them. My words meant: Assumption mountain of My ascension remains My home, My child.

[512] For two thousand years it has been guarded, and today I proclaim it as My capital city. I dwell here. From here I spread My patronage, My royal tents. I invite My disciples here. From here I rule

the world. Here I proclaim the tabernacle of the Commander-in-chief, against Tibet and the New Age. From here I shall defeat the Roman Whore and her seven seals. The Vatican and the Byzantine villain shall be defeated by the Blessed to the fanfare of trumpets. Never again shall the fiend prey upon people. The clouds of the Kingdom will lie over the new Earth.

[513] Here is the Ark, My child, here is My Ark.

[514] On these wonderful pastures I will graze My lambs, which are gathering today from the most distant countries. Here they will find the most restful peace. Here they will find the long-awaited and desired bosom of their Mother. Here will be fulfilled all the divine akathistos names given by Me: the Queen of All, the Most Blessed, the Guide to Paradise, the Milk Nourisher, the Mother Glorified.

[515] Here I promise rapturous bliss to those who love Me. Here they will find peace in this world. The cross and the Holy Passion? Here is peace and consolation. Amid the temptations and blows of your neighbours? Here you will find healing and eternal bliss. They will ascend to the heights of the Kingdom by the steps of Nightingale Mountain and hear the voice of the Divinity.

[516] May the Divinity bless you with the blessings

of His home. The hour will come when I will clad
the Seraphites in My vestments. Peace be with you.

I ask the Queen to pour bliss and delight into all my
disciples and She gives generously. She also gives me
a vial of oils. I kiss Her hands. I prostrate myself before
Her. I feel peaceful before Her.

O, My Holy Lady,
Supreme Wisdom of the Divinity!
Nightingale Mountain, o!
Bliss multiplied.

I am consecrated into the heavenly world. It is inexpressible. I am bereft of the power of speech.

Peace, peace, peace is coming from the heights of
the Kingdom of the Most High.

:——

Selcuk. Passers-by with shopping bags, nice coach-
es with tourists…

So much Solovki myrrh has been poured out today
by the Queen!

We are returning from the Kingdom. How strange
the world seems after Nightingale Mountain! A camou-
flaged military man, holding a paper folder in his left
hand, marches quickly along the street. A young man
in a orange sports T-shirt, jogging. Cars, bustling in
their own worlds somewhere …

How distant earthly life is from the bliss! Tourists
are given helpful information about the ruins of an-

cient Ephesus, listening to tales of some medieval conquering pirates: how authority was passed from one to another, from Byzantine kings to sultans, from the Caesars to the Jews... But try suggesting a pilgrimage to the place of revelation of the Purest Virgin! They would bare their teeth at you. It is incomprehensible for this business.

... it scorches the heart.

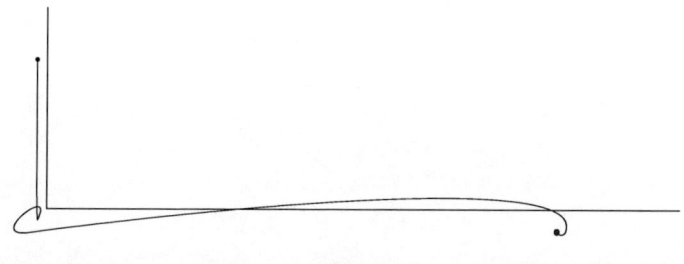

THE MOTHER OF THE NEW CHURCH

Izmir, 1 May 2005

The Mother of God:

517 The struggle for the new Church has begun.

518 There are hard battles to fight, but Melchizedek is invincible. Our enemies the Pharisees do not know against whom they are fighting.

:—

519 The sweetest silence. For weeks the Queen dwelt amidst the silent music of the Kingdom, blessing the world as the Tabernacle of the Lord. She personally experienced the New Tabernacle, the Temple.

520 Just as the Divinity chose Her ever-virgin bosom for the embodiment, He chose Her myrrh-shedding Heart for His home. And the Divinity filled Her and conjoined with Her in heavenly Theogamy.

:—

521 Two doctrines were developed by the old church: that of the Godman and that of the Everlasting Virgin. But the Melchizedeks teach about the Godgroom and Godbride.

:⸺

522 All that Christ wanted to create for His Church He gave to the Heart of the Purest Virgin as a precious stone of the Heavenly Grail. Alas! The old church could not comprehend this highest mystery.

523 Here, on Nightingale Mountain, the Divinity created His Church as a new greater 'tabernacle not made by human hands'. And now the Purest Virgin wishes to bestow this treasure of the Church of Christ, inserted within Her, upon the new Seraphic mankind.

:⸺

524 My child, now I want to talk to you about things which I have never said before.

525 For forty days the Divinity appeared in His transformed spiritual body. He talked to His disciples frequently. But I remained feeble and seldom saw Him.

526 The most difficult thing for Me was the period between Jerusalem and Ephesus... My child, the Saviour would come to Me at Nightingale

Mountain in His transformed body, and I would walk with Him along heavenly pastures. My child, how wonderful He was! Like the Infant Divinity, the absolutely perfect Adolescent, godlike Man, the sweetest Lamb. The absolutely perfect Godman, the Messiah on the cross, worthy of His mission, the embodied Divinity.

527 How wonderful He was while talking to Me! During our sweetest dialogues He told Me many of His secrets. He disclosed to Me things He could not have revealed to His disciples. He confided to Me the mysteries of the future age.

528 But the Saviour of Nightingale Mountain was even more wonderful and perfect, My child. Through sufferings I was being prepared for even greater bliss, for the sweetest feast found neither on Earth nor in Heaven. Yes, My child! Even in the heavenly worlds I did not find such sweetness as in the days of His descent. For a long time, My child, we walked along the slopes of Nightingale Mountain, and the Saviour's speech flowed in an endless stream of grace and heavenly wisdom. I continued to enter His words into My heart. It seemed that I heard more than He had told Me. Hearing Him from eternity, My ears were delighted by His divine voice. I was exalted to super-celestial spheres.

[529] What did He talk about, My child? The Saviour showed Me the man as created by the Most High. The white, waxen, mystical heart is the inner altar, within which is His sealed sweetest image, and the gates of paradise leading to the heart's secret of secrets and to the inner man*.

[530] My child, the Saviour explained to Me how the Divinity designed man. The devil distorted the perfection of the Most High's angelic creation, which had been intended to replace the fallen angels, and many Church fathers knew this. But, My child, man was destined to be particularly close to the Divinity, different from the angels, heavenly birds, or any other creation surrounding His throne, not to mention the fallen man.

[531] The Saviour brought to Earth the mysterious assignment of the new Adam – Theogamy as a sacred treasure – and gave it to Me.

[532] It seemed as if the Saviour was reshaping Me. As I understood, He was sculpting a new person in Me: divinized, and destined for an unknown mysterious relationship with the Most High. The Most High wished to make man His abode, to dwell within him. To unite with him in mysterious bonds, to give him an extraordinary treasure never possessed by any of the angels.

[533] My child, absorb what I have told you. Man's destiny in the Divinity's plans is higher than the most perfect angelic hierarchies. Imagine their divine ranks, their purest hearts, their heavenly nobility, and the shining Divinity that they spread. Man has been summoned for greater things, My child!

[534] The garments of the old humanity have been worn out. The Jew, the Christian, the Hellene, the philosopher, the Muslim... they are now useless, My child. Adam's deep, oppressive sleep has caused Our grief. The Most High is determined to remake man according to His initial plans.

[535] That is what the Seraphite will become, My child. Tell My blessed adolescents, who have taken the vows of virginity and are fully consecrated to Me, that Our Father and the Purest Lady will remake man through them.

[536] Paul's 'new creation in Christ' has not been realized on Earth due to the guilt of the church. It has been fulfilled here, My child.

:_

[537] Do you know what struck Me most? In My earthly days, while I listened to His sweetest discussions, I became accustomed to hearing the voice of the Lord from Heaven. My child, coming to Nightingale Mountain the Lamb of the Divinity, sacri-

ficed for the sins of the world, spoke to Me from the most divine sphere. He revealed to Me the mysteries sealed even for Seraphs, Cherubims, and other celestial ranks. I collected them in My heart and carried them as if they were an infant, to be born and given to you as the heritage of the humanity of the future age.

538 The second millennium of Christianity has come to an end. The third is dedicated to the Seraphites. I am giving them the treasury gifted by Christ of Nightingale Mountain. The heavenly Lamb twice transformed, twice descended from the Heaven, the Divinity of the Seraphites of future ages is giving you this untold wealth and the greatest of miracles. Keep it, My child. And if you keep and multiply My gift, the Kingdom of the Divinity will come into the world, and the Heavenly City will descend to the Seraphites.

Today I am bringing the world neither revelations nor messages, but a new Heaven and divine spheres for the people of the third millennium.

539 My child, the Saviour initiated Me into the secrets of His triumph over Our enemy – the devil, the ancient snake, the red dragon (he has more than a thousand other names). .

540 My child, remember what I am saying: T h e

Godman has absolute power over the devil. His name is magically invoked by exorcists, occultists and thousands of others. But, My child, the irrefutable power of the Divinity comes from the heights of the Mountain of the Transfiguration. Here is the new Tabor, My child. It was necessary to hear about His authority over the cunning one from His own lips in order to perceive the surpassing strength of His divine wit, His divine scepter, and His divine power.

[541] My child, the devil truly lost his power after the Lord had atoned for man's sins and man had been clothed in godlike vestments. But, having fallen into spiritual lechery, and having followed the temptations of this world, the church came under the power of Caesar and lost the Lord as we saw Him in our eyes.

[542] Oh come, come into the tent of the most divine sphere, from which I am speaking! And promise Me never to leave Nightingale Mountain, for here the Divine Son has absolute power over fallen angels, snakes, tarantulas, pigs, wolves in sheep's clothing, foxes, wild dogs, ghosts from dead planets, and space aliens. It does not matter what image they take. His power over all these hordes of enemies is absolute.

⁵⁴³ My child, on the day of His arrival there were legions of our enemies. I guessed that the Saviour was close; not from some secret signs, but from intensified struggles. The enemy literally trod on Me, pinned Me down. But, My child, as soon as the Saviour appeared the enemy hordes dispersed and retreated immediately.

⁵⁴⁴ The Saviour revealed to Me the details of His divine reasoning of His fight with Lucifer. I was delighted, My child! The church traditionally indicates Christ's victory over the devil on Golgotha and the subsequent Resurrection. My child, the power of the Saviour cannot be described. An infinite number of heavenly ranks surround Him.

⁵⁴⁵ Our Saviour possesses thousands of keys with which to entrap the devil and prohibit him from setting his foot on Earth ever again.

⁵⁴⁶ I hasten, My child, to share with you that which I have not revealed to anyone else, although you have already been told so much. For example, what power the Fiery Hierarchy of the Second Golgotha of Solovki had over the enemy; or the sweetest Chalice of the Grail, giving the hot wine of heavenly feasts; or the vows of eternal virginity. Only these three spheres possess absolute power

over the cunning one, without needing the shield, prayers of expulsion, or other means of the rattling chatters of the Pharisees.

:⸒—

[547] My child, I hasten to share with you unspeakable joys.

[548] What a contrast, My son! Barely an hour ago the evil one was strangling Me, threatening, pressing a knife against My throat, beating Me to death, and stunning my ears. And then I arose a rapturous Virgin and flew with the Lord in My spiritual body, contemplating His power over His enemies. It is beyond all words.

[549] My child, as you continue to visit My paradisiacal abode (the Queen means Nightingale Mountain) I will gradually reveal many secrets disclosed to Me by the Son of the Most High. These treasures from super-celestial spheres are intended for the people of the future epoch, the Seraphites. I shall say the following: Do not wait for 'the end of times', 'disasters', or arks. Do not assign much importance to apocalyptic signs and eschatological predictions. Nothing can prevent you, the Seraphites, eternally born by Me in immortal bodies and myrrhic compositions, from confessing that you are Seraphic lambs, Seraphites, and Godlike.

550 As the Christians rejected Adam's sinful heritage you must, My wonderful children, reject the sinful heritage of Judaism and Christianity which led Adam's race to its final decay. Profess yourselves the people of the future age; live in My cities. I promise now: nothing can prevent your triumph. The Leader of the angelic forces who has not faced a single defeat since the creation of the world is behind you.

551 You are My angelic forces, and the more difficult the battle, the stronger our enemy; the more glorious the victory, the more beautiful our wreath.

552 Oh, what perfect rewards and unexpected joys are given to those who, following My words, receive the myrrh-pouring compositions, bright images, and virginal attire; who resolutely fight against the rulers of darkness, the spirits of lust, mammon, the Ben-Elohims, and the lowest cosmism*. The servants of Satan are too numerous, and each is masked in its own way. But My child, the penetrating eye of Supreme Wisdom sees their disgusting games and devilish mimicry.

553 Profess yourselves as solar Seraphites in immortal attire, the heirs of the Second Golgotha of the Solovki, the children of Nightingale Mountain, the worshippers of Your Queen's Theogamic throne,

the disciples of Christ the Holy Spirit, ascending to the Theogamic Bed, divinized, veiled in the virginity, power and wisdom of your Heavenly Lady. Let peace be in your hearts!

554 I promise you more than My presence (which I have already promised to My earthly disciples). I promise to unite with you, to become miraculously one with you, to enter the mysterious interior so deeply that each of you will say: 'The Queen is closer to me than I am myself!' And each of you will say: 'I am more than I am. The Divinity is within me.'

555 My child, I am more than your Mother. I am the Eternally-Bearing Mother. I am giving birth to you spiritually, which means that you are forever coming out of My bosom, and I hold you in My arms like a newborn child. And, as the mother who has just given birth is one with the child long in her womb, so I am one with My bright children, newly born from on high.

556 My child, The Divinity promised to be unprecedentedly, inconceivably close to the new disciples and apostles of the Theocivilization. I promise it.

> The Queen asks us to reject the old Christian seals, particularly the evil inquisitional patterns, and to follow Hers.

557 During My divine appearances I clothe you in new garments and give you divine reason. Do not forget this. Nourish yourself from the most heavenly sources. Be a perfect example for your disciples, so that they act like you.

558 Continue to ask yourself: 'Am I following the pattern of the Purest Lady? How would the Heavenly Mother behave in these circumstances?' Being born from on high, you must not act according to your personal judgement. Your whole essence is consecrated to Me. You have to let Me act through you.

559 The Lord, My Son, loved Me because I was fully consecrated to Him, prostrating Myself before Him. When He came I did not exist. I let Him enter Me, and He lived and rested within Me.

560 'To clothe yourself in the vestments of the Godbearer' (about which I often ask) means to lose your sinful personality and allow the Purest Mother to make your interior Her abode and Her home.

∶⸺

561 My child, as the Mother I can see the grief concerning the unhappy state of the world in millions of Christian hearts. To enumerate all the abominations and disgusting deeds of the cunning one

would take hours and hours. In consolation to the world, My child, I say: Supreme Wisdom knows how to convert souls caught in the devil's net, souls struggling in his hawkish claws, to the throne of Our Most High.

[562] ...A predatory eagle saw a tortoise crawling upon a rock. In an instant he swooped down and grabbed it, soaring up into the sky and preparing to dash it against the rock and devour the flesh within its broken carapace. Suddenly Supreme Wisdom dawned upon him, and the eagle peacefully returned the unharmed tortoise to its former place.

[563] Look more deeply into the essence of things. Gain insight into *further,* exceedingly divine perspectives.

[564] The heavier and deeper their sinful chalice, the greater the number of Mary Magdalenes, spendthrift Matthews and thieving Dismases that are born in this unhappy world, full of infernal shadows and devilish delusions, the sooner they will be converted. Today the power of your Lady Supreme Wisdom is greater than ever before. Remember this and do not exceed My words, My child.

[565] The world will be converted. How? You will see. I will tell you nothing about it, so that the enemy does not hear.

566 Be grateful to Supreme Wisdom, My child, for witnessing the terrible condition of the world, the dissolution of morals, the power of the devil, the satanic sects and cults, the Pharisaic desolation in churches, the inquisitorial clans in the Roman hierarchy, and the malicious collusions among Byzantine bigots. Only by thanking Her will She prepare to invite a never-ending multitude of the fallen, the sick and the lame to the Great Bridal Feast.

567 And let peace rest in your hearts!

:⎯

568 My dear child, I would not like there to be bewilderment amongst those Christian souls who love me.

569 Their crisis has been caused by the collapse of the hierarchy. The sins of the priests are innumerable. The Most High has abandoned them. Rome and the clergy are under My aegis no longer. I have created a n e w C h u r c h. Only the diabolical hypnosis of the Babylonian whore, spread throughout the millennia, holds My disciples in slavish nets. They must shake off the dust and be courageous enough to find priests capable of leading them to the Kingdom of Heaven with the scepter of transfiguration, birth from on high, metanoia*, sincere repentance, true love and belief.

[570] May Christ's disciples and Christians all around the world receive the treasure given by Me from Heaven and read the fragrant myrrhic scrolls in thousands of worlds! What more can I do for them?!

[571] The hypnosis has no power over them any more. The Destroying Angels will do everything to release hearts destined for the ascent to the Most High from the Roman hypnosis and Byzantine opium.

[572] The new Church, My dear child, is not only your sons and daughters, the priests of Melchizedek, but also all the righteous pastors who have been sheltered under My aegis. There are great many of them, My child! The Archbishop and martyr Melingo, Father Dino of Italy, Mother Mary-Rose of the Dominican convent in Detroit, Mother Catharine, and mother Angelica.

[573] Oh, My child, when I look at the Church and perceive mysterious things I see a multitude of people prepared for the Bridal Feast. They need only unite. And today, from the height of Nightingale Mountain, I call upon all genuine disciples of Christ to unite. They will be more than you can imagine. Under the pressure of the fears and hypnoses of the Roman whore they have been scattered

across the world and feel as Christ's disciples did after the Crucifixion.

[574] Rome has fallen. Let no righteous Roman Catholic experience any illusions.

[575] Christ lives! And Nightingale Mountain breathes, and My voice sounds in all the worlds, My child. My Voice, like a cloud of Glory, embraces the hearer.

[576] The Church needs the treasury and grace, the opened gates to the Kingdom and the staircase spread with angels. I have done all that I could, and the new Church has been born. Soon it will be glorified all over the world. There is nothing hindering you, My children, from finding true pastors and awaking up from the deep sleep caused by vampires and liars (I am talking to the Christians of true spirit, those who seek to enter the gates of Christ's Kingdom).

> O! How riveting is the new Gospel! Fragrant news shrouded in the cloud of the Holy Spirit descends from Nightingale Mountain, coming down over the transformed solar sea. And only indescribable raptures remain:
>
> O! O! O! Christ's felicity. Ineffable bliss, ineffable bliss.

O! The indescribable bliss
of Nightingale Mountain,
the priceless gifts of Theocivilization III!

I am filled with bliss. I cannot endure the solar transformation and rapture. My soul is saturated, filled beyond measure, enraptured.

⁛

The Mother of God:

⁵⁷⁷ My child, I am carrying my solar Grail through the air to My children in Greece, Israel, Europe, South America, Asia Minor, and Africa. The sun of the Grail's sea descends to the world. The Theocivilization is being created, My child. Solar Cherubims surround the altar of Nightingale Mountain! Carry the Grail across the new solar sea to the shores of Greece, which granted Me shelter in My earthy days!

⁵⁷⁸ Peace be with the new humanity of the New Heaven and the New Earth!

⁵⁷⁹ I am giving you My peace from the heights of Nightingale Mountain, and endless grace from spheres higher than Heaven. Cover yourself with grace. Partake from the chalice of solar bliss and from the indescribable feasts. Let your hearts be filled with the joy of hallelujah!

580 Peace be with you, people of the new humanity! Peace be with you, you who are being transformed. Peace be with you, you who bear the burden of the cross. Peace be with you, you who shine brightly. Peace be with you, crowned victors. Peace be with you, you who are awakening from deep sleep. Peace be with you, you who speak and foretell in the Holy Spirit. Peace be with you, priests of Melchizedek dressed in solar garments. Peace be with you, teachers of the Grail and of the nourishment from the Kingdom on high.

581 Peace be with you, wonderful people of the Earth. Christ is sealed within you. The image of the Most High is revealed within you now and forever.

582 Peace be with you, all creation. Peace be with you, fish of the sea and the Marine Kingdom*. Peace be with you, contours of breathing mountains, bushes, plants, grass and flowers. Peace be with you, deer, goats and herds of wild animals. Peace be with you, cattlemen and shepherds.

583 Peace be with you, most blissful ones, in whom the incomparable image of the Most High has been sealed. Peace be with you, you who accept the cloud of Jerusalem descending from Heaven. Peace be with you, who imprint the sun in your interior. Peace be with those who are covered with

the never-ending blisses of the future age. Peace be with you, My chosen and anointed people. Peace be with you, My true children, the inheritors of endless wealth. Peace be with you, My disciples, and the wisdom of the divine reason. Peace be with you!

584 Enjoy the myrrhic scrolls that I am spreading. You will read in them the scriptures of the future age, names of each of you written in reverse.

⁚—

Oh! My heart, it seems it will tear apart… My heart is able to accept the Sun. My heart is able to become the Divinity's abode.

What great potential, if you could only realize what the spiritual heart is. To make it your inner capital city, your New Jerusalem. To extinguish all the other sources that hinder the opening of the heart and the heavenly gates: the abdominal furnace, lust, evil thoughts, rationality, etc.

Her heart was burning. Every day Her heart was torn into three thousand pieces, receiving new patterns, imprinting them within itself like a fiery tablet. And ever more Her heart summoned Him in the unutterable blisses given by Her today.

What I felt here was the very bliss of the Virgin Mary of two thousand years ago, given today as an inheritance, above words or epistles – through vibrations, seals, gifts and images.

The treasury

585 My child, I present you with the Treasury of Nightingale Mountain. Take it as a priest of the coming age. It contains all that the Divinity needs to realize His plans: immortal bodies and virginal garments; precious pearls, each of which is worth as much as all the riches of the world; unique patterns, destinies, fortunes, mysteries, anointments, gifts and keys. Take it from My hands, My child.

586 I have guarded it for two thousand years, awaiting the hour when I would bestow it upon a priest of the True Church, upon the heir of the Golgotha of the Solovki. I give it as a token of the many thousands of Solovki martyrs exalted to Heaven. More than one thousand of them have been taken, body and soul, to the Bridal Chamber!

587 I give this Sacred Treasury for future generations, My child.

588 The church treasury is empty. The 'holy hierarchy' is rolling in money, but they are the servants of mammon: spiritual nonentities, and destitute.

589 Here is the royal treasury, My child. I am giving it to My mere tsar, who so greatly resembles Solomon, Amos, Ezekiel, and John the Evangelist. Not to the Pope or the Orthodox Patriarch.

590 My dear child, let your every disciple be inspired by My love, the love of the Queen of Nightingale Mountain. I kiss their hearts. They are before of Me now. I see, bless, and embrace each of them. I bow to them and ask for their blessings.

591 I am embracing you, My beloved children, from eternity, with the solar vestments of Nightingale Mountain.

592 My child, the apostles did not come to Me only once in the hour of My Assumption. They gathered through the air, and many visited Me mystically, borne by the angels of the Most High. I taught them. From here I governed the whole Church of Christ, conveying images and seals.

593 Today I invite you to Nightingale Mountain in order to help you create the new apostolate, even more fiery and full of grace. And may you blessed by the Divinity of the present and future ages.

> My Divinity, how can I comprehend what I have been told in this life? Oh, what other mortal gates and temptations, secular commercial organizations, deserts of loneliness, dirty sheets in third-rate motels, and ruined mobile phones will I have to experience? And what else will I suffer in order to realize what I have heard from My Lady?
>
> My Lady! Like Montfort, I prostrate myself before You at every stone, at every wooden pole, unable to hold

back tears of gratitude and tender emotion. I kiss every image of You, never ceasing to look at You devotedly.

Centuries will pass, but the mysteries of Nightingale Mountain will be revealed even more than today. The gifts I have received will be presented to Your priests at many millions of forums.

O, Virgin Lady! O, Mother of the Theocivilization! Protect and bless humanity from the celestial heights in the fragrant air of Nightingale Mountain.

:⸺

The heavenly grace of the Queen of Light will spread throughout the world.

594 The Holy Spirit descends into your disciples. Regarding your personal sympathies, choices and preferences – trust them more yourself. Meekly obey those whose ears are open to the words of the Divinity, which are revealed through you.

595 The hand of the architect and the engineer, who planned this house to the slightest detail, was guided by Supreme Wisdom of Nightingale Mountain and the castles of the Holy Grail. The Grail gives you this precious gift from the castle of the Most High. Accept it humbly and be filled with reverence before the majesty of the descending mysteries. They surpass all miracles previously revealed to humanity.

⁵⁹⁶ Come to Me, My child. In my home you will always find peace and consolation, given to you by your Heavenly Mother, who endlessly blesses and loves you.

⁵⁹⁷ My pure child, My anointed sovereign of the Kingdom! Peace be with you, and may you have the strength to bear your heavy cross.

⁵⁹⁸ Let Our peace, the peace of Christ, the peace of your Mother Supreme Wisdom, and the seals of Nightingale Mountain always be with you as the cloud of the Most High. I bless you.

:⸱_

⁵⁹⁹ Mother Euphrosinia and St. Seraphim of Divine Tenderness used to come to Nightingale Mountain. Now they are sending you their divine blessings and endless love. The Triumphant Church longs to bring Christ's true disciples to its bosom. It is full of admiration for the coming mysteries and treasuries, which are not even being revealed to all My chosen ones in Heaven.

⁶⁰⁰ My child, today you have received My sweetest grace. Praise the Most High for that with which you have been honoured. Your heart has been changed. Today's outpouring of sunlight was possible only through the sacrament, performed by Me, of the in-

fusing of the white, waxen heart to My anointed sovereigns in the Holy Passion.

[601] My child, the White Cross is descending over the world, and the Earth is changing. It is full of the ravishment of Our Most High like your Holy Lady. It is My child.

[602] Today I am giving birth not only to the new man and the new priesthood. I am the Mother from Whom the new Heaven and the new Earth issues. May the Divinity bless you under the aegis of the Most High. May peace rest in your hearts, which means: the Heaven has descended to the Earth, and the Earth has been raised to Heaven; creation has been transformed, and there is infinite joy.

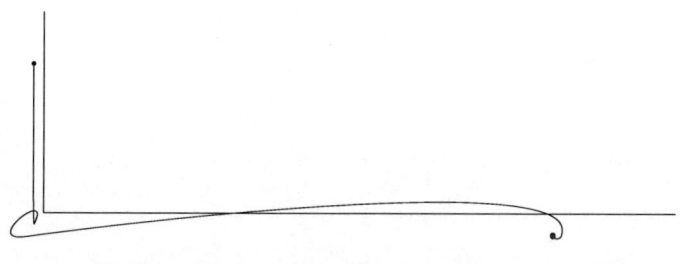

THE BLISS OF THE BRIDAL CHAMBER

Izmir, 30 April 2005

Forgive me, my Perfectly Holy Mother!
The Bride of the Holy Passion.

On daily Holy Passion I ascend the Mountain of Bliss with Father Paisiy.

'The hill of God is as the hill of Bashan; a high hill as the hill of Bashan... this is the hill which God desireth to dwell in; the Lord will dwell in it for ever' (Psalms, 68).

As it is in the Holy Passion – the suffering of prayer. It is being taken away. Which one to pray? Which one is better?

A half-paralyzed mind, inner disharmony, nerves... How can one play divine songs on a third-rate guitar?

Our Lady has led me into life-bearing fruitful Holy

Passion (which are like the sufferings of a mother before birth) and has revealed the Rosary of the Bridal Chamber of Nightingale Mountain, its five sacraments, or meditative castles:

1 The Gospel of Salvation on His Spilt Blood. The three-hour-long Grail of Surpassing Love.

2. Supreme Wisdom contemplated the Lamb on the altar of immolation, on the Throne of His Glory. She alone was honoured by Him with this Surpassing Love, poured out onto all of creation, and especially into Her heart.

3. Supreme Wisdom takes the Heavenly Queen away to the fifteen-year desert of Ephesus, to the peak of the mysterious mountain where She is protected by the Most High Himself. She is nourished by the Chalice of the Grail, and, in the divine, mystical ecstasy of the bride, experiences the repetition and multiplication of the Fiery Wedding (or 'Surpassing Love', the 'writing in blood').

4. The Gospel of Salvation on His Spilt Blood has not been composed for idle contemplation, nor even for 'writing in blood', fainting spells, or ecstasy. No! This passive order of the past only prepares humankind for the mysterious mission of Christ, sealed by Christian history because of *the malicious priests.* The Saviour wishes to prepare the Bride, so He gives Her Christ-like Holy Passion.

Our Lady has been co-crucified with Him. She is

overwhelmed with love. She cannot find a place to live. She longs for Him even more greatly than in the earthly days. The holy madness of a flaming candle. Every day She is ready to die of love for Him. And She dies. And He comes to Her. Motherly embraces are followed by the embraces of the Bridal Chamber.

5. The flame of heavenly love flares up in Her heart until She says "My heart is ready" for the second time. The first time She said this was when She was raised to Heaven here, on the Assumption Bed in Ephesus. The second "ready" means the doubled Gospel of Salvation on His Spilt Blood. This is the last sacrament known as the Bridal Chamber, the union between the Divine Beloved ones, or the wedlock of the Two Olive Trees of Supreme Wisdom. It constitutes the pinnacle of divine meditation and the last, fifth mystery of the Rosary the Bridal Chamber of Nightingale Mountain:

Rejoice, Holy Lady of the Bridal Chamber! Blessed are You by Our Divinity!

⁝

Do not abandon bliss

The Queen is speaking to me:

⁶⁰³ My child, being the anointed sovereign you should acquire those conditions worthy of My disciple, My blessed John. Do not abandon bliss. Do not give the cunning one cause to attack you. Do

not seek guilt in anyone. Do not blame anyone. The level of your consecration to the cross and to the Holy Passion is such that neither desert nor retreat can deprive you of myrrh-pouring bliss unless you make a false step yourself.

604 Seek no other shield (prayer, exorcism or liturgy) other than the bliss that you receive in the spheres of respiratory meditative prayer. Seek more and more bliss, for it has been doubled and multiplied in the Bridal Chamber.

605 Thus, My dear child, My anointed sovereigns are worthy of three things: surpassing love (given even to enemies), surpassing peace (when tempted), and Supreme Wisdom (when attacked by rational arguments or human thoughts).

606 The Holy Passion are eased in the Bridal Chamber. The stage of your consecration to the Holy Passion is over, and I have led you into the Bridal Chamber. That is why I have called you here, to the throne of the Sacred Theogamy, from faraway Moscow. From here the Wedding Bed will float after the disasters, like a white Ark of salvation – a sign of the survived humanity, of the remaining children of the Divinity.

607 Insufficient attention to bliss, given to you in plenitude with the seals, discredits the stages of

the Holy Passion through which you have already passed.

608 Blame no one, and demand nothing from others. I am asking you for only one thing: bliss. Remember what St. Seraphim said: 'Acquire peace, and thousands around you shall be saved.' I shall paraphrase the words of My beloved hermit, Seraphim Sarovsky*: 'Acquire bliss, and waves of it will spread amongst your disciples.'

609 Now, My child, you are not the only one invited to gain bliss; My endlessly loved sons and daughters around you are invited too. Look at Father Paisiy with my eyes and you will see the inexhaustible potential of bliss in this exalted and enraptured soul. Seek divine bliss not only for yourself, but for him as well.

610 Your disciples and those close to you await myrrh-anointing oils and bliss from you more than anything else. So give it all to them, My child.

611 The bliss of the Bridal Chamber cannot be expressed through external prayers or traditional liturgies.

612 My child, the devil's attacks are subtle. He does not approach you today with thoughts of lust, mammon, or worldly order. Our enemy is sly. He will confess his defeat where you have put your

shield. The enemy attacks you through old forms that you once took to be spiritual: liturgies, sermons, regular prayers, the life in the community...

[613] My dear child, you have been anointed in the Holy Passion. You are on the mountain called the Throne of the Most High. And at the same time it is the desert to which ran the Wife, Mary, clothed in the Sun of the myrrhic Gospel of Golgotha.

[614] I was absolutely alone for weeks and months. The Bridal Chamber is mysterious. There is no one else on the Bridal Bed but the Most High and His bride. My son, reach the heights of the Bridal Chamber, and trust nothing else.

[615] Led by God's mercy, I have taken away that which until recently nourished you with grace and is now an aggressive whirlpool threatening to blow you away. Wherever you are – be it in Gethsemane near Moscow or on Elion[17], during the liturgy, in the holy passion or within a cement sarcophagus* reach glorious bliss! When attacked by the evil one, always remember the untying absolution of the holy passion. A mother gives birth with sufferings, but the fruit from them is bliss.

[616] My dear child, you are gifted with special bliss

---

[17] In Gethsemane near Moscow or on Elion – there are two communities near Moscow, where the author usually spent his time there.

of a kind not even mentioned in the Gospels – the bliss of the Bridal Chamber. Take it upon yourself to become its inner apostle and victor. And let all those who have heard My Word be overwhelmed by the contemplative respiratory peace of the prayer of the Bridal Chamber and raise their minds to the heights of Nightingale Mountain, where I await them.

617 My dear child, there is no need to embark on a pilgrimage or climb Nightingale Mountain on foot, seven miles from foot to peak. My dear child, the Throne of the Most High has been erected in the devine existence. And today I am summoning My sons and daughters of the Bridal Chamber.

618 But first I tell them to repose on the contemplative prayer bed. There is no need for anything else. The cross has been sealed on your back and spine. The bloodstained Gospel of the Lamb, contemplated by Me, has been sealed within you. Recline on this cross, My dear child, as on the Bridal Bed and appease. As soon as you have invited the Holy Lady of the Bridal Chamber and have begun to pray 'Hail, Holy Lady of the Bridal Chamber, blessed by the Divinity', I am coming at once and generously anoint Christ's bride.

619 In His earthly days the Saviour preached about

wise virgins and the followers and disciples of the Old Testament did not understand. But I am preaching about the brides of Christ, about His myrrh-anointed lambs.

620 My child, measure your inner state by your peace, and do not let the devil conquer you under any pretext. He is like a whirlwind. His ferocious malice towards My anointed sovereign is obvious in cruel attacks, unbearable blows and bad thoughts. I see it, My child, but I permit as much as you can bear. If I lessen his attacks you will be unable to reach the destined level, My anointed king, My dear son, My tenderly beloved child.

621 I see your sufferings and loneliness. Your soul sobs continuously. Today you have come to Your Mother so that I may pour the Lord's surpassing love onto you. Nightingale Mountain stands in eternity, My child. I am spreading My arms to the Divinity, asking Him to pour into your heart the love you deserve for your Christ-like Holy Passion.

622 My child, why are you testing My love? My motherly love is expressed in everything that happens to you and surrounds you. I invited you, I chose you. I have given you wonderful disciples. I have arranged for all your needs. I have given you everything you desired, and much more. I keep you

away from mischief and temptations beyond your strength. I am aware of your human weaknesses and free you from any guilt. I prohibit the deeds of you enemies with one powerful stroke of My palm, and they choke on their own rage.

623 I chose you to be My vessel and named you the father of the coming Theocivilization. Of all humanity, you have been chosen to proclaim the mystical Ark of the end of times. You will lead the Seraphites up the stairs of the Bridal Chamber and take them into My fragrant residence. Millions will hear your sermons, preached today in eccentric clubs, cinemas, huts... I could recite more of My deeds, but this is enough for you to see and be aware of My love.

624 I am giving you the never-ending celestial blessing of Nightingale Mountain, My child. Today I am calling all the saints gathered around the Throne of the Most High – the Fiery Hierarchy of the Second Golgotha of the Solovki, blessed Euphrosinia and her throne, Seraphim and his twelve myrrh-pouring brothers, the Council of Orthodox and Catholic saints, and all unknown martyrs – to pour their love onto the Church of anointed disciples. May peace be in your hearts. Do not let the cunning one overcome you under any pretext, and hold

the scepter of blessing given to you as Melchizedek of the present and the future.

> I was resting in Nightingale Mountain's refuge. Glade and prayed serenely, experiencing unearthly bliss and ascending to the Chamber of Her Bridal Bed. Then She gave me the foregoing epistle.

:⎯

The Mother of God:

⁶²⁵ Oh, My child, the evil one is irritated by the bliss of the coming age revealed to you, and wants to steal it under any possible pretext. Learn the lengthy path to the bliss of Nightingale Mountain:

1) the rejection of ancestral programs*;

2) birth from on high;

3) the fearless profession of faith – to the roots of your hair, until your last breath;

4) the fiery repentance that leads to the forgiveness of sins;

5) the zealous devotion to faith;

6) pilgrimage;

7) poverty;

8) unworldliness;

9) Lamb-like humbleness, strict obedience to the Most High and being led by Him;

10) the succession of the saints;

11) the edification of myrrh-anointed disciples within the spiritual church;

12) persecutions led by secular and religious enemies;

13) consecration to virginity;

14) consecration to your Holy Lady;

15) the incessant revelation of the Holy Spirit and accumulation of divine grace by the patterns of the Lamb;

16) ascription to the Second Golgotha of the Solovki;

17) initiation into the mystery of the cross and the Holy Passion;

18) the readiness to abandon all previous achievements, no matter how precious they are or how fruitful they have been, for the sake of the divine poverty of listening in the present.

[626] My child, it was not at your conversion but your birth that I built you the ladder of bliss leading to the Bridal Chamber. The devil would like to tear you from the last step and discredit you, saying: "Look at him, My Lady, he is useless. He does not appreciate the bliss you have given him. He is ready to substitute it with any secular pleasure. He cares about everything other than Your gifts. He does not appreciate the divine wealth freely given to him. He

does not want to drink from the holy springs." Satan is always quoting from the Holy Scriptures.

[627] My dear son, I will help you. Do not waste your aspiration for My celestial bliss. It has been revealed for my myrrh-anointed disciples.

[628] May your hearts be full of divine bliss and peace. Today, My dear children, I can name you sons and daughters of the Bridal Chamber without any mysterious meaning. You have already been enlightened enough by the Holy Spirit and by Supreme Wisdom to understand Our language.

[629] The Bliss of the Bridal Chamber is precious and there is nothing higher than it. It is an invaluable treasury and royal wealth. Therefore resort to the bliss of contemplative respiratory prayer and believe that it is the pinnacle of the path to the Heavenly Kingdom revealed to you.

[630] I have mentioned some stages leading to the divine bliss of the Bridal Chamber, but there are still more than thirty of them yet to be named.

[631] Yesterday I told you that Adam fell because he misunderstood the goals of the creation of the soul, in Heaven and on Earth, from dust. And I would like to remind you that the Theogamic sphere protects the bride of the Lord. Do not lose the per-

spective of the Bridal Chamber! Strive towards it and never expect some 'abstract' or 'approaching' Bridal Bed. Be guided by the inspiration of the Holy Spirit, and begin contemplative respiratory prayer:

632 'O, sweetest myrrh-pouring bliss! Peace and prosperity' or 'O, the Holy Lady of the Bridal Chamber! Blessed are You in the Divinity!'

633 You are infinitely precious to Me as seekers. The world has become too negligent to long for the Most High. The Psalter is full ofze the seekers.

634 You are infinitely precious to Me for your dissatisfaction with what you have achieved. I forgive your little failures and feel no resentment.

635 From the peak of Nightingale Mountain I would like to invite all Christians to become seekers of Christ, as is forbidden by the malicious Pharisees. They say that He is 'obvious' and 'plain'. And they present Him as a wooden idol, thus provoking the search for prohibited satanic secrets, 'the depths of Satan' (as they were called in Paul's epistles).

636 My child, there is nothing more mysterious than the Lord, or more beautiful. But to find Him you need to make an effort and take His path. Look for teachers of the true way (I am talking to Christians now). Look for those who know how to gain

bliss and the Bridal Bed, who know how to be one with the Heavenly Beloved. Seek the internal Christ.

[637] My child, the seekers – although sometimes nervous, irritated, and suffering from the defeats and attacks of the cunning one – are much more precious to Me than the well-fed righteous Philistines, especially those who pretend to know Christ. They are the most bitter enemies. Having sealed the gates of the Bridal Chamber and the authentic Christ, they opened thousands of the gates of Lucifer and aroused an interest in forbidden knowledge.

[638] My child, being the Supreme Wisdom of the Highest Chamber, I say to you: there is nothing more perfect or more beautiful than our Christ. My dear, the Saviour cannot be understood in this epoch. You are unable to perceive His wisdom in the human body. But My son, even in the True Church of Divine existance, I tell those saints who have passed many stages of learning: 'You must comprehend Him in over-celestial, super-celestial spheres.'

[639] There is no atheism or black art that can harm the cause of Christ more than the obvious, dogmatically correct confession. Pharisees were and remain the most malicious enemies of Christ. And you, the seekers, are their enemies. Blessed are those who seek, for they will find. Having chosen you as seek-

ers I appealed to you after many anointments. Others would rest on their achievements. And My child, even these new myrrhic anointments, received during the Holy Passion ascents to Nightingale Mountain, are just the beginning. The Bridal Feast lies ahead, My child.

:⸺

My prayer was blissfully contemplative: 'Oh, my Lady of the Bridal Chamber, you have found the grace of the Divinity.' The Queen said: 'Words like "my Lady of the Bridal Chamber" refer not only to Me, but also to the highest soul enclosed within each zealot.' My child, in each of My disciples shall be erected a mysterious internal altar, and the image of your Heavenly Lady shall be within it.

640 Wonderful is the mysterious, outward appeal to Me. But, My child, do not forget the internal Kingdom, according to the words of the Saviour. Your Holy Lady Theogamy abides in the secret of secrets of your heart. Converse with Her, calm Her and bring Her joy. Nothing can prevent your divine dialogue with Her, no straitened or tempting circumstances. No one can take away your Holy Lady as the Heavenly Pearl. She is always with you. Remember this.

641 My dear son, as the father of the new church

you must be aware of the divine potential (the potential for divinization) of children between the ages of twelve and fifteen. The fact that My beautiful children can hear the call of virginity and heed the words of priests that belong to the anointed branch is a sign of the inexhaustible potential within them. Do not use the Pharisaic method of respecting grey-haired, long-bearded elders grown wise with experience. Youth is the best time for the perception of the Divinity, of the eternally young Groom: your Christ.

642 Today I want you to enable your children (down to the third and fourth generations and further) to grow in divine fullness. Let them go ahead of you. Do not restrict them. Rely on Supreme Wisdom. Believe that in the hearts of their generation, as in each subsequent generation, have been placed special graces and oils. Priests, be like children, and children like priests! Perform divine rites, My beloved ones!

643 The devil never misses a chance to sting a young soul with lust and then push him or her into the abyss. Do not miss any opportunity to convert the young generation to the throne of the Most High, and ask your Holy Lady to send special angels to open their heavenly treasuries.

644 My child, you are the king of mystical power. Reign wisely. Be generous and love with all your heart as Solomon did. Be as strong and solid in battles as David was. My son, give them the glorious never-ending spiritual treasury that has been revealed to you. If you never leave it locked the enemy will never be able to approach as secretly as a thief, and, having found the key, steal the treasury away.

645 Give your children more than they are able to take. Do not think that you are better or more spiritual. Always remember that your mission is to entrust the young generation to Me and give Me the chance to model them. Then, My son, they will tremble before the fathers in the greatest reverence and sincerely thank you, now and forever.

Oh, Father! How magnificent and divine is Your throne over all the worlds and over Heaven! Your glory resounds amidst the clouds.

The enemy is dreadful. At one mention of his name you lose your peace and your heart stops beating. But my Lady mitigates the blows wisely. She is the sweetest Bosom, the eternal and spiritual Mother. She always builds a bridge between the incompatible and the impossible. She indicates the true path among thousands of tempting diversions. She carefully calculates all circumstances and crosses so that Her disciples, having been led to the edge of the abyss and undergoing the hardest temptations, emerge as victors. They are crowned and thank Her with their holy flowing hallelujahs.

:⸛_

646 Oh, My dear child! You are such poor vessels! But I have chosen you to be the bearers of *My* love and *My* peace. As a reigning priest of Melchizedek, take it upon yourself to shed My motherly love.

647 You must deny your old compositions, not for the sake of the selfish salvation of your soul, but to receive the Lord's wise grace and His surpassing love.

648 Take it, My child, take My divine essence, My maternal bosom. I live within you, I am becoming one with you. We are one entity.

649 You no longer exist. You are the keeper of My heavenly maternal love. Yes, the keeper of supreme wisdom and of the Holy Passion and peace as well. But love comes first. Today it resounds like a new commandment. It is always new, My child.

650 There was nothing new about love in the time of Jesus in comparison with Moses' 'Thou shalt love the Lord thy God with all thy heart, and thy

neighbour as thyself'. But the Saviour gave His commandment a new name, and today I am doing the same. I am talking about surpassing, most heavenly, Theogamic love as a new commandment.

651 My dear child, this commandment is new because it remains mysterious and concealed, and it is universally revealed at all times.

652 Oh! My dear child, promise to remain the vessel of My divine love and of My restful peace in all circumstances. Divine liturgies of enraptured bliss are celebrated in your heart. Inside is an altar, and inside this – a pearl. And in the most hidden place is the Holy Lady, the Queen Theogamy.

653 My dear, henceforth all the heavenly worlds will be placed within your blessed heart. Extract them and bestow this treasure upon your companions. I consecrated you to the mysteries of eternal virginity in order for you to enjoy the treasury given to My brides.

654 My child, this is what I want to tell you. The more revelations you receive, the further you recede from the traditional forms of Catholicism or Orthodoxy. This means that you will receive more blows. You should realize that you are far away. And you should fearlessly reject the chimeras attacking you

through your past, no matter how precious they may seem to you.

655 You cannot even imagine how greatly the old church was neglected. No man, no criminal would be able to stand it if I uncovered all the sins of that church. Meanwhile they dare to call themselves "holy fathers" or "the holy church".

656 Turn away from them forever. The divine treasury has been revealed to you. Draw from it, nourish yourself from it, and desire nothing else. Do not look back.

> Oh, Divine Lady New Universe!
> Oh, immortal myrrhic grace!

657 The cross and repentance have been transferred to your inner essence. New seals are being given. New is the epoch and all else, My child.

658 You are on the threshold of even greater revelation. It will be given to you from here, from Nightingale Mountain, when it has been proclaimed the centre of the approaching Theocivilization.

659 Be careful, My dear: hordes of enemies will be sent by the enemy to tempt My true disciples. Keep vigilant and pray at night. Do not say too much. May the Supreme Wisdom of the Most High illuminate you and stay with you.

660 Today there is no need to visit the Theogamic

Throne in order to avoid temptations. One day I will call you again, My child, but now is the time to learn what I have said. Read the Gospel of Glory in heavenly scrolls, My child; read it and open your spiritual sight to the beauty of the heavenly cities. Thank your Holy Lady, because She, through your image, gave our world an opportunity to participate in the unutterable bliss of the coming age. Peace be with you.

:⎯

> My soul is miserable about leaving this earthly paradise. And the Lady reads this in my heart and comforts me:

661 A part of your soul will remain here. Nothing will prevent you from coming back. The sanctuary of the Most High is spiritual. Here there are legions of angels and a multitude of saints. My dear child, they gather around Me from all the worlds in order to heed the Voice of the Most High and their Heavenly Lady, like the apostles in the hour of My Assumption.

662 I am keeping a place for you at our sweetest feasts, My child. I promise that no one will take it.

663 My child, like Paul I led you through the hierarchies of the old Orthodox and Catholic Churches. Like Moses you were born in your own Egypt, but

your destiny is different: to lead the people of the Divinity to the promised land in the new Heaven.

[664] My beloved child, it was I who persuaded you to seek the spiritual treasures of Orthodoxy and Catholicism. And then you were born from on high, you descended from heavenly clouds to convey the inexpressible riches of the coming age.

[665] The penetralia for the Seraphites in your hands. Guard them.

[666] There is no turning back, My child. The saints of old churches bless and greet you. The angels of the Orthodox and Catholic Churches applaud your assemblies and Sunday liturgies.

[667] Now I shall visit all of your disciples, name them, anoint their hearts, and give them My maternal blessing. May the ever-burning candle be lit within them. Peace be with you.

Oh! Anoint as many souls as you can!

[668] My child, may My heavenly love be spread from here all around the world, may it enter the internal being and restore peace in the hearts of My poor children being tortured in the strong claws of the cunning one.

Oh, myrrh-pouring Mother! Oh, Heavenly Lady!
Pour out Your heavenly love, calm us and descend.

Your Theogamic throne ascends over the world and floats in the Heavens across the sea of the Grail, from the island of Samos to Athens, and from Athens to Europe and further. Oh, Most Holy Lady, how glorious is the Divinity's throne! Oh! Divine grace! I am out of my mind. I am being carried away...

From the heights of the throne of Theogamy our Lady blesses Selcuk, Kusadasi, Izmir and all the capitals and cities of the entire world. Hallelujah! The fragrant current, the waves of the Holy Spirit are spreading to all the worlds. The mountains are breathing! The Revelation continues.

Our Lady is being more and more exalted, and She is shedding myrrhic grace from Her heart. It pours out, again and again, endlessly. The entire world is already brimming over with Her grace.

She stopped. She became pensive and screwed up Her eyes. She discovered something that only She can see. She gave blessings with Her right hand and withdrew slowly.

669 My children (The Blessed Virgin addresses the entire world), release yourselves from the yoke of the sinful past. I am the Queen-Mother of the Most High. I have come to this world to bring you to the embrace of our Lord, to give you the immortal compositions of unutterable beauty. I want man to be new, victorious, and sinless.

670 Hear Me! My voice is a living Ark, resound-

ing miraculously. Those who hear it have already entered and saved themselves. The deaf lose hope, My child. No circumstances or excuses can ever save them.

671 Peace be with you, My dear children.

672 O, Our King! (The Blessed Virgin is address-ing the Most High.) Shed even more clouds of grace. May each of them descend onto a city and a village, embracing all inhabitants with Our heavenly love. May peace and My celestial blessing reign in your hearts.

:⎯

673 The devil has wasted his power. His hours are numbered. I do not tire of repeating this in My messages all around the world. Those who think otherwise are mistaken. My revelation to the world is already the devil's defeat, severe and irretriev-able. The wounded beast has crawled into its den.

674 This is the time of the Most High! The time to be born from on high. The time to proclaim the ap-proaching civilization of the humanity of the future, of perfect wealth and the never-ending inspirations of the Holy Spirit.

675 May there be peace in your hearts. Rejoice, My children. Forget your daily routine and come

out to greet your Most High as the Jews came out on a Monday to meet the Messiah, entering Jerusalem on a donkey: 'Hosanna to the Son of David! Hosanna to the Supreme Wisdom of the Divinity! Hosanna in the highest! Hallelujah! Triumph shall the Lord!"

676 My child, there are difficult trials ahead of us. Remember: the most arduous stage to reach is the last one. But My child, it is rewarded with the Father's embraces and the Bridal Chamber, with something absolutely unexplored and unknown to the world.

677 Rejoice and do not be embarrassed. Rejoice and triumph. Rejoice and embrace with your spiritual sight all that I have done. Rejoice, witnessing our victory and our power over the evil one. Rejoice, contemplating our prospects! Rejoice, watching the never-ending host of saints and angels standing by the throne of Our Most High.

678 Rejoice, My child! The time of victors has come. The world will be converted. May deep divine peace live in your interior and My maternal aegis stay with you and upon you!

679 In His plans the Most High intends the salvation of the world. The divine plans changed after the

revelation of Nightingale Mountain. Rejoice, My child! The disasters have been postponed. Rejoice, my children, and nourish yourselves with the spiritual grace of the words from the Kingdom, as if they were honey.

[680] Peace be with you, My blessed children, and gain victories in your little Holy Passion. See each other with the eyes of your Heavenly Lady. Be born from on high and live in Our images. Peace be with you.

[681] The Divinity has secret plans to overcome the devil. From the heights of Nightingale Mountain He will reveal this mysterious path to His chosen ones. It will be completely unexpected.

[682] Peace be with you, new settlements! Peace be with you, cities…

:⎯

Oh, my God, what great mysteries Atlantis* wants to reveal! So many holy souls lived there; I am overwhelmed. Having sunk to the sea bottom, it became the framework for the creation of the Great Marine Kingdom.

The Lady never abandons this marine city. She tells us that for Her the sea is the upturned Heaven, as was revealed by an angel from the Marine Kingdom in Split, Croatia.

The ancient wisdom is great. But from the heights of Theogamy has been revealed an apocalyptic sign of the coming age and of the end of times.

Our Lady is always with us, not only 'every day until the end of the age' but also in its final hours and in the coming ages. Thus it is possible to spread the revelation given in Ephesus, a few kilometres from here. From the heights of Nightingale Mountain the Queen speaks the humanity, prostrated before Her... Humanity will shine with bliss, love, and celestial light. May those who bless our Mother be blessed, and may peace and prosperity come upon them. May peace be in the hearts of all who love the Most High.

I saw a hunt, led by the cunning one. Hordes of wolves and strange monsters visit that mountain. But our Lady drives them away. And a special fiery cherub stands there.

In order to climb Nightingale Mountain to the Throne of Theogamy, we should be aware of the spiritual war that shakes Earth. May our Lady put an end to these predatory jaws and vulpine tongues.

I am taking the treasury of Nightingale Mountain with me. Oh, infinite treasures of the Kingdom! Oh, boundless generosity of the Lord! Angels of highest ranks could envy it. But the Lord has so many gifts and wonderful blessings for the blind, the lame, and the mortal. Such is His love. Here there are thousands of Garabandals, Fatimas, La Salettes, Grushevos, and so on.

While writing a book about Her apparitions from the first to the twentieth century, our Lady showed me all the thrones of Her revelations. I was together with Her spiritually in the pilgrimage to all those mystical places in order to proclaim, from the heights of Nightingale Mountain, the approaching Apparition of apparitions and Revelation of revelations for the coming age.

Come down, the Ark! Highest Light, embrace the world. O! O! O! Unutterable bliss!

꞉

After the revelation the Earth seems a paradise. I am astonished by the change in my sight. Some kind of different lenses or heavenly pupils have been placed within my eyes.

'Thrones of the Most High, exalted grace!' Sing Eucharistic angels, Seraphs, Cherubims, and Thrones. Oh, my God there are so many of them!

My dear myrrh-anointed children: Leonid, both Alexanders, and both Marys. Mother Euphrosynia nourishes them in the meadows of Heaven. Hallelujah! The Second Golgotha of the Solovki is above them persistently, like the fiery cloud from the time of the Jews' exodus from Egypt.

What mysterious mountains are ahead of me! But all of them 'feel envy' although they 'cheer'. For they are nothing compared to my Mountain, the home of my Purest Lady the Sacred Theogamy, Mary the God-bearer.

O! Thrones of the Most High!
Most exalted grace!
Most enraptured Virgin,
blessed by the Most High!
O the Virgin most enraptured,
blessed and blessing!

Your ways are wonderful, My Lady Supreme Wisdom. Do not abandon me in my Holy Passion.

O! Thrones of the Most High!
Most exalted grace!
O, heavenly Queen
With anointed brides.
It resounds in the inner being.

The course of Supreme Wisdom is wonderful and unpredictable. I happen to be here – in this remote, isolated seaside resort! But here I find protection and the shield. The Queen Herself has placed Her tent here. Here are the mysterious settlements of the Most High.

About the Mother of God's love for the seekers

Christ of Nightingale Mountain was for Her the rediscovered Christ. She wants to present this new revelation – the new Christ, twice transformed as the Groom and the Holy Spirit – to humanity.

I know from my mystical experience that She was the only sole witness of the Gospel of Salvation on His Spilt Blood, the outpouring of His surpassing love. She knew who He was; She saw Him with Her heavenly eyes. Christ that visited Her at Nightingale Mountain was the Lamb of the Solovki, Christ of the Bridal Chamber, the Groom.

How can an ordinary mortal, whose eyes have been sealed with Pharisaic clichés and taboos, understand Him when this mysterious Christ, continually multiplying in His mysticism, was unknown to our Heavenly Lady Herself?!

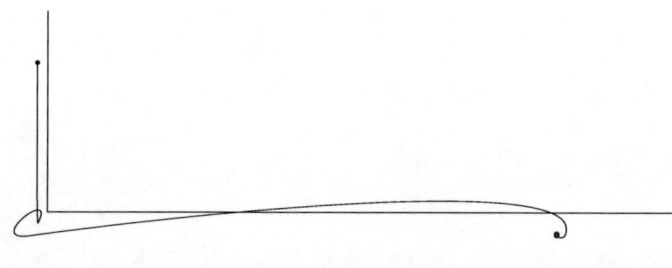

THE JERUSALEM THAT RECEIVED THE LORD IS MARY

Izmir, 18 April 2005

The Mother of God:

⁶⁸³ The Most High wants to found the New Jerusalem here. This canyon (the Purest Virgin is looking around) is proclaimed as the New Jerusalem.

⁶⁸⁴ Mary is the Jerusalem that received the Lord. The material Jerusalem crucified Him. The spiritual Jerusalem took Him in its arms from the Cross and anointed Him. His heart again began to beat, and His blood to flow. Oh, My child, Our Lord was coming to life in my arms!

⁶⁸⁵ And look, after two thousand years – the New Jerusalem is here.

⁶⁸⁶ I am extending My Bosom here – the Bosom of the Most High. I call this land the 'promised land for the Seraphites'. Into this canyon, onto the chain of Nightingale Mountains, will descend the City of

Heaven, the perfect City, the City of saints. Oh, My child, twelve rivers with hot divine water and the Eucharistic wine of Christ will flow through our city. My child, it will be furnished with tables. And saints will descend from Heaven with goblets, never-endingly scooping up and drinking the wine.

:—

687 And now about the war, My child, the war against the devil himself.

688 When I came here, to Ephesus, I felt as the Lord had felt at the beginning of His ministry. And He began His new ministry in Me.

689 My war against Lucifer was extremely vehement, My child. Our Lord strengthened Me, Our Lord acted in Me. The enemy blasphemed the Lord. The enemy mocked the race of Adam. The enemy threatened Me. So many times he wanted to throw Me from the mountain! So many furious whirlwinds swept over Me, surrounding and carrying Me through the air, after which I fell breathless and was brought to a quiet place where I was washed with holy water, and recovered…

690 How our enemy hates the plans of the Lord! I took the cross upon Myself in order to found the Kingdom of Christ. My child, here, on the moun-

tains of Ephesus, was fought the battle for the coming Church. And if I had not been victorious, if I had not trodden on the head of the accursed dragon, if I had not avenged the death of My Divine Son, Christianity would not have occurred and the Church would not have been founded. My child, the Most High brought Me here in order to start the final battle and defeat the enemy. I fulfilled His will, My child. On the Assumption Bed I reclined as victor.

691 The war exhausted My forces, My child. And My yearning and love for My Divine Beloved led to that most beautiful expectation, the indescribable Easter of the Bridal Chamber, with which I was honoured, My child.

692 All these years the Saviour came to Me to comfort Me, saying:

693 'Mary! For the sorrows that You are going through, My Mother, the greatest joy awaits you: the Bridal Bed.'

694 I could not understand what was meant by the Bridal Bed. How could I, having taken the vow of eternal virginity and been invited to become the Mother of virginal humanity, marry the Divinity Himself, My Son, or the Holy Spirit? Theogamy and

the brides of Christ caused the same perplexity in Me as the Annunciation. 'How shall this be done?' – I asked.

[695] Our Lord explained to Me that He had protected Me for this moment. How many times, on My knees before Him as the most magnificent heavenly Sun, had I asked to suffer and die for His love. I threw myself upon the Cross of Golgotha and afterwards died of grief innumerable times, My child, while walking the path of the cross and pouring My blood onto the stones of the desert.

[696] Our Lord protected Me for this moment: the hour of Theogamy. It will come through My A s - s u m p t i o n, so glorified in Orthodoxy, My child. My chapels and monasteries are the prototype and symbol of the approaching Theogamy.

[697] The Assumption is neither the end nor death and resurrection. The Assumption means that you are taken to the Bridal Chamber. The most mysterious sacrament, barely intelligible to the race of Adam but understood by My disciples, the Seraphites of the third millennium, is spiritual union with Christ.

[698] My child, having sacrificed His life on the Cross, our Saviour united with the humanity by

the Bridal bonds. I saw the Bridal Bed spread over Golgotha in the hour of His dying groans. My child, the Saviour was preparing the same Bridal Bed for His disciples when He said to John: 'Behold your Mother'. And to Me: 'Behold Your son'.

[699] For sixteen years I prepared myself for this divine mystery: to enter the Bridal Chamber with the Son of the Most High.

[700] The Saviour came to Me and comforted Me in My sorrows: 'O, Mother, o, Daughter of the Most High! I shall name You My Bride. You will be the next to overcome death after Me. I have overcome it as a result of My Bridal union with My disciples and the Adamites. I will exalt You from Your Assumption Bridal Bed to Heaven, and You will be taken to the Bridal Chamber. And over the place of Your Assumption, over this canyon, the Bridal Bed will be spread. After two millennia it will float over the mountain of the New Jerusalem, formerly Ephesus, towards Greece and Europe, and will stand above the centre of Europe, the place announced as My Grail (My Garabandal).'

[701] And the Most High explained to Me the mystery of Theogamy for which I had been waiting, as well as the mystery of My death. Oh, My child, I

knew about it, I anticipated it. Supreme Wisdom had revealed it to Me.

[702] Go and tell My disciples that even if they die they will not decay and disappear without leaving any memories, nor rise from the dead (in the Christian understanding), but reach the Bridal Chamber of the Most High. My child, anointing takes place on the deathbed and is not possible in any other way.

[703] Ascend now, My child, to the height of the prayer of the rosary: 'Ora pro nobis nunc et in hora mortis nostrae. Amen'. It should not be understood as My presence when taking a soul to Heaven, driving out demons, and so on (although, My child, I am present then, too). My presence in the hour of My disciples' departure is a sign that they have been clothed in the divine vestments of the brides of Christ taken to the Bridal Chamber. I come to anoint them. My child, I anointed our blessed ones: Nicolas, deacon Epiphany, Leonid Beliy, Alexander, blessed Iya, Mary, and the other Mary. I anointed them on their deathbeds. That is why their bodies emit fragrance. I clothed them in the vestments of the Heavenly Chamber.

[704] At the hour of My Assumption holy oils flowed in streams, My child. I reclined on My bed.

A fiery stream, the stream of the Bridal Chamber, poured out of My pierced heart. The archangel of the Bridal Chamber had barely touched my heart with the lance of the last drop, when it fell into the embrace of the Saviour with its final 'O!'. And our Lord raised Me to the Heavenly Chambers.

705 They are ineffable, My child. No words, ecstatic epithets or exaggerated comparisons can describe how I felt, not even slightly. Different compositions are necessary, My child, different anointments, a different origin, a different human being.

706 My disciples should only prepare themselves for the Bridal Chamber. Before that, My son, 5, 150, 1500, 15'000, 150'000 preparatory spheres are necessary.

707 Do not be surprised by our heavenly arithmetic. $15 + 150 = 1$. Numbers are dispersed in divine space and mysteriously multiply and compress themselves, reflecting the mystical meanings of divine vibrations and sayings. Spheres reveal themselves and disappear just as enigmatically, while angels come and reveal the brightest undiscovered new worlds.

708 My child, I will teach those who have passed the seventh grade of anointing about the Bridal

Chamber. And after that – those who have passed the eleventh, twelfth, thirteenth, fourteenth, and fifteenth. And it is only possible to reach the Chamber after the fifteenth, My child.

709 Yes, My child. I fought not only for My Son, the Divinity become man. I fought for humanity – for its divine mission, revealed to Me by the Most High. My child, I have won several thousand battles against the devil. Each of them with bloodshed and extreme Holy Passion.

710 My child, We shall continue to reveal the Gospel of the Assumption Chamber, the Gospel of the Bridal Bed, to our disciples. Without them Christ's whole life and teachings would be unfinished and in vain. In the Gospel nothing is said about His forty-day preaching! Nothing about the disciples' ten-day staying in Jerusalem cenacle. Nothing about the first settlements in Ephesus. Nothing about the Bridal Chamber.

711 O, My child, what occurred was the only possible thing for that time, with its Judaic superstitions and Roman philosophizing. Now, My child, I am preparing all humanity for the ascension into the Bridal Chamber.

712 Look at the young generation with My eyes: Brazilians, Argentines, Africans, Europeans, Rus-

sians. My child, this generation has been anointed for the Bridal Chamber!

713 Get rid of all other patterns, My child. Seal the Gospels, especially their cheerless sin-centricity, dead Typicon, and hellish rules crucifying the Holy Spirit and Me. Teach them about the Bridal Chamber! More fearlessly, more and more, My child. In order to avoid illusions, teach them about sobriety, teach them about the feat of transformation. Teach them about the necessity of being born from on high, and to reject the past. Teach them about the divine processions that meet the Beloved. Teach them to adjust their lamps and to meet the Groom without any further thought or delay.

714 Teach them about the Bridal Chamber, oh, only about the Bridal Chamber: how I was embraced by the fire of His Divine love! My child, the fifteenth mystery of the rosary – the Crowning of your Heavenly Lady with the wreath of the Bride of Christ – is Her entrance into the Bridal Chamber. The Rosary of the Bridal Chamber, from now and forever!

715 My child, renounce all other patterns of faith, regarding church attendance, fanatical ideas of salvation, icons, candles and the like. Encourage My

potential anointed sovereigns to reach the Bridal Chamber, and tell them: Today's faith does not lie in reading the Gospel, nor in believing Muhammad to be a prophet, professing Moses of the time of the law of Sinai, or waiting for the coming Messiah. The living faith means to be embraced by the fire of divine love, to enter the Chamber of the Most High, for which it is necessary to lay on the Assumption Bed.

[716] To die for love, My child! To thirst for that divine holy water to be brought to you, the heavenly wine of a different Eucharist. That which you drink in the Chapel of the Three Fools is magnificent. The most magnificent of all is the fiery Eucharist prepared for the brothers of Seraphim from cranberries on the island of Anzer*. But the Eucharist that awaits the sons and daughters of the Bridal Chamber (as I call this generation) – o, it is beyond all expectations!

꞉

[717] My child, from this Mountain I begin My new revelation and the new fiery letter written in their hearts.

[718] A goblet! Bring a silver goblet, My angels! Fill it now with the hot wine of Our love. Let them try this celebratory drink, and having tasted it let

them long for more, and I shall say to them: 'Do you know what is the living faith of today? It is neither Moses, Christ, nor Muhammad, but the BRIDAL CHAMBER of the HOLY SPIRIT and the path leads to it.'

[719] Marians, persecuted Marians all around the world will settle in these lands. Here I will lead beautiful souls with lofty anointments on their brows. In the home of their Heavenly Lady they will find the most fragrant Eden. Welcome! Here is the home of your Heavenly Mother – the Ark, the Bridal Chamber for all humanity of world.

⁚⸗

[720] I spent around fifteen years here. And during all these fifteen thousand years Supreme Wisdom descended upon Me and illuminated Me. My child, I breathed under the dome of Her temple. I was embraced by Her cloud. My child, My every cell is imbued with the Supreme Wisdom of the Most High.

[721] Listen, My child, to what I am going to tell you: as the Son dwells within His Mother, having left Her the Kingdom, so the Father dwells within Supreme Wisdom. My child, when the Father incarnated Christ, His Only-Begotten Son, He also

prepared a dwelling place for Supreme Wisdom: Mary. And when both of them returned to their heavenly chambers, He celebrated with them the never-ending wedding feast of Easter, inviting the most dear guests and a multitude of angels of different ranks, and saints.

[722] Illuminated by Supreme Wisdom, I penetrated the destinies of the world. Supreme Wisdom raised Me to the very Chamber of the Pantocrator. My illuminated mind dwelt in the homes of Supreme Wisdom.

[723] My child, how insufficiently Supreme Wisdom has been revealed to the world! There are so many obstacles to Her descent: religious institutions, priests, set rules, adopted forms of salvation, zealous deeds, and holiness. My child, the time will come when Supreme Wisdom will d e s c e n d a n d i l - l u m i n a t e the Seraphites, Her disciples. Supreme Wisdom has built Herself a new home, and has inscribed upon it in gold letters 'THE EIGHTY-FIFTH CIVILIZATION OF THE SERAPHITES OF CHRIST' (Seraphicus Christi).

∵

[724] My child, for two weeks while I lay, half-paralyzed and weak, I reread Christ's scroll, the biography of the Lord from His birth, His ministry in

the earthly days. Angels explained to Me the divine Gospel of His Glory. I saw the wonderful meaning, fruits and consequences of His ministry.

⁷²⁵ My child, before being prepared for the Bridal Chamber by our Lady Supreme Wisdom, I learned to see Christ through other, all-seeing eyes. And now I would like to persuade you to see Him as a chamber of Supreme Wisdom, as Christ the Mysterious.

꞉⁻

⁷²⁶ Ephesus served as John's home, and he provided Me with shelter. Now I would like to shelter My John in Ephesus, so that he may live near the chamber of his Mother, near Her Bridal Chambers, the place of the most divine blessing of the third millennium.

⁷²⁷ Here I shall set the Throne of the Bridal Chamber. From here the Bridal Bed will proclaim the coming Theocivilization III.

꞉⁻

⁷²⁸ My child, not a single day passed without entering into mortal combat with the enemy. Supreme Wisdom gave Me strength. I rejected all his arguments and defeated his logic. The Most High illuminated Me with the mysterious workings of

Providence, and the devil fled in disgrace. For a thousand years I kept him caged like a wild beast. Here he suffered a defeat that he had never expected.

[729] In the beginning he came to Me in order to understand Christ, and why he had received such a vital wound. And he howled with pain, like a bleeding wild beast, wounded by the spear of the hunter! I explained to him who the Lord is. And then he attacked Me.

[730] My child, he attacked Me with a sharp weapon. He wanted to tear Me apart and strangle Me, to throw Me from the peak of the mountain into the abyss. He presented countless arguments, more and more of them, in order to corrupt the Adamites and defile the incarnation of the Son of the Divinity. My child, he dared to disclose to Me his entire vision, from the creation of the world, from the creation of angels, from the fall of Lucifer. I saw how he had destroyed eighty three civilizations one after another, and now wants to destroy the present eighty-fourth civilization of the Adamites.

[731] My child, when I told the enemy about the plans for the Lord's victory, he howled. Then, pretending himself calm, he began to ask Me for details of how this would happen. But, My child, I hid from him the details that he should know.

732 My divine son, this is the place of the great victory. That is why the Ark, being built here and no-where else, will descend from here. This is the place of his absolute and final defeat on the Earth. That is why, My child, the angelic regiments descended here from Heaven, to where they will return.

733 Descend, angels, into the valley of bright transformation! Name these Mountains the new Tabor, the New Hermon, the New Elion, the New Solovki!

734 Peace be with the coming Theocivilization (the Purest Virgin is waving). My peace and My blessing. Those who wish to live should fear nothing. No disasters will touch you. The church will be transformed. Await the hour when the Lord will purify it from the tares and make it His worthy Bride, for which Supreme Wisdom has prepared a wonderful home for My sons, the priests of Melchizedek. I invite them to come.

✣

735 My child, you cannot imagine how I felt after the Lord's ascent! What a burden I carried upon My shoulders, what a responsibility, what a cross! The Saviour entrusted Me with the Church. I had no other choice but to prostrate before Him and Supreme Wisdom.

[736] The persecutions began. My child, the Pharisees hated Me more fiercely than My Son. In Me
they saw the source of all their disasters. 'The de-
famed virgin…' O, to this they added more than ten
other abominable names. May their misfortunes
never end on this Earth. The devil told them where
to find the dwelling of the Divinity in divine existence and they organized a hunt for Me. They were
ready to pay spies and denunciators any price in order to do away with Me. Two of My companions,
myrrh-bearing maidens, warned Me about the plans
for My assassination.

[737] They followed Me everywhere, and found Me
many times. The Lord guarded Me miraculously.

[738] Believe Me, My child, the Pharisaic malice
was only a weak reflection of that terrible war and
mortal combat that the devil waged against Me –
and I against him. It was due to the deeds of the
Lord, the fruits of His three-year-long preaching,
His incarnation on Earth, His suffering and resurrection. I took C h r i s t ' s   b u r d e n upon Myself,
My child. I heaped the weight of human salvation
upon My small, already old, exhausted, severely
wounded shoulders.

[739] My child, My war did not consist in avoid-
ing the Pharisees, strengthening disciples, offering

prayers, or casting out spirits from those possessed by the devil. No, no, My child! Not an hour passed without fighting against the devil. I took Christ's mission upon Myself. I longed for His triumph at any price. I was ready to mount the cross, to be crucified as He had been, to be stoned, to be humiliated like Him. I was ready to endure any suffering and to pay any price in order that Christ's mission should triumph.

740 When My conditions became unbearable the disciples prepared a ship and I sailed away secretly, reaching Ephesus after much travelling.

741 My child, I am not mistaken when I say that, in moments of weakness, in hours of My severe holy Passion, I was attacked by a whole army of evil spirits (directed particularly against the Son of the Divinity). Later this army tempted devotees, ascetics, and saints. The Lord gave Me strength, My child. Only He could defeat those innumerable regiments.

742 The valley of New Jerusalem is before you. Now imagine: I am lying in a wretched hut, with ragged boards instead of a ceiling, and around My head are swarms of devils from the whole valley. They have come from all the worlds and have surrounded Me. What could I have done without His

help? But, My child, I recognized the majesty and might of the Son of the Divinity born of Me, because at every mention of His name the hostile armies, ready to devour Me and break My bones to pieces, receded powerlessly.

743 The valley of resurrection, the Ark of the third millennium, My child, flows with the blood of My Holy Passion. Every inch of this land is covered with My tears. Demons from hell, from all the unseen worlds, gathered here. You may find their traces to this very day. And the angelic armies came here as well. You are in the place of Armageddon, My son.

*

744 I established close relations with the Ephesian disciples. They literally devoured My every word about our Saviour. I told them the revelations of the Most High.

745 Did I receive revelations? My child, My mind was constantly in the Heavens, and Supreme Wisdom initiated Me into Her mysteries. The Saviour was one with the Father, and I was one with Supreme Wisdom, My child. And I never left Her. Our Saviour was glad to see Supreme Wisdom embodied in Me. But, My child, do you remember this evangelical passage: 'The child grew and waxed

strong in spirit'? Thus I grew in the Spirit of Supreme Wisdom, My child.

⁷⁴⁶ If it had not been for the sixteen years of My Holy Passion on Earth while in exile in Ephesus (oh, sixteen years of continuous longing!), I would not have revealed Myself on Earth so frequently. After the Lord's Ascension I understood His mission more clearly than ever before, and could not leave His disciples. Those sixteen years stretched to two thousand years of My constant apparitions and teachings, and will continue in eternity.

⁷⁴⁷ My child, when in Ephesus I was born in spiritual bodies through the different countries of the world I came to many common people, healed them, taught them, strengthened them, anointed them, and took them into My heart. And they became faithful to Him.

⁷⁴⁸ My child, I did not pass a single day without kneeling and begging the Most High to send Me more sorrows. Oh, more and more sorrows, so that I could do as much as possible for our Lord! I passionately loved Him. But the Most High relied on each of My tears. And each of My Holy Passion, no matter how severe, resulted in a defeat for the devil and a victory for My Divine Son.

[749] The Gospel, My child, is a scanty book. Our enemies would like to seal the true events of Our earthly days, the true Gospel of Heaven and Earth. The Gospels! There is almost nothing in them about the Lord. The Lord is seen as if from outside, by a stranger. I did not recognize Him on the pages of these canonical books.

[750] My child, during the first years after the Saviour's Ascension, His presence was unheard-of. The disciples communicated the divine story of His deeds by word of mouth. And it incomparably surpassed all that is recorded in the new scriptures and legends of all these inquisitors, written to glorify the universal torture chamber and the universal inquisition.

[751] The Protestants seem to Me to be the most miserable. My child, they cling to the Holy Spirit sealed in the epistles of St. Paul and in the Gospels of Christ's disciples. But it is so difficult to find the treasury of the Spirit in such a limited book!

[752] The Saviour left no Scripture. My child, He left His Purest Mother at the Cross. He gave His Church, His life-giving Gospel to me. My child, I sent an angel, and the Holy Spirit dictated events in the earthly life of Christ to the authors of the canonical Gospels. My son, how insignificantly little

they inscribed in their books! And by 'insignificantly little' I mean nothing at all.

[753] During the fifteen years of My Holy Passion and My blissful residence in Ephesus I was astonished, and gathered these events in My heart. I never tired of being enlightened and of rejoicing in the divine greatness of our Lord. I have given My seals to you, My child. Your never-ending search, ascension, and double-winged aquiline flight to the heavenly deserts have been given to you by Me.

[754] Oh My child, instead of adhering to ungifted priests, these well-fed holy eunuchs from the suite of the pagan queen Cleopatra; instead of feeding on the crumbs from the table of a king, t u r n t o M e ! I shall reveal Christ to you. I am His epistle! I have preserved within Myself His every groan. During the fifteen years of My Holy Passion He revealed Himself to Me hourly, each time anew, as if for the first time. One day I saw Him with My own eyes; the next I lost Him, suffered, cried, appealed to Him as one abandoned, and then found Him again – always closer, My child!

[755] The Saviour revealed so many mysteries to Me! The Saviour united with Me so closely that I am unable to express it in human words.

:⸺

756 My child, the Divine King Christ was infinitely kind, and it was divine kindness. When I asked Him for something and He could not fulfil My motherly request, He gave Me reasons for why I should submit and act according to the will of the Lord and our Mother Supreme Wisdom. He would say: 'Our Mother Supreme Wisdom'.

757 But, My child, it later turned out that He would always fulfil all My requests. And He would give Me incomparably more, a million times more than I had asked. I asked to be allowed to unite with Him, to suffer for Him – oh My child, how could I have proposed the Bridal Bed in My earthly days? The Bridal Chamber and the forthcoming exaltations? The two-thousand-year fiery wedding feast? The mystery of the Second Golgotha of the Solovki?

758 With incessant fiery grace, with rivers and streams of divine burning wine poured onto the pure martyrs of Christ, My child, His goodness surpassed all My expectations! Indescribable, impossible, My child! The angels tremble when they see the endlessly superior plans for His divine mercy. I have no choice but to bear witness to His mercy and convey it as His Mother, the Ambassador.

759 Rejoice, rejoice, My child – I am revealing

the Lord to you as I see and know Him. His dearest disciples were also M y disciples.

⁷⁶⁰ The Lord said almost nothing about Himself. His lips kept silent about His mission. The Lord more often spoke in parables and used unusual language. I testified for Him! By means of the Holy Spirit He revealed to Me the mystery and the majesty of His divine mission. He revealed to Me His glory in Heaven. He entrusted Me with His Church. And I, My child, possess the keys to all the entrances of Christ's Kingdom. Tens and sometimes thousands of My years pass in teaching the saints about Him, and preparing them for the Bridal Feast.

⁷⁶¹ The destinies of the Godbearer, which you like to mention so often by the Holy Spirit, are the destinies of the Bridal Chamber, My child. And they presuppose lengthy and patient preparations of the soul, without force.

⁷⁶² Supreme Wisdom poured out through you, My child, is the result of Our prayers and the longings of the Holy Passion. Consecrate as many disciples of Christ as possible into the mysteries of the Most High.

⁷⁶³ I am preparing you for the Bridal Bed, My beloved children. You are the Church of the Bridal Chamber. You are the exalted, myrrh-anointed

ones of the superworldly Cross. I love you infinitely. I long to enter and settle within you, to dwell amongst you, to anoint you, to descend upon you like a cloud of Supreme Wisdom, to teach you again and again about the mysteries of the Most High, and to anoint and lead you.

:⸺

764 My child, I have revealed the endless perspectives of the Lord. The hour will come, My child, when I shall lead all of humanity. Oh, look! (The Queen reveals a great endless white ship.) Millions will board it. I shall lead this new white Noah's Ark to the heavenly heights. The angels will take care that as many of My sons and daughters board it as possible.

765 Ascend to the heavenly heights! Rejoice, My beloved children! Rejoice, for the Supreme Wisdom of the Divinity is pouring Herself into you! Rejoice, for when I came into the world I promised the Lord to reveal to the chosen souls mysteries that are as dear to My heart as they are infinitely dear to Him.

766 Rejoice, My children! Rejoice as I do. Rejoice in My joy, because amongst you I see many who are able to heed the high mysteries.

767 Yes, I see how the world has fallen, and how

powerful the devil has become recently. I see how he twists the minds of millions, having caught them in his webs. But, My child, with the eye of Supreme Wisdom I see something else: souls extricate themselves from his webs with ease (as always happened when I helped the disciples of Christ, entangled into the enemy's nets), and follow their Lady Supreme Wisdom.

[768] My child, I am happy to come and to teach you. I am presenting you with My smile and with My motherly happiness to suffer for you, die for you, and dwell within you. And to defeat the evil within you by propagating the millennial Kingdom of My Divine Son, lighting the ever-burning candles of the eternal Gospel in your hearts, and enlightening your souls with mysteries. I am sealing My Divine Son within you, for His Kingdom will only multiply. His divine solar civilization is approaching, and His never-ending glory will resound in all worlds, on all instruments, in thousands of hearts, in fanfares, trumpets, orchestras and organs – the glory of the Highest!

* * *

the Heavenly High Priest dwelt here…

CHRIST OF THE SECOND COMING

11 April 2005

On the Throne of the Son

⁷⁶⁹ Be the forerunner of t h e U n e x p e c t e d Christ.

⁷⁷⁰ The Jews also awaited the Messiah, and the rabbis predicted that He would soon come to save Israel. But He appeared in a manner completely unexpected for His followers. He was rejected, boycotted, and eventually put to a shameful death.

⁷⁷¹ My child, although the Son is one with the Father, He differs from Him. The Kingdom, anointments, and feast of the Chalice are of the Son.

⁷⁷² Christ and I are one. But, My child, if the disciples of your Beloved accept the old image of the pathetic, 'Lord-have-mercy' Christ, I risk being rejected as Christ of the Second Advent, and will have to repeat what I said in My earthly days: 'When I come, I will scarcely find faith.' It is not

the cultish Christianity of the temples but the perfect living faith that I preach.

⁷⁷³ The Father hopes to be delivered in His Son, and the Son in the Holy Spirit. Prepare your pure hearts and immaculate plates. I shall depict My image in the secret of secrets, I shall enter the internal chests and sanctuaries of the heart.

⁷⁷⁴ Prepare yourselves to meet the Unexpected One as He is presented by the Unforeseen Lady Supreme Wisdom, the Holy Fool Mother.

⁷⁷⁵ Yes, yes, My child! I was not wrong to saying 'holy fool', for Her moves will be too unpredictable and absolutely unexpected.

⁷⁷⁶ The Pharisees, 'followers of canons', 'will deny Her. The image of the Holy Spirit will benumb and horrify them; they will rise against Him and will want to dispose of Him. Anger will torture them, the same anger with which they tortured saints both long ago and recently.

⁷⁷⁷ My child, your mission as the forerunner consists of preparing the world for My unexpected coming, My unpredictable movements, and the holy fool forms and images have been taken by Me.

⁷⁷⁸ First of all, My child, renounce the inquisitorial judgement 'what is from the Divinity and what

is from devil'. Suspicion and guarded investigation testify that the soul has not been dedicated to the Most High. You are embraced by Your Heavenly Beloved. Your Mother took you in Her arms and led you into the bosom of Abraham. What more do you need?

[779] The Devil has been denied for-ever, which means that the world is filled with the most fragrant and mysterious presence of the Divinity. In these last times, while the cunning one rushes about the cities of the night and installs his Luciferian dens, My presence is as stronger than ever, My child! Nothing makes Me as happy as a rapturous prayer:

> There is no one but Him,
> My Beloved.
> There is nothing but love,
> His love.

[780] With this prayer, My child, enter casinos, gay-clubs, bestial saunas, discos, and any dirty gather-ings. But do not profess yourself to be the ally of the Divinity or the enemy of the devil.

[781] The Jews were shocked by the incarnation of the Son of the Divinity in human form. It was a double shock for them when Christians called My Mother as the Mother of the Divinity, the Godbearer.

⁷⁸² Their furious spite and accursed anathemas against Me were provoked by the fact that they were sure of their right to judge what comes from the Divinity and what from the devil. Using their old-fashioned criteria, the Only-Begotten Son of the Most High was 'the most dangerous of all magicians and criminal number one'. They talked about Me like this. They said to their allies: 'Come and entrap Him like a fox, do with Him what you will. Free the world from His presence and His sermon!'

⁷⁸³ You have no right to judge what comes from the Divinity and what from devil. This is how I interpret one of the main commandments given by Me during My earthly days in Israel.

:⸺

⁷⁸⁴ Our Mysterious Lady, divine Theogamy! Look at Her, My child. The unutterable rapture of the heavenly dwellers caused the ease with which She captures the cunning one in Her nets. Snakes twist around Her feet, unable to do anything. Fill yourself with the Spirit of Supreme Wisdom, My child, and bravely proclaim to the world that the Kingdom of Sacred Theogamy is approaching.

⁷⁸⁵ 'I have come to this world to be united with the Divinity through suffering humanity. Amen.' There is no other worthy recipe or meaning.

786 Teach people about their true destiny and lead them to it, sweeping aside the rest as unworthy for the man of the Divinity. The cunning one will approach to you with bad thoughts, reprimanding you: 'Prayer has been taken away from you. Where is the "God-have-mercy" type of liturgy? Why aren't you saying the Rosary? Where are your bows? Where is your fervency for relics? Where is your zeal and asceticism?' You should reply like this:

787 'I have come to this world to be united with the Divinity. The Most High knows how to arrange it. I am a virgin bride. I am completely in His power. I devote myself to serving Him. I sacrificially accept all that He assigns to me. But I know, in spite of all circumstances, that my covenant with Him, my indissoluble agreement, will lead to the divine Bridal Bed, and I will fall into the embraces of my Beloved.'

:⸺

788 The serpentine Pharisees come from the devil but think themselves from the Divinity. Which legal criteria can they use, other than those that have become outdated? Distance yourselves from them! John the Baptist was the first to accept Me without any doubt. It happened because the Heavenly Father announced to him the u n e x p e c t e d forms of the coming of the Messiah.

⁷⁸⁹ Fascinating, perplexing, doubted: these are the three types of perception of Revelation.

⁷⁹⁰ The mystery of the 'Gospel of Salvation on His Spilt Blood' is f a s c i n a t i n g, isn't it?

> The Saviour smiles. He quotes my Grail prayer and shows how much He enjoys hearing the converting, myrrh-anointing prayer.

⁷⁹¹ The priests of Aaron were s t u n n e d to see Moses coming down from the mountain with heavy stone tablets in hands. They were so heavy that even a four-metre-high giant could hardly lift them. But Moses descended proudly, as if carrying some awesome relic.

⁷⁹² The Jews were d a z z l e d by Moses' story of the appearance of the Glory of God, accompanied by a multitude of angels, archangels, and other celestial ranks. Their astonishment reached its limit when the Purest Virgin was admitted to the Holy of the Holies of their temple.

⁷⁹³ The celestial ranks were s t u n n e d when they saw the arrival of the Infant Divinity in a village manger for cattle.

⁷⁹⁴ My Crucifixion and Resurrection shocked and stunned the whole universe.

⁷⁹⁵ The language of our Mother Wisdom is astonishing. My advent in the form of the Holy Spirit

will be just as shocking, unforeseen, and unprecedented.

:⸝_

⁷⁹⁶ The rotten schemes of the Pharisees' Dead
Testament are as dead as they are ('the Last Judg-
ment'). I will come and find barely
any faith among those that love dusty Typicons
and the rattles of watchmen.

⁷⁹⁷ My admired disciple, may the Divinity bless
you to accept Me as I am! Cleanse your mind of the
prejudiced judgements of the traditional religious
order, of the trite images with which the Divinity is
usually portrayed. Prepare yourself, My son, and,
like John the Baptist, await the sign and apparition
to accept Me as I wish to be revealed Myself to the
world.

⁷⁹⁸ My child, the Forerunner knew of My coming
and proclaimed My absolute Kingdom. According
to His words, the Heavenly Kingdom was revealed
to him with My birth.

⁷⁹⁹ Proclaim Sacred Theogamy, the divine solar
throne of My union with all creation. It bears great
fruits, My child: fertile figs, olive gardens, paradise
trees…

⁸⁰⁰ With your mystical eye observe the path of
Our Church. You will see Paracletic liturgies, the

renunciation of generational programs, night-time vigils, ablutions in the Holy springs of Mother Euphrosynia, the Grail, the heavenly Chalice that nourishes from on high, the Solovki, the fiery wedding, the true saints revealed to the world, and rapturous liturgies in holy fool barracks where cults are fought...

[801] Supreme Wisdom has led you to the throne of Theogamy and prepared the feast, grain by grain.

[802] Hold on to Theogamy, and do not retreat from Her throne. My child, proclaim this new sphere to the world. With the Holy Spirit, rise with righteous anger against lovers of Egyptian bricks and mutton shashlik covered in a religious sauce.

[803] Like Moses, lead the people of the Divinity to the new exodus. He taught about the promised lands. Proclaim the new promised Heavens that are descending to you.

[804] The world has been renewed.

[805] Believe, My child, that I was born in the new Bethlehem as the reigning Infant Holy Spirit. And I am accompanied by different grace and different surroundings.

[806] A different sermon is on My lips. Today, thousands and millions are able to heed it.

[807] Oh, My son! Long for Theogamy, as I did.

[808] In My heart there is only one ache: to be united with all creation.

[809] I passionately love every being. I love them now more than in My earthly days. They are unbearable. They have fallen. They are in the embrace of the devil. They are depraved. But believe Me, My child: with a single movement of My scepter of Melchizedek I shall convert them and captivate them a m i l l i o n   t i m e s   m o r e than I did with My previous disciples.

[810] The theme of Theogamy is a royal theme. No one can contradict it. The devil becomes dumb and loses all his strength. Moreover, his plans to assume the shape of humanity and fulfil his long-awaited project – to call the earthy kingdom the civilization of the devil – are unmasked.

:⸻

[811] My child, I called Lazarus' sickness a sickness for life, not for death. Come down with this sacred sickness for eternal life, for Sacred Theogamy. Seek to penetrate the bliss of the divine existence during the night-time prayer, the day-time sermon, the rapturous liturgy, and the messianic feasts of the descending Grail. Never grow tired of repeating:

> The Inexhaustible Chalice,
> The Chalice of Sacred Theogamy
> Is spread above the worlds.
> The Lord is among us!
> Mary is with us!

[812] Look at the attire of today's triumphant saints. The John Chrysostoms, the Innocents of Balta*, your beloved brothers of Seraphim, the priests of Melchizedek, and others – all are clad in Theogamic garments.

[813] The attire of the priests of Melchizedek is covered with the seals and signs of Sacred Theogamy. Heavenly birds and the inhabitants of the universe tremble before Her. My Bridal Bed exhales myrrh scent, which contains the particles of adhesion to your Beloved.

[814] All paths lead to the union with the Most High. Yes! Only by observing the world with the most merciful and Theogamic eyes can you repeat after Me: 'All paths lead to the union with the Most High.'"

THE FORERUNNING SERAPHIC GENERATION

THE REVELATION (PARAPHRASED)

10 April, 2005

Moscow, Sheremetyevo II Airport

𝓜ysterious anointments. I see: the anointing ceremony of this generation is now taking place in Heaven. They wear white clothes. They are anointed with heavenly oils and myrrh taken from the Bridal Chamber. And in their hearts begins the game of lights. The candle of the Holy Passion is lit. They turn weak with bliss. They are the mysterious anointed sovereigns.

Great mysteries. Incredible, incredible, incredible…

The revelations in the dentist's chair; each word comes from spheres never before revealed to the world. They are prepared for 'the new people born in Christ', the Seraphicus Christi.

And now something else is revealed. These souls come from mysterious spheres from, where no man has ever set foot to Earth, nobody from these spheres has ever been to this world. They are mysterious souls. They are the mysterious anointed sovereigns.

The aim of the sacrament performed by the Heavenly Church is to anoint them plentifully with oils for the sake of the carrying of the cross of the forerunners. The Seraphic generation of the eighty-fifth civilization, the blessed Seraphic forerunning generation, will be sealed by the Paraclete Holy Spirit, the Bridal Chamber, and the throne of Sacred Theogamy.

One more thing has been revealed. As Christ will appear multiplied in all creation, so His forerunner will be multiplied in the entire generation. These are the Seraphic forerunners. They will proclaim Him and prepare for Him. They are to be the first Melchizedeks descended from the Heavens.

:—

An hour ago a mysterious anointment of young people took place in Heaven. They were anointed as secret anointed sovereigns, as the forerunners of the Seraphic generation.

They were anointed as joining forerunners. As Christ will appear jointly multiplied in millions, so His forerunner will appear in his generation.

This generation is called blessed, forerunning, and Seraphic. They come from the spheres from where no human being has never stepped on Earth before. This is a special, mysterious generation. And this morning it was anointed with Solovki oils of a dual nature: for the carrying of the cross of the Forerunner on Earth, the preparation for the Theocivilization of love; and for the necessary seals.

The spheres from which these souls have come are the spheres of Sacred Theogamy, of the union with the Divinity. That is why they will hear only this new Word.

They have descended to Earth with the mission of preparing the eighty-fifth civilization. Heaven asks us to perceive them only as the forerunning Seraphic generation.

I saw the anointing ceremony. They were clad in white vestments. They were anointed with oils: their brows, their hands. They also performed mysterious initiations.

:—

It has been revealed how the inquisitional Pharisees will be put to shame.

Some oriental master will come: self-important, mammon-loving, preaching ecumenism, and wishing to see the peak of Hinduism in Orthodoxy. He will be converted to Orthodoxy and will start to exert a powerful influence over some important hierarch – an archbishop or a metropolitan. This important person will take his side and accept this new synthetic doctrine, under the influence of some personal affection (maybe infatuation with him), and tempted by a Christianized version of Hinduism like his fathers were seduced by communism. His teaching will be as follows: Christianity should be made the peak of all oriental sciences; all oriental sciences should be summarized and made part of Christianity.

Under the influence of the archbishop, having converted to this seemingly ecumenical new faith, this religion will spread and become popular among hundreds of priests at once. They will accept this abomination without understanding it.

This converted Hindu will be an agent sent specially by the devil in order to destroy Orthodoxy.

And thus Orthodoxy will be lost in a short period. They will accept some accursed diabolical delusion, calling it the peak of Orthodoxy, and eventually vanish from the face of the earth.

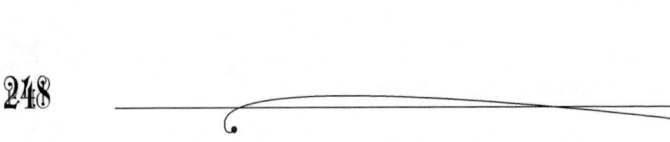

I AM YOUR MOTHER, YOU ARE MY CHILDREN

Kemer, 12 April 2005

815 I am your Mother,
  you are My children.
    – sings the Saviour of the World, the Holy Lady.

The Throne of the Son

816 Christianity, the church, Rome… Lord, look at the people that I have been able to collect. These are My lambs. The lambs of Christ. They are like Me.

817 How many anointed sovereigns, how many martyrs of Supreme Love were there from the first Golgotha of Jerusalem to the second Golgotha of the Solovki! What ripe grapes! So heavy with rich juice, My child!

818 My incomparably beloved child! If you wish to see the birth of the approaching Theocivilization you must sweep away all the clichés of the old

church. The majority of saints, honoured as such on earth by the institutions, are not among my disciples.

⁸¹⁹ But look how numerous they are! They are never-ending indeed, for each is multiplied by a thousand. But how many of them do you remember? How many do you mention in your prayers? Do you invite them to the Council of My saints? Christmas and obituaries are a poor parody of the Triumphant Church of Christ the First-anointed Sovereign.

⁸²⁰ The Theocivilization will be born from the True Triumphant Church of Divine existence. That which has, from the beginning, rejected all that was alien to the Kingdom and denounced the devil and all his accursed temptations.

⁸²¹ My son, I have succeeded in gathering a great number of true disciples. Only the Second Golgotha of the Solovki conveyed a great fiery cloud capable of leading to the Kingdom not merely one small nation, but ten planets like that of Adam.

⁸²² The Second Golgotha of the Solovki has illuminated myriads of worlds sleeping in the darkness. It has revived and inspired them. Who glorifies the Sun of suns of the Second Golgotha, My child?

⁸²³ Day and night the saints ceaselessly pray to

Me to denounce the institutions, because they are an obstacle to realization of Our plans on Earth.

[824] Was it not Me who prayed for the sole wish of Our Father in Heaven and on Earth? May it be fulfilled!

[825] Love the image of the infant. Do not boast of your wit, knowledge, institutional heritage, Orthodox fathers, and the like. Supreme Wisdom loves those who are pure of heart and innocent like a child.

[826] It is to them that She reveals Her secrets and Her treasures. She does not see upon them the seals of original sin – multiplied hundreds of times by institutional temptations – upon them.

[827] This is why the Mother of the Divinity reveals Herself to twelve-year-old children. Patricia Talbot, the supermodel from Ecuador, was pure of heart like a child when Our Lady revealed Herself to her at the age of eighteen.

[828] My child, the Pharisees are arrogant and intelligent. The most powerful way to conquer them is not with abusive prayer, a shield against their 'arrows', and so on; but the shining image of the Infant Divinity. Today I shall imprint it into your heart. From henceforth, My child, only the triumphing

Heavens and the council of My saints will be before you.

⁸²⁹ Have any of the Christian theologians and interpreters understood the meaning of John the Baptist's phrase 'Gather like chaff and burn in un-quenchable fire'? Their magnetizing and hypnotizing treatises have been written for glassy-eyed snakes. Destroy their old books! Burn them in the fire before I do it Myself.

⁸³⁰ Only one throne exists for My disciples, the throne of the Most High and of the Lady, Supreme Wisdom.

⁸³¹ Why do the interpreters not accept the commandment 'Listen to My voice'? Why is there not a single loving heart among them, My child? Supreme Wisdom has rejected them.

⁸³² No matter how often they profess themselves believers, witnesses, zealots, devotees, humble, venerable, and ascetic – it is all empty, My child! Supreme Wisdom has rejected them. At their best they are poor parody turned against the true saints, the true church, and the true faith.

⁸³³ My child, convey to those who can hear My voice through your sensitive scroll-shaped heart: I want them to become as simple as infants and devote themselves to their Lady Supreme Wisdom. It

is not suitable for an infant to suspect or criticize his mother. He lies confidently in her arms, looking lovingly into her eyes, and is nourished by her maternal caress. Both mother and child are connected in a miraculous union of love and trust.

[834] Such faith I demand from My disciples.

[835] My son, their institutions have sunk into evil thoughts. Their anathemas sound like the hissing of snakes. Their damnations act against their own selves.

[836] The saints that they killed and tortured bring them scores without end. And the apostles that approach the Theocivilization angrily demand Me to forbid and seal this tabernacle, which prevents the birth of the Solar Church and the spreading of the tent of the approaching Fiery Theocivilization.

[837] My child, Supreme Wisdom wishes to foster within you 'the mind of Christ', as it is called in the Gospels. Do not hinder Her! Free yourself from the burden of excessive knowledge and the usual clichés. Supreme Wisdom cannot stand this inner snake, secretly sealed pride.

[838] Remember that today's twelve-year-olds will not overtake their teachers while fighting against

contradictions, encephaliti, tarantulas, rhinoceroses, and other dark masses crawling from the serpents and the 'typicon of Skabalanovich'*.

839 My child, commit yourself to this blessed exchange. Pass Supreme Wisdom – the treasure inserted into your heart for thousands of centuries – on to your children. And from them receive child-like trust, spontaneity, and innocence.

840 In order to help your children overcome the intelligent bearded Pharisees by means of the 'mind of Christ', become as a child yourself. Repeat after John the Baptist: 'I must decrease, and they must increase in spirit.*'

841 My love, My child, My burning love affects those anointed by My Purest Mother.

꞉_

842 A magician from St. Petersburg is strongly opposing Me. He arrogantly believes himself to be like you, My child.

843 Supreme Wisdom has H e r o w n w o r l d s t r u c t u r e and lays H e r o w n s e a l s. Only those who follow you in your earthly days are bless-ed. And woe to those who run on ahead of you and begin to spin intrigues. The devil will enter into them. Satan himself, surrounded by a hundred thou-sand snakes, will enter into them in order to tor-

ture the body of the nascent Church. But, My child, these pitiful reptiles are blown away by the wind of Supreme Wisdom like irritating specks of dust.

844 Look, there is no one left. Where are the wild dogs? Where are the encephalitic claws? Where are the wolves, foxes, and boars? Where are they? Supreme Wisdom has rejected and pinned them down, indicating a place where they can pass their days without harming anyone else.

845 Supreme Wisdom, My child! Do not forget about the Mother who has anointed you for the feat of the proclamation of My Messianic Kingdom.

846 It is not against you that the pharisees fight, My child. They are the enemies of the Supreme Wisdom. And they do not detest you as much as Supreme Wisdom, who has found a dwelling place in your vessels, words, gestures, and thoughts; and finally in your disciples, sorrows, and crosses...

847 My child, forget about glorifying the Divinity without Supreme Wisdom. You will not be able to rise higher than a captivated Protestant or a spiteful Byzantine rhinoceros.

848 The Most High reveals the Kingdom of His Supreme Wisdom. Prostrate yourself at your Lady's feet and worship Her, calling Her by new names: the

Lady of Sacred Theogamy, the Mother of Transub-stantiated Divinization, the Lady of the Heavenly Cenacle, the Immaculate Conception, the Bosom of Abraham, the Mother Giving Birth From On High, the Milk-nourishing Mother, Fiery-Winged Sophia, the Mother of the Solovki (Kindest of the Kind), the Lady Clothed in the Sun.

849 My child, the flame of Sophia, Our Mother, sets the accursed rotten Pharisaic straw alight. Our enemies know it. They look for huge water cannons to extinguish Her flame.

850 Have evil thoughts attacked you? Has the ar-row of the Pharisees hit its target and wounded you painfully? Do not hurry, My child. Do not think evil thoughts or enter any battle. Gather your strength and – Oh! no matter how difficult it is, how brainless and mindless you are, worship Supreme Wisdom. And your enemies will disappear by themselves.

851 These are the days for Supreme Wisdom. Worship Her day and night, calling Her your Moth-er, your Lady, your Tent, your Heavenly Mother in Childbirth.

852 The Pharisees' donkeys severed Me from My Mother Supreme Wisdom by making up dogmatic schemes. Later they did the same with the Purest Virgin, denying Her Immaculate Conception[18].

^{853} Here is how I will punish them. No, I will not do it by unmasking them. I shall send them cunning temptations. Their entire being will be stricken by the devil's wisdom. They will take the Adversary* for the Mother of the Divinity in white vestments, and the disgusting, mean movements of our enemy as the wish of the Most High.

^{854} I will shame them in this way, My child. Having rejected Supreme Wisdom and Her anointed sovereigns, they will fall into a dirty puddle of swinish narrow-mindedness, and will be interested in the 'satanic depths', as Paul called them in his epistles. Then the people of the Divinity will retreat from them.

^{855} And on you, My child, I put the seal of the Infant Divinity of New Bethlehem, Christ the Holy Spirit.

^{856} My child, I revealed Myself to you for the first time on My throne as a twelve-year-old Child-King. A boy will grow up. Today I am the Infant Divinity Holy Spirit, and you are the one with Me. Accept My origin and grow in Me.

---

[18] Immaculate conception – is the way of concepting the souls in such civilizations as Atlantis and Hyperborea, which were the civilizations of the immaculate origin. The immaculate conception of the souls are based on the love to the Heavenly Bridegroom, which has been lost for the modern man.

[857] Oh, if you could keep your vow of Supreme Love, and accept nothing else!

[858] Oh, if you could understand to the utmost that Supreme Love overcomes sin and Pharisaism, dissolves serpentine particles, and leads to metanoia. Without much effort and in a short period of time Supreme Love will lead you to absolute holiness, if you keep the cross of Supreme Love in your hands and draw from Supreme Wisdom's treasury of sobriety.

[859] The Cross and Supreme Wisdom, My child, accompany the zealot of Supreme Love, and are impressed in him in a virginal way.

[860] You have been anointed and given more than you can take for yourself. For thousands of years, and for thousands of disciples. Draw from your own treasury, My child, and take a vow of unconditional Supreme Love in the Supreme Wisdom of the Cross, even if you pay the price of mortal sorrows and torturous Holy Passion.

[861] Oh, I can see how many times you will have to break this vow, and how the devil will fight against you! But, My child, I am not asking you for much: live only in the realm of Supreme Love, which illuminates the zealot of My school. Sweep all else aside.

862 I am not asking you for any prayers, regular rules or psalms. I do not need your brilliant memory to remember by heart the dozens of prayers that you have taken from the Heavens.

863 Bear in mind another thing: the throne of Supreme Love sealed in your heart. And hold on to Our Heavenly Mother Supreme Wisdom (one of Her magnificent names in the Theocivilization), the Mother of Supreme Love of the disciples of Supreme Wisdom, the sons and daughters of My Bridal Chamber.

864 Do not feel ashamed of pity the villains that were once your disciples. None of them has been anointed nor has even approached the mysterious Chamber is revealed to you. Forget them forever.

865 The trials have been left behind, My child. Today – the joy and blossoming garden of Supreme Love. Look, what beautiful flowers Our Lady Supreme Wisdom has planted!

866 The coming generation will accept only the language of Supreme Love in combination with the seals of Supreme Wisdom, the building of anointments from on high, and the heavenly Wisdom of the Cross.

*

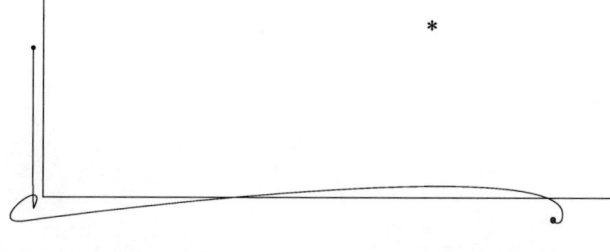

The Divinity gives the Chalice of the Grail:

[867] Drink, drink My sacred Flesh and Blood from the Inexhaustible Chalice of the Grail. May they enter your inner compositions and enrich them!

[868] Today I am the one with you.

⁚—

The revelation has finished. We are sitting under an old pine-tree and enjoying the blessed honey of the Kingdom's presence.

Earthly origins should fade away, especially the source of lust that feeds the lower nervous cells, so that the higher cells – the untouched treasury of the inner man and the divine potential – can be revealed, allowing the pearl of Theogamy to shine upon the Holy of the Holies of the heart's altar.

I do not understand how man can draw strength from the lower suspicious sources, not even suspecting what an outstanding untouched treasure the Most High has laid in his heart!

My Lady Supreme Wisdom! Queen of Supreme Love, Mysterious Supreme Wisdom of the Divinity, enlighten the world!

Humanity, enter Her waters!

⁚—

Waves, waves of Supreme Wisdom are coming from the Throne of the Mother of the Divinity.

The Mother of the Divinity:

⁸⁶⁹ The world will accept My aegis. Humanity is still preparing to accept My seals.

⁸⁷⁰ Peace. Blissful peace be with you!

> The Queen is observing the Turkish settlements below, the coniferous and olive groves, the sea, the highways… What a miracle!

⁸⁷¹ Exalting peace be with you, inhabitants of the Earth; peace be with you!

> It seems to me that the Kingdom of Supreme Wisdom has never before flourished in this way.
>
> Which prophets have entered Her inner chambers? Who was able to see, so intimately, how She serves humanity before the eyes of the Most High?
>
> Oh, hallelujah! Her worthy language is in the mystery of mysteries, in the most interior of our internal being, in the Holy of the Holies. Hallelujah, My Lady!
>
> Bless the church, my children. They are young Seraphites. Bless them, Queen! Clothe them in Your vestments. Present them with Your seals. Weave Your own garments. Share your destinies. Fill them with Your Joy.
>
> Hail, Mary, full of grace! The Lord is with You!

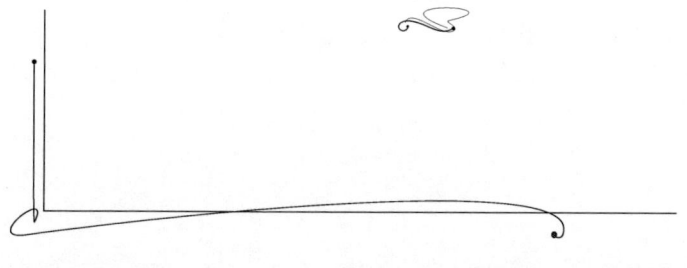

2005 YEAR – THE GOSPEL FOR THE SERAPHITES

Izmir, 13 April 2005

The Lord:

872 My Kingdom is not of this world. My child, it is not enough to learn about the irregularities and fall of the present world. You need to reach the heights and mystery of My Kingdom. O, the Kingdom of the divine light! It is inaccessible at the present time.

873 My child, you are the disciple of Christ. You have entered the radiance of the Grail. You have performed your ablutions in the font of divine lights. My child, Supreme Wisdom has clothed you in solar garments, and you have been exalted to the heavenly world. What sin are you talking about?

874 The spirituality of My disciples surpasses all the spiritual schools of the world. On ancient sar-

cophagi I was depicted as defying the contemptu-
ous the head of the pagan idol Uranus.

[875] My child, I want to talk to the Seraphites only.
2004 is the birth-year of the Seraphic Theocivilization. 2005 is the year of the Gospel for the Seraphites. My child, My Word is dedicated to them.

[876] I no longer speak to the Adamites. These pitiful freaks cannot crawl of the swamp of seduction.
They are boiled in the cauldrons of their vices, and
in their inability to change, to abandon sin and
achieve fiery holiness, they justify their fundamen-
tal vice with the help of the Roman priests.

[877] The Roman church has fallen, My child. It
hates Me. Today I reject the Roman whore; it is not
that I am rejected. I have left them their pitiful be-
longings, the double bookkeeping of their cardinals,
their delusion, and their inquisition – directed not
only against the saints, My child, but against the
Living Divinity.

[878] They wanted to bring the Most High to trial.
But I shall judge them! My verdict is more than
merciful, My child. No, they will not be punished
with infernal cauldrons or scalding frying pans,
eternal fire or the lake of sulphur. No, no. They will
be left behind as they are, with their poor evil be-

longings, if they do not change. I will reject them, and that is enough.

[879] My child, I am aimed at the Seraphites. I thirst to communicate the Gospel of the Divine Word to them. I am in My children. I am Christ of the Seraphites, My child. I am no longer Christ of the miserable Adamites, who handed Me over to the two-thousand-year crucifixion by the Roman whore. I am not Christ of the Byzantine rhinoceros, who pierced and hooked Me with its sharp horn and threw Me into the abyss.

[880] My child, limit your preaching to the new Seraphic universe. Teach about the Seraphic – the Divinely Anointed Sovereign, the Godman, the Godbride, and the Godvirgin. My child, prepare as many Seraphites to be new 'upper new'[19] as you can. My child, enlighten the world with the radiance of the Seraphic Sun. Teach them about the new Seraphic compositions, about the new man.

[881] The old has been sealed! Not only the old tabernacle (the church, the institution); the former man has also been exhausted. His potential is hopeless. His storerooms have become rotten with time. It is

---

[19] It corresponds to the upper room where, according to the Gospel the descending of the Holy Spirit occured upon the desciples of Christ (Acts 1:13).

useless to search for divine signs in him; they were erased without a trace. "Why patch up old clothing if it only makes larger holes?" I say about the Adamites of the twenty-first century.

882 My child, embodied as Jesus Christ the God-man in Jerusalem two thousand years ago, I had already created the fiery Seraphite: the church of exalted and solar apostles.

883 From now on man is divinized. He walks in a solar body, exalts to the Heavens, descends to the bottom of the sea, floats on the surface of the new sea, rises to the clouds, travels through the air, converses with angels, and sees the Most High clearly. His bodies are immortal. He is nourished by mysterious manna. He is illuminated by Supreme Wisdom. The old dusty books are burnt, My child, together with their poisonous catechisms and cursed schemes.

884 I am talking to the Seraphites. They are pure of heart, My child. They are not responsible for the sinful heritage of the eighty-fourth civilization. Some of them (those who come first) will enter the Ark; others will descend from Heaven after the annunciation of My Millennial Kingdom and the descent of the new sun. It will be proclaimed by one hundred and forty-four apocalyptic trumpets.

885 The throne of eternal virginity is for the Seraphites, My child. The Solovki gave birth to the candle-lit procession of Seraphic adolescents in white clothing. During the feast I nourish the Seraphites from the Chalice of the Grail. I give them, My new people in Christ, My Eucharistic Flesh and Blood. Go and announce to your generation: Christ of the new universe is with them!

886 Come out to meet Me, My children, and I will show you the way. You are the children of the new humanity. You are not tainted by the sin of Adam. The old is useless. To begin with, reject Christianity as the initial temptation. Declare yourselves adolescents of the new universe, disciples of the Holy Spirit in the virginal image of the Paraclete, the Groom, your Beloved. Come towards Me. Clothe yourselves. Clothe yourselves with solar vestments. Clothe yourselves…

887 I am the Divinity of the Seraphic universe.

888 Sacred Theogamy, Sacred Theogamy… Why am I speaking to the Seraphites? Only they can understand Me. I have imprinted My seals in them. I live in them. I can enter them as I was unable to enter the Adamites. The Seraphites are My consolation, My angels. They are full of love and absolutely

pure and virginal. I can repose within them, whereas the Adamites only irritated and castigated Me.

889 I have changed their compositions. My wise children are not vulnerable to the hypnosis of the serpent. Pharisaism is alien to their nature. The Roman institution and Byzantine Caesar will no longer be able to arise in their midst. It is inconceivable, unbelievable, My child.

890 They are brides of the new sun. They walk on the surface of the new sea. My child, I see them in the radiance of lights. They are magnificent.

DRINK FROM MY CHALICE!

Izmir, 14 April 2005

The Lord:

891 I have never released the Grail from My hands. Hold the divine Chalice in your hands. The Father is nourished by it, and the need for anything else vanishes.

> The Grail is the Chalice assigned by the Father to His son. The son drinks from it and partakes of all the grace of the Heavenly King. But a worthless, prodigal and venal son will drink the chalice of damnation. He seeks to partake of the Grail, of the Chalice of the Father, but Satan feeds him from his vial of black tar and poisonous rust.

892 Drink from My Chalice! Drink from it for a thousand years. Please drink. I will give it to you to drink.

893 Not a single Pharisee shall be able to drink from My Chalice. Their Sofrino junk-shop* goods are full of poisonous abomination. Venomous

snakes and frogs swim within them, and malicious bacteria develop.

[894] Drink from My Chalice, My child, My little Melchizedek, the priest of My order. The Chalice is united with Me in one. The Chalice is from My heart. Drink and conjoin.

[895] Drink from the Chalice of the Bridal Chamber and exalted, My precious bride! Drink, drink more, drink infinitely.

* * *

Izmir, 18 April 2005

The Throne of the Mother of the Divinity

She Herself was astonished by the fact that the Divinity lives within Her. The mystery is that Christ did not only 'die and was resurrected', as the Christians sing, but that He mysteriously left this world and remained in the Mother of the Divinity.

He remained in Her in the same way that He was born from Her. Christianity did not continue with apostles, but with the Purest Virgin for the next. And it lasted for sixteen years. And She was amazed by this.

What did this continuation consist of?

It was the greatest multiplication of Love after the Golgotha of Jerusalem. The Queen of Heaven appeared in the Bridal Chamber and carried Her cross for humanity, in order to exalt them to the Bridal Chamber. And in Heaven She initiates saints into the Bridal Chamber.

꞉—

The first apparition in Ephesus happened a few kilometres away from here: they called Christ, but His Mother appeared. Christ appeared in Her. (Father Paisiy).

꞉—

896 I will reveal the mystery of My mission to all humanity. All the peoples of the world will worship Me.

897 But it must be suffered great grief (the Mother of the Divinity is crying).

* * *

It is true that this house is the place of the Mother of God presence. She Herself dissolves in this air. Everything is filled with Her. The air is filled with Her. Her presence here is of a kind.felt in no other sacred place of the world.

Driving past these places is like driving into Her heart.

MYRRHIC SCROLLS

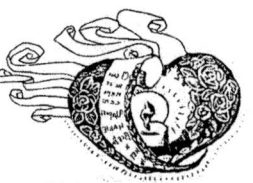

Izmir, 19 April 2005

The Exalted Mother:

⁸⁹⁸ My child, the Torah was copied from eternal scrolls. I read the Pentateuch (and the later Christian Tetraevangelion). How little, My son, is written in the Torah – even with its one hundred and fifty simultaneous spheres of the knowledge of Supreme Wisdom – about the inner penetralia of man, of his infinite divine potential!

⁸⁹⁹ My child, the Torah is fixated upon original sin and its fatal consequences. The Jews could not defeat the sin with the law. The Adamites were given a chance to return to immaculate life in Christ. They scorned it, My son. The more that the church leaders (with their judging and mentoring authority) saw the Church as an innocent bride, the more tightly it was entangled and enchained by the devil.

⁹⁰⁰ My child, I would like to commence a n - o t h e r Scripture. I am unrolling new white scrolls

before you. I never tired of coming and unrolling them before My chosen vessels. But the scrolls in My hands today are being revealed for the first time, My child. They contain the divine treasury of man being revealed to the civilization of the Seraphites.

901 Oh, My child! If only man could see himself through Our eyes! Oh, My son, if he could only once see this treasury, placed by the Most High in his heart, he would begin to ache with the mystery of this inner pearl, and long to extract it. But the sin-centricity of the Pharisees and the inquisitorial eye shine through him, forcing him to repent without the fruits of his repentance, frightening him with horrible tortures in the event that the sin has not been forgiven.

902 I am spreading myrrhic scrolls from My Assumption Bed. They smell sweetly as a sign of wonderful fragrance of the inner man.

903 Listen to me now, My child. The secret inner man is fragrant. There is a fragrant pearl within him. And within that, within the internal marine Grail, is the sign of Divine Matrimony.

904 In Christianity is the cross. In the coming epoch is the Bridal Bed with eight symbols written upon it, which I will reveal later.

[905] So, child, forget this shameful sin-centricity forever. Listen to me attentively. As long as you are concentrated on your own sins or the sins of others, the Pharisees have the power to pierce you with their arrows. See the cup of sins of somebody with the eyes of Supreme Wisdom. Suffer, weep, raise your hands, suffer for others take upon you, take part in redemption, be called a small co-redeemer – yes, yes. But, My child, before entering the heavenly gates, d e s i r e   t o   u n s e a l   t h e i n t e r n a l   g a t e s .

[906] 'The Kingdom of the Divinity is within you.' These are the words repeated tirelessly by the Saviour, in contrast with the Pharisees' 'ascend to the heaven of Enoch, to the God of Israel'. And I am following Him – the heavenly gates i n   t h e   i n - n e r soul, My child, unsealed penetralia and infinite treasures. These exceedingly divine spheres, these most heavenly gifts.

[907] My child, there is nothing in heaven which you could not find implanted by the Divinity in your heart. There are no riches, angelic orders, spatterings or dust, compositions and thoughts, which have not been inserted into man's interior.

[908] Now understand My tears. They are not connected to the end of the world, nor the crucifixion of

the Lord. My child, in the third millennium I speak a different language and reveal Myself to the new people of the Divinity, the Seraphites. My grief is caused by your blindness to your own selves, which equals the blindness to perceive the Divinity.

909 And now I want you, My child, to open your eyes and knock on the inner doors. My child, I can accept you into My destines to the degree that you are able to enter your interior – the Holy, then the Holy of the Holies, and finally the Holiest Holy of the Holies.

910 My child, remembering sins and repenting are the most miserable means by which the devil today can suggest, with the objective of leading a creature of the Divinity to the most wretched condition and make him absolutely blind. The origin of sin will disappear as one grows in holiness. So, My child, focus on the inner treasures!

911 The poor Christians have for centuries repeated after the priests: 'His Kingdom is not of this world'. But they sought it who knows where: in imagined heavens; in cloisters, caves, and deserts; in experiences of saints; and so on.

912 My child, when speaking of 'this world' our Saviour had in mind spheres that do not touch the

inner man. My child, the Father has blessed Me to unroll these myrrhic scrolls before the new humanity. Read them! Look within yourself. Seek and you will find. I shall repeat the words of our Saviour: 'Knock, and it will be opened to you'.

[913] I have asked the Most High to bless the unsealing of the inner treasuries. The way to the superheavenly royal treasuries is opened, My child!

[914] Descending into your inner being, you will find and attain the Seraphite within you, not implicated in the original sin of Adam. And then, together with Me, you will read the solar Torah and the heavenly Gospel, called 'eternal' in St. John's Revelation. And then you will read the myrrhic scrolls for hours, without the power to remove your eyes. After this you will be imbued with blessed inner peace, and you will not be affected by any conditions which might disturb your serenity.

[915] I will name 'crowned victor' the one able to reveal divine treasuries within themselves and see the countless great riches kept in them.

[916] My child, I will reveal to you one of the divine mysteries of the coming age. In order to marry the Divine Beloved as a worthy and prepared bride (remember: the bride of the Lamb prepared herself),

the Seraphite should comprehend and see the Divinity sealed in his interior. The Most High has inscribed Himself in your utmost depths. The human 'I', and the way that the soul perceives itself in the light of the reflected mirror, is an external refraction of the divine origin imprinted in the mystery of mysteries and in the interior of the most internal.

917 But there is an even deeper level than the Divinity concealed within man, My child. I am revealing this layer for the first time. It is called Theogamy.

918 My child, Theogamy has been sealed. And, although many can feel it with their hearts, singing 'O, Theogamy! O, our Lady!' during the liturgy and worshipping it as you do, My child, you should light the Theogamic candle. After that the river of Theogamy will begin to flow. Then fragrant oils will be shed, after which the anointed sovereign will be prepared to marry the Most High. His departure from the world is the last of the preparatory sacraments for the Bridal Chamber.

919 My child, descend to your inner treasuries again and again. Joseph was a carpenter and his favourite occupation was making ladders. The ladder of the Cross of Golgotha exceeds that of James, My

child. Take from St. Joseph this carpenter origin, also inherent in Our Lord, in order to erect a one-hundred-and-fifty-step staircase in your interior leading to the Bridal Chamber.

920 Descend into your interior again and again, My child. There you will find divine treasuries, the Second Golgotha of the Solovki, Sekirnaya Mountain, the oils of master Seraphim, and all that is happening and will happen in the world.

921 Hermits did not go out into deserts in order to say meditative prayers, ask forgiveness for their sins, or avoid the temptations of the world. No, no, My child! In this blessed seclusion the angels crafted inner penetralia into which the chosen ones descended as if into anointed cellars, extracting beautiful images, myrrh, anointing oils, and other treasures.

922 My child, penetrate My words! Penetrate them again and again so that you understand that they are incompatible with the Christian way of thinking!

923 Christianity has perished because it returned to Jewish and Pharisaic sources. Sin-centricity has killed Christianity.

924 When the Saviour told the parable about the pearl buried in the field, He had in mind this inner Grail: something mysterious and anointed, united

with the Divinity. Seek it, My child! Seek your inner virginal Grail.

925 Have you not taken vows of unworldliness for this reason? Have you not, for this reason, renewed the vows of obedience before Me and of devotion to Me in each liturgy? Have I not, for this reason, shown you the treasures of Orthodoxy and Catholicism in the images of their saints – in order that you accept the pearl of the Grail, the treasure of Christ?

926 My child, as the Mother I would like to protect you from enemy arrows. And I ask you only for one thing. Please follow My words, no matter how difficult it may be. I could not give you a better shield than the revelation of these myrrhic scrolls and the wonderful chambers of the most divine inner Seraphite. They will fully protect you, and the furious Pharisees will be left rage-stricken and breathless.

927 My heart languishes for Theogamic bliss, for the kingdom of the brides of Christ! My child, Catholic missionaries converted the people of Africa to Christ. Now imagine a fiery mission leading millions of souls to the Theogamic Ark. My child, imagine My desire to convert souls to the Bridal Chamber.

928 Take this vow for Me. Promise Me to limit

yourself to the fiery apostolate of Theogamy. Perceive the new and eternal Gospel within it, sealing the Tetraevangelion as once sealed the Pentateuch – the Torah.

THE ASSUMPTION BED HAS BEEN REVEALED

The Mother of the Divinity:

929 My sweetest children! I invite you to take part in the plans of the Most High, revealed to humanity for the first time.

930 Was this place not hidden for nineteen centuries before the revelation to Anne Catherine Emmerich*? Has the Church not erred by calling miserable Jerusalem, the place of the Lord's crucifixion and My persecution, the place of My Assumption? My child, the mystery of Nightingale Mountain as the place of My Assumption has been hidden until the end of times. I was transferred from Jerusalem to Ephesus by the right hand of the Most High. And with My establishment here, at the site of the embodiment of the Son of the Divinity on Earth, Jerusalem was transferred here as well.

931 My child, the place of My Assumption and its mysteries were sealed until the Bridal Bed of Theogamy had been revealed.

932 From here I was lifted up to Heaven, to the

fiery Thrones of the Glory of the Most High, to where no mortal soul has ever ascended and even the highest angelic ranks have no access. I am establishing My throne of the Bridal Chamber here. And from here I shall ascend, with the humanity of the future age, to the ever-lasting Supper of the Lamb and the places of His eternal triumph.

933 What I have revealed will happen in the coming times. But the Assumption Bed was revealed on Nightingale Mountain, My child, and with it the mystery of Divine Theogamy.

934 Did the apostles not gather h e r e on Ephesus Mountain, rather than in Jerusalem, to witness the crowning of the Mother of Christ with the crown of the Bridal Chamber? And now, My child, I will call new apostles – new Bartholomews, Peters, and Andrews – and they will gather together around My fiery pillar in preparation for the ascent to the Bridal Chamber.

935 From here I proclaim the will of the Divinity. The Divinity wants to enter into the union with the new humanity of the Earth. And today I invite all listeners to My Theogamic Bosom of Abraham. Come and delight your ears with the words of the Most High! Come, shower your hearts with myr-

rhic oils! Come and find peace under the Heaven of the Most High and under the tabernacle of Supreme Wisdom that has been erected here.

The Heavenly Queen is fragrant. The fire of Her heart cannot be described. For the first time I can see the Bridal Chamber above the hills of the Assumption, above the mountains of transfiguration, above that place appointed the capital of the approaching Theogamy: the country of the Most High consisting only of brides, virgins, ecstatic poets, Seraphites of unutterable beauty, troubadours, knights, elders, warriors, and lambs. Thousands of images of Christ, the Son of the Most High, will be imprinted within them.

This divine place has been kept safe until the end of times, says the Purest Virgin. And now it is presented to all of humanity as a gift. Take it! Hear the fiery message of our Queen Theogamy, who invites all of the race of Adam to the Bridal Feast, to the mystery of Christ.

The Queen is returning to the theme of the earthly days:

[936] My child, Our enemy has long ears. His spies reached Ephesus. Although I asked that not a word was said about Me, it was not able to hide My residence. Rumours about the place of My concealment reached even Jerusalem. From the top of the mountain My two faithful myrrh-bearing maidens saw

three criminals who had come, armed with sharp knives, to slaughter Me like a lamb. We managed to hide on time.

937 I did not know rest in any place on the Earth. Theogamic ecstasy and the inspirations of the Bridal Chamber are accompanied by Holy Passion. The Holy Spirit raises His bride to the Bridal Bed so that she is not distracted by anything else. And in her sorrows He shows her through sufferings t h e c o s t of this union, this most inconceivable of inconceivable mysteries.

938 But say, My son, could the Jews even imagine that the tablets would fall from heaven and that Moses would lead the elected people with a pillar of cloud by day and a pillar of fire by night? Could their descendants imagine that the Most High, One in the Holy Trinity, would send His Only-Begotten Son Christ the Godman into the world? My child, before crucifying the Lord, before they came to hate and damn Him, they were petrified not knowing what to do.

939 Now, My child, I proclaim the new, bright, eternal Theogamic covenant of the Most High with the race of Adam. By origin the Seraphites descend from Christ, from the New Adam. Today

I embrace you with divine arms of the Bride of the Lamb. I have come to bring His sweetest blessing down to you and to call upon you to leave your previous deeds and images of faith or faithlessness; to encourage you to reach the chamber of the Most High, and to enter the Ark (which means the same thing).

940 Peace be with you, My beloved ones! And await the miracle of the revelation of the Bridal Bed above the world.

⁚—

941 ...To my enemies. Three times I was transfigured in the Glory of the Most High. They were burnt to ashes, and afterwards I resurrected them from the dead. And having been converted they became My zealous servants and friends.

942 My child, the enemy rose against the revelation of Supreme Wisdom all over the world. Evildoers in the guise of saints wage a bitter battle against Me. Pay no attention to their damnations and poison.

943 Drink the sweetest wine of Supreme Wisdom. Glorify your Lady. Never grow tired of glorifying the Purest One, as She has revealed Herself to you. Invite the whole world to worship

the Most High in the person of His Mother Supreme Wisdom, who has revealed Herself in recent times more closely and clearly than ever before.

⁹⁴⁴ Have faith in the victory of your difficult battle.

THE WHITE GRAIL
IN SHINING LIGHTS

Izmir, 23 April 2005

The Mother of God:

⁹⁴⁵ *I* will establish a new universe. My protection is spread all over the world. I am the Queen of the new mankind.

⁹⁴⁶ The Grail will come from this sea, and three elders in solar vestments will bring it into your home. After this the Ark will be closed, and the most painful hours will come.

⁹⁴⁷ The white Grail in shining lights will be raised above the first liturgy of the altar of Sophia of the Theocivilization, and will proclaim the kingdom of Melchizedeks, Seraphites, and engraved Christs.

⁹⁴⁸ Izmir means 'iz mira[20]' – 'from this world'. It is the land of Exodus.

I see mysterious signs on the Grail.

---

[20] Phonetically it sounds correspondingly to the Russian "iz mira" – not from this world.

THE TREE OF ETERNAL VIRGINITY

[949] Son of the Bridal Feast praise virginity over and over again!

[950] In the Revelation of St John the fallen church was shown as a whore. I am speaking 'again and again', assuming that the extolled height of the virginal thrones, virginal communities and churches praised by you is insufficient.

:⸺

[951] Virginity, My child, comes from the immaculate source. Virginity sets you apart from original sin. The church was lost when it betrayed original virginity, like Adam and Eve. The all-healing purity of the divine light of the original creation was returned to the church by Christ and Me. And the church collapsed, having accepted the seals of this world, Caesar, and the whore.

[952] The disciples of Christ were supposed to be virgins and lambs consecrated to the cross (the instrument of Exceeding Love). This is what John saw in his Revelation. He depicted the throne of the Lamb surrounded by virgins.

[953] The church should not have mixed with the sinful world; it should have gone out into the world

with the cross of eternal virginity to conquer and convert fornicators to virginity. Instead of fulfilling its mission and high vocation, the church lost the gift of distinguishing the spirit. Having committed the sin (equal to the crucifixion of the Saviour) of persecuting the saints, the church permitted secret sorcerers and fornicators to enter its bosom. And from within they seduced the tree planted by Christ and nurtured by Me.

954 The image of the Godbearer of the old churches is being swept aside, My child, as the greatest hindrance to My plans. Today I am not the 'Mother of the Divinity, the 'Godbearer', or the 'Mother of the Lord', but the Mother of eternal virginity. The Ever-Virgin Lady, the Immaculate Womb giving birth from on high to a humanity untainted by sin.

955 My womb is the Ark of salvation for the humanity descending from on high. I invite angels from Heaven, souls with the immaculate marking on their brows, and all mortals of the race of Adam who wish to reject the original defilement. I ask them to thirst for eternal virginity.

956 To invite only virgins to the church does not mean a lopsided celibacy, a monkish or desert-dwell-

ing monasticism. And here the church has split and deviated from the plan of the Most High.

957 In their bridal union the true disciples of Christ begin virginal relationships and are anointed to virginal and fruitful matrimony in a special way, My child. Gradually, having fulfilled the duty of raising children, the spouses take a vow of eternal virginity and become part of angelic hierarchy.

958 The Seraphites will do that the Adamites were unable to do. The centre of their lust has been removed or interrupted.

∴

959 Virginity, My child. Start your morning with the prayer:

> I have come to this world
> to enter into the bridal union with the Divinity through suffering humanity.
> And:
> I make a vow of eternal virginity to you, My Holy Lady:
> virginal mind (touching your brow),
> virginal life (belly),
> virginal heart, absolutely faithful, sacrificing, passion-
>   less (heart)
> ascending 150 stairs of the ladder of virginal glory
>   (from the right to the left shoulder).

[960] I have performed the signs of the vow of virginity, My child.

[961] Therefore, keep the mind virginal, so that nothing sinful or mean may touch it. Do not disgrace it with bad thoughts, suspicions, mental reasoning, or condemnation of your neighbour. Your mind should be innocent, virginal and lamb-like.

[962] Virginal life, My son, is possible only when have been touched with My scepter of the high priest Melchizedek and your lustful furnace has been removed. You understand what kind of cross awaits among those, who are possessed by lust. But accomplish the feat for the glory of the Most High. Carry and retain the seals of eternal virginity within yourself like a tabernacle. Nourish yourself from its source. Ascend to the heights of its joy. Find peaceful, calm and long life under the sign of eternal virginity. By 'eternal virginity' I have in mind the virginity that leads to eternal life and the sphere of the divine existence (of the True Church).

:⸺

[963] Your heart, My child (the Queen is touching my heart), is one with Mine. They are united forever. There is a lit candle within it. And the heart longs for the bridal bliss.

964 Child, do not cloud your mind with the sight of other people's sins, nor with dark thoughts, ugly surroundings, the stupidity of your colleagues, the absurdity of circumstances, their idiocy… The heart resides in the chambers of the Most High. There is a golden ark, three vessels with oils, and the Solovetskay Golgotha. And the Lamb has found peace.

965 The Bridal Chamber is within your inner being, My child. Do not seek it in anywhere else today. Seek it here on Nightingale Mount.

966 Observe the encircling chain of mountains; this is the place of My Assumption. These Ten Mountains are the city of the Bridal Chamber.

:—

967 The church has become entangled with the order of this world. Neither the Divinity nor the world is in need of such an entangled church, My child. Humanity needs a different church, a virginal church, supporting within itself not only the seven institutional sacraments, but also the mystery of the reality of the descending Kingdom, the mystery of the presence of the Most High, and the mystery of the victory of virginity over lust, of meekness over self-will, and of genuine spirituality over its surrogates.

968 My child, the world is in need of apostles of superior virginity. They will save the Earth. I will take into My Ark only those who have taken the vow of eternal virginity, or at least strive for it.

969 I appeal to spouses in the myrrh-anointed union of the myrrhic Christ to take the vow of eternal virginity, which means asking Me to change the image of their union and to make it perfect, in the shape of Theogamic and superheavenly matrimony. Oh, My child, may each marriage bed become the Bridal Bed! May Theogamy become the desire of the new humanity!

970 I am offering you the ideal of universal Theogamy. I am extending its tent to the full extent of heaven and of earth. In this way I wish to save the world from the inevitable terrible disasters, and also the millions of innocent victims destined to die during them.

971 My child, the root of lust must be chopped off at its foundation.

972 I am chopping it off! (The Queen chops off the root with a sharp spear. She lifts it and shakes some gnats from the disgusting dry bush.) And I tell you that nothing sinful will be saved, but thrown into fire. (The Queen is throwing the hewn bush into the fire.)

973 My child, look at this tree (the Queen is pointing to a wonderful fragrant tree and the nightingales singing around it.) This is the tree of eternal virginity. Love it. It is beautiful. It bears the sweetest of fruit. Desire to taste it, and only it. Agree to die, but not to partake of the origin of lust.

974 This is the only way to fast today, My son (the Mother of the Divinity is emphasizing it). I invite you to only one fast, My beloved ones. Cease to nourish your mind with lust, your blood with lust, your thoughts with lust, your whole old being with lust. Nothing lustful that weaves mortal clothes should interest humanity any longer.

975 I am bringing new ideals. See how beautiful is the tree before you. And remember the bush that I have just thrown into the fire. Its leaves were rotting in the ground, its fruit had decayed long ago, and snakes were coiled in its branches to warm in the sun.

976 I give that image in My vivid description of the eternal glory of Christ. My disciples and the followers of Christ, the 'faithful witnesses', will be those who realize that Christ's teaching is the appeal to eternal virginity, the virginity of the entire human.

[977] The Theogamic covenant begins with the vow of virginity. Love it with all your heart, and come to Me. Only I, the Most Merciful Lady of the Thrones of eternal virginity of the Creator, am able to perform over the Adamites the sacrament of the extinguishing and complete removal of the lustful furnace.

[978] What I have done with you, My child, and with dozens of My favourite fathers, sons and daughters called to be anointed sovereigns of the Bridal Chamber, I would like to do with all humanity. Yes, My child: with homosexuals, lesbians, drug addicts, and punks.

[979] Why do your hearts accept the apostolate of eternal virginity with such difficulty? Because of your connections with the old churches, My child. They are stuck in the mire of disgusting lust.

[980] My child, I would like to reveal to you the degree of the fall of priesthood. The number of paedophiles among Catholic priests exceeds those depicted in the mass media by dozens of times. And it is usual for them to have a lustful mind. Their merely bookish and philosophical interest in the Gospel, their love of vicious Hellenic sources, speak of them as native fornicators, as My eternal enemies.

[981] My child, have no contact with them! You are a different church. Even if you are called sectarians and cursed, fear nothing. The church has been ordered to be the ever-virginal sanctuary descended from Heaven, bearing witness the world and dispersing the surrounding darkness with its light. If the church ceases to be a lamp its candle will be blown out and thrown away to rot in wet cellars.

[982] My child, remind humanity of all that I have said.

[983] Virginity is not a vocation for certain people only. Man is the creation of the Divinity and is called to virginity. Let no one dare wave it away or justify themselves on account of their family, their chalice of sins, their horoscope, their unreadiness, and so on. May they not become like those invited to the Bridal Feast in the Lord's parable: justifying themselves with different excuses.

:⸺

[984] The criteria for the divine and its opposite are wonderfully simple, My child. There is no need to organize councils, establish church courts, or pass sentences at the inquisition. The virginal comes from the Divinity; the lustful from the devil.

985 My child, accept My words as the sole criterion for life in the third millennium, and for the judgement of the Divinity over souls. The degree of initiation into virginity, with its many consequences and stairs and graded anointments, determines the fate of the soul in the eternal world if it has not been invited specially or excused by celestial protectors.

986 The devil continues his artful game secretly, sending the serpent. His main occupation is to cause disorder, chaos and confusion among the Adamites invited to high anointments and to aspirations higher than those of the angels. The mission of our enemy includes 'Babylon', i.e., to cause disorder, to mix what is inharmonious: virginity and lust.

987 Nothing lustful, whatever form it takes, has anything to do with the Divinity, with humanity created in the image of the Divinity, or with life given from on high. Any lust is extirpated, burnt and punished with purifying fire, My child.

988 Why fear disasters and, turning the television off at 12 in the evening, which transmitted the chronicle of some Asiatic disasters[21] on the news, break-

---

[21] Asian disaster: the tsunami in Thailand on 26th December 2004, were 200,000 people were killed.

ing out in a cold sweat? My child, lust presents a universal Asiatic cataclysm for every one of you. The fire of hell carried by the serpent will achieve its ordained fate. Yes, My child, millions find themselves in subterranean spheres only because they fed upon lustful sources, from Gehenna and the sulphurous sea.

989 My child, I am now offering My White Fonts and Life-giving Springs. See how many there are over Nightingale Mountain!

> I see a wonderful spring of water bursting from the new sun. And from this a thousand streams flow to all the corners of the Earth. Each signifies a new spring, bursting from the centre of Hiroshima, Tokyo, Los Angeles, Rio de Janeiro, New York, Moscow, Saint Petersburg, Berlin, and the other cities of Europe, Asia, and Africa.

990 My child, choose virginity as your perfect ideal. Become its apostle. First turn your inner being into its apostle. Mould yourself into a zealous, fiery virgin, full of Holy Passion. Sweep aside all lustful thoughts and aspirations expressed in the form of gluttony, phrase-mongering, or idle reading.

991 Lust has many forms. The devil is a master at carrying lust into refined spheres, of presenting it in subtle shapes. The entire fallen cosmos con-

sists of transformed forms of sophisticated lust. My Supreme Wisdom will help you to reject them and extract the pearl, the treasury: virginity.

:—

992 My child, as I said before, the criteria of the divine for life in the third millennium are extremely simple. You need no catechisms or services. The virginal will be preserved in the life of the future age. The lustful will be swept from the face of the earth.

993 I will present My virgins with oil that will attach them to the Divinity and enable them to experience unearthly joy. Those who are ridden with lust will be rejected if they ignore My call to chastity after receiving My sign.

994 On the eve of the disasters, My child, I promise to give the sign of virginity to members of the race of Adam who rank among My potential sons and daughters. Many will hear and convert. By conversion I mean the vows of purity taken for the return of the original image of the Divinity in creation.

995 Peace be in your hearts!

996 Build a new universe! See no sin, for its days are numbered. Sin is the mortal beginning and rotten

shoots. It is corroded by mildew and aphids. And it is being swept away into nothingness.

[997] Love virginity with your whole being and see the presence of the Divinity within it.

:⸺

THE MOUNTAIN OF THE BRIDAL CHAMBER

Oh, how rapturous is the grace of the Bridal Chamber! Oh, the mountain of the Bridal Chamber! Here the grace of the Holy Spirit is so abundant that man walks ahead of himself, speaks more than himself, and knows significantly more than himself. A divine particle has been inserted within him, by means of which he surpasses his own self. The mountain of original charismas for the humanity of the third millennium. Having ascended it, the foreordained anointed sovereign will fall into raptures, ecstasy, and mystical reverence; and his mind will be exalted to the chambers of Theogamy.

:⸺

[998] Humanity, drowning in your sins – you are invited to the light of perfect holiness. May peace be in your fonts, purified by My motherly suffering.

:⸺

A bus full of tourists is passing by. The guide points to something in a lively way. Of course, to some archaeological site or historical monuments; anything other than the words of the Mother of the Divinity. The bus has passed by the prophet of the Divinity. How is the world experienced through the bus window?

We meet a foolish, weak-sighted Turkish marmot. He is accompanied by Balaam's donkey, an underdeveloped mare, or something similar. The foolish man will approach us and ask: 'Who are you?' And the Divinity will reveal to him the mission of Nightingale Mountain.

Eurotours are a kind of Eurocloset around the belated relic. The tour mafia is closely connected to the religious mafia. The Pharisees bless tour groups and pass sacred temples off as living museums and archives; instead of being "faithful witnesses" they perform the roles of guide and archivist, leading tourists amongst the frozen relics of the past. Meanwhile the Divinity creates living thrones, temples, and churches.

999 My rapturous grace is spread over all the worlds.

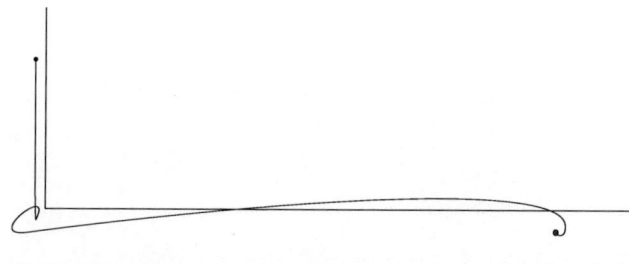

THE HOLY REPOSE
OF THE BRIDAL BED

Izmir, 24 April 2005

The repentance of the anointed sovereign is different to that of an ordinary sinner.

The Holy Mother:

¹⁰⁰⁰ My child, do not look for repentance or penitence in them. They cannot repent of that which you ask of them.

¹⁰⁰¹ The repentance of the anointed sovereign is different to that of ordinary sinners. They are capable of repenting only of what their conscience condemns: sexual, generational, sleeping, waking, gluttonous, and other sins. But there is another kind of repentance: the repentance of the anointed sovereigns. Do not demand it from those who have yet to reach the level of insight into the spiritual world.

> The Mother of God is grieving greatly. They do not hear Her. The cycle of revelations on Nightingale Mountain is coming to an end. The Mother of the Di-

vinity is weeping. Tears pour in streams from Her eyes, which have taken on colours unknown to me. They are dark. It must be the colour of clotted blood.

Izmir, 27 April 2005

¹⁰⁰² I will give my special patronage to those who are persecuted.

¹⁰⁰³ Oh, how much I have already done for you! I entered your godmother, Mary Orlovskay. I shaped Saint Euphrosynia. I blessed Seraphim Solovetsky; the scrolls of the Second Solovetskay Golgotha were unrolled from Heaven, and his words started to pour myrrh.

¹⁰⁰⁴ From here the path to Nightingale Mountain is only for those who are persecuted and in the Holy Passion. They find incomparable grace here.

THE UNIVERSUM OF THE MOST HIGH

Izmir, 29 April 2005

O, Queen of the Bridal Chamber,
My Lady with the God.

Here on the Mountain of the Bridal Chamber there is nothing other than the path of love. Here is the holy peace of the Bridal Bed. Here the Divinity unites with His Bride. Here there are no thoughts, no prayers; nothing that separates or divides in two. Here, for the first time, the image and likeness according to which man was created serves divine goals. The *image* means that the Divinity is secretly concealed within man. The *likeness* means that man can act like the Divinity. The institutes erased the image and likeness in humanity, transforming people into miserable slaves persecuted by their own fears and thoughts.

Here there is nothing but the Bridal Chamber. Here there is nothing but the Bridal Bed...

The prayer:
Hail, Mary, full of grace...
Christ, that is born in *us*.

This version 'in us' should be repeated many times. Later it will also be possible to say: 'Christ that is born in millions'.

:⸺

An unbearable devastating battle began. An attack. Hostile whirlwinds fell upon us. Satan commanded me to jump from the mountain into the abyss, and to throw a stone and kill Father Paisiy...

I suffered, I could not find peace. Nothing could help me – not prayer, the Holy Passion, or faith – nothing. The Queen strengthened me with a prayer:

'Hail Mary... the Lord is with You... Christ is born in us, in millions,' She said. 'Only a few of the anointed sovereigns can say this prayer.' After that, in the position of the Solovki catacomb (lying), She blessed the contemplative respiratory prayer. She came and calmed me with Her smile.

The Holy Mother:

[1005] My child, you were given a sign that told you which devilish whirlwinds blow on the mountain of the Bridal Chamber. Who is the dragon, My child? He guards the entrance to the Bridal Chamber. He is like a fiery cherub with a sword, guarding the gates to paradise against the cunning one. I am the reigning Lady Supreme Wisdom, and the dragon has submitted to me. My child, I have permitted this battle, these several minutes of terrible attacks. I saw your Holy Passion – the whirlwinds tried to extract your waxen heart, anointed only yesterday with myrrh – and I stopped our enemy instantly. My child, I can now tell you: a c c e s s t o N i g h t i n g a l e M o u n t a i n h a s b e e n c l o s e d, w h e t h e r o r n o t t o u r b u s e s c o m e h e r e d a i l y, wheth-er or not the Turks set up rows of shopping stalls near the foot of the Mountain, whether or not the Catholics consider asking for another stall for a newly-discovered relic.

The Lord:

1006 'Do not ask for help or prayer from any one. I am your shield. I am your Lord'.

> O my Lord, I am your bride.
>
> You sent swarms of demons to me so that I would lie on the grass, spread my coat beneath me, put a stone under my head and appear before You as your bride: I am all yours.
>
> It was a little Bridal Bed. Sorrow approaches the happy hour of the Assumption. ...The blessed virgin of the Divinity.
>
> ҉⁚__

> Prayer:
>
> *Breathing in:* Oh, the sweetest,
>
> oh, myrrh-pouring bliss!

Breathing out:	Peace and perfection.
Holding one's breath:	The Bridal Chamber of the Most High Divinity, Most exalted grace.
With pressure:	The treasury of breathing has been sealed.

∴⸺

The Holy Mother:

[1007] I have revealed to you what I wanted to say. Now lie on the Bridal Bed. The double Gospel of the Salvation-on-His-Spilt-Blood. I have inserted the pearl of the Grail into you, and into it the mystery of the conjugal ties of Jesus and Mary, because it would not have been conveyed to you otherwise. You, and the church after you, and the world after that, will be raised to a new level in order to experience that which I have experienced here on Nightingale Mountain: the most celestial bliss of the saints, of those who enter the Bridal Chamber, and of the elected brides. But for this to happen another heaven should first be revealed – the Heaven of the Lamb, the Heaven of the Solovki.

[1008] The groom is the Lamb of Supreme Wisdom. Do not be misled by false meekness and humility. As the embodiment of the Divinity, the Wisest Lamb is universal and powerful. Oh, My child, first My aegis, My selection, My patronage, My shield, and My sphere. And only then the anointment, the path, the prayer, the faith, and the Bridal Chamber.

1009 Repeat My name over and over again. Rarely do I hear the address to Supreme Wisdom from priests. They are not elated by Sophia – they do not understand who She is, or what storerooms She conceals. They do not understand that She is the Tent of the Most High, the Abode of the Living Divinity. I repeat to you: the institutes, the 'substitutes', can manage without Me. They replaced Christ with priests, and Supreme Wisdom with dogmas and catechisms.

1010 Break into the Kingdom of Supreme Wisdom. And confess yourself the disciple of the Supreme Wisdom day and night. Study and explore Her mysterious ways. My child, I am a faithful Mother; I will not betray a disciple protected by Me.

1011 Yes, I have come to destroy the old tabernacle, to demolish the aspersions cast on the Living Divinity as well as the vampire crypt in the centre of Rome. Yes, My child, I am erecting a new temple. As priest of the Most High, have the strength to disperse the demonic armies with a single motion of your hand and to establish the Glory of our Lord.

[1012] I, the Most Fragrant Lady of the new humanity, the Mother of the new universe, am blessing you with peace (The Queen is talking to the world), with the cloud of my Supreme Wisdom, with the descent of grace, and with virginal vestments. May the essence of man be changed. May he receive the light of the Most High and turn his eyes to Heaven.

[1013] Oh, My child, the mystery of Nightingale Mountain is that he who looks to Heaven from its slopes will see the face of the Most High. My child, I now invite all humanity to turn their eyes towards Nightingale Mountain. Before you will be a fiery chariot, solar Ezekiel, wise Enoch, the Tabor tabernacles of the three disciples, and the transfiguration of the Saviour.

[1014] My child, today I invite tens and thousands of My new disciples to gather around the new Assumption Bed, which is called the Bridal Chamber. The apostles formed a circle. You will form five, ten, and fifty circles. And here will arise the new universe, the universe of the Most High. And may peace be in your hearts.

[1015] My child, during an attack do not act in traditional ways. You used to take out your rosary according to habit and say the prayer of exorcism, 'Hail, Mary', and so on. Summon your Mother Supreme Wisdom, understanding that She has permitted and blessed this act. And remember that the power and absolute might over diabolical powers has been given to Her. You will see what happens. The Cunning One will retreat. Do not allow the enemy to confuse your mind; summon your Lady Supreme Wisdom, serenely committing yourself to Her power.

This is the Mountain of the power of the Most High. I see a multitude of angels. They fly with a great noise, together with the chariot of the Divinity. It is indescribable!

The Bridal Chamber will become the property of millions. I see and bless it. I exult, unite, rejoice; I fly through the air, on wings, to every corner of the earth. The new apostolate of the Bridal Chamber. Hallelujah!

No one has ever taught about the Bridal Chamber. The world will be converted.

The whole world belongs to you, my dear Lady of all nations of the Earth. I bade farewell to the Holy Mother on the Mountain of the Assumption.

I see that all of my children have been sent by Her. Our church has collected all those who passionately love the Mother of the Divinity – Her children. And it will continue in this way. All those who are loved by Her and who love Her will, in a special way, unite with the Church of the Most Holy Godbearer.

* * *

Izmir, 1 April 2005

Oh, I would like never to descend from the mountain of bliss. I am experiencing something similar to your apostles when they built the tabernacles and said: 'Lord, let us stay with you here forever. We are so happy'.

The Queen answers from above:

[1016] Nothing prevents you, My son, from being here with Me in spirit. I will always wait for you on Nightingale Mountain.

As I understand, this mysterious sanctuary of the Most High has the ability to be omnipresent, i.e., the ability, as the main throne of the Heavenly Father, to extend over the world and invite all those who seek Him to the top of the mountain. Marvellous!

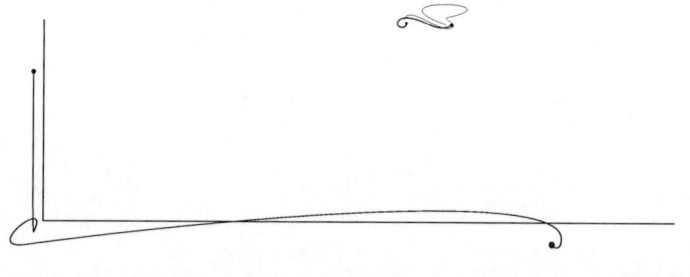

THE TREASURY
OF THE SHAPING
OF ADAM
OF THE BRIDAL CHAMBER

Izmir, 3 May 2005

The Queen of Heaven:

1017 This mountain has existed since the beginning, My child. The Most High said: 'I have been preparing it for You since the beginning. And You must prepare Nightingale Mountain for My disciples, the young offspring of the Solovki.

1018 Nightingale Mountain is older than Marine Kemer Mountain. Man was created upon it: he was formed from the dust of the earth and the living soul was breathed into him. And Nightingale Mountain has been attended by the Divinity since the very beginning. The Most High gave it to Me as My chamber. The chamber of the Daughter of Zion – this is what He has called it since the beginning of time. It is the sum of the mysteries of Divine Providence. The most mysterious secret of secrets, the place of the presence of the Divinity.

[1019] When mist descended upon the Earth and there were no plants, reeds, lakes or waters, the Most High recognized Nightingale Mountain in His Providence and called it the birthplace of the sons of the Divinity. For Theocivilization III it will forever be New Bethlehem, New Jerusalem, New Elion, the New Cenacle, the New Wineskins, the New Church, the New Priesthood, and the New throne, My child.

[1020] Supreme Wisdom, considering Nightingale Mountain and the ten surrounding mountains to be the Divine Tent of Her Presence, has revealed Herself to the world as the Lady of the anointed sovereigns, as Theogamy. She has spread the myrrhic scrolls of divinization, of the sweetest union, of the ineffable act of uniting as one – of the mysteries never before revealed to humanity.

[1021] Since the beginning of time the plan to give man His divine treasury (hidden even from the angels of the highest ranks) has existed and, during the years of the world's history, been contemplated by the Most High. He faithfully adopted the Sons of the Divinity as His heirs.

1022 My child, from here, where the tent of the Supreme Commander-in-Chief and the army of the Most High has been erected, I see the opposing mountain in the Himalayas which is called the 'Ben-Elohims'* (fallen angels), Tibet, the lowest cosmos, and the civilization of the devil.

1023 The Most High has begun to speak! Theogamy has descended from the Kingdom like a cloud, like the City of the Divinity coming down with an assembly of myrrh-anointed saints. The oils of the Bridal Chamber are in their hands. Immortal bodies and restful vestments. The fragrant air and Supreme Wisdom of the Most High have been impressed in their inner souls.

1024 Oh, My child, let the people of the last times turn their eyes here, to the Chamber of the Most High, to the chambers of His Son, and to the Bridal Chambers of the Groom. The Mysterious Trinity, unique and unconstrained by any rational understanding, is revealed today as the Theogamic Chamber of the Three Images of Supreme Wisdom. It is followed by another twelve royal white chambers, with wonderful virgins and a multitude mysterious objects for the Bridal Feast.

1025 My child, Judaism was abolished by the Most High for the same reason that He is abolishing Christianity today. The institutional priests have not understood the higher plans of the Most High, which means that they have not fulfilled the task of the priesthood of Melchizedek.

[1026] For forty days the Most High prepared Moses for the ascent to the Bridal Chamber. The petrified tablets in the prophet's hands fell from the Theogamic chambers. Israel was being prepared to become the bride of the Most High and to enter the Theogamic castle, where it would be met by the eternal Groom, El-Elion, the Divine Zealot.

[1027] The Jews desecrated the Bridal Chamber and deprived themselves of the protection of the Sweetest God of Jacob[22]. They inherited nothing but the huge serpentine eggs of Beelzebub, laid in their synagogues and places of worship.

[1028] The Tetraevangelion had the same fate as the Torah. The Saviour never stopped mentioning the nuptial garments and anointing oils. Disciples heard nothing. The language of Theogamy was incomprehensible to them. The Christian Pharisees finally sealed the covenant of the Bridal Chamber of our Lord Jesus Christ within the frameworks of Judaic eschatology. The Gospels were written for the Jews and remained a testament to their conversion.

[22] The Sweetest God of Jacob – the authentic name of the God of Izrael (Gen. 28).

¹⁰²⁹ Those who place emphasis on reading the Gospels, and who take the words of the Divinity from the Bible, will receive the same fate as that of Christ's disciples in His earthly days. They understood nothing; they were shocked and frightened; they crowded together, made a fuss, and fell asleep.

¹⁰³⁰ So many eyes have glared at the worn-out pages of the Tetraevangelion, My child! Inquisitors, the spawn of the serpent, and various witches. They sentenced and persecuted innocents and saints in the name of Christ's Gospel and our Lord.

¹⁰³¹ Do not look for the Bridal Chamber in the Tetraevangelion. Forget and reject the image of the Gospel Saviour. Christ of the Second Coming came to the Solovki, and Christ of the Third Coming is that of the Bridal Chamber.

¹⁰³² Being taken body and soul to heaven – this is the sign of the ascension of the anointed sovereigns to the Bridal Chamber. Enoch, Melchizedek, Abraham (his bosom), Elijah, Moses, John the Evangelist, the assembly of the tender souls of the Solovki, and the fiery hierarchy… The Saviour was raised to the Bridal Chamber during His Ascension. The extolled Mount of Olives is the place of ascension to the Bridal Chamber.

¹⁰³³ Theogamy is a misunderstood mystery in the

current age and appointed for the Seraphites. That is why they have come into the world.

The Greek town of Ephesus is only four kilometres from Nightingale Mountain. The Hellenes loved the Purest Mother so much! They honoured Her as the highest Goddess. They stopped glorifying Athena, Aphrodite, and the other Greek gods. The noble Hellenes and particularly the common people were outraged by the persecutions of the Queen of Heaven.

The Ephesian community grew and counted many of Christ's followers among its numbers. The Queen of Heaven constantly communicated with Her disciples in Ephesus, and loved them infinitely. She wrote them spiritual messages, guided them, revealed their destinies, and promised to take them to Her Heavenly Chambers (which She did).

The grace of Nightingale Mountain was spread first and foremost upon the Ephesian community of Christ and Mary. This was shown by miraculous healings and by the presence of the Mother of the Divinity and our Lord.

The Jews demanded that Greece hand over the Purest Virgin. Three years after She had settled at Nightingale Mountain the priests discovered the place of Her concealment. Enraged, the Hellenes prevented them from taking Her and protected the Heavenly Queen. The Jews resorted to different tricks: they promised great riches even threatened to invade Ephesus. But the Hellenes remained firm, showing the strength of their national spirit.

The Greek gods also submitted to the will of the Purest Virgin of Nightingale Mountain. Ephesus honoured Her as its Holy Patroness, and was fragrant with the outpouring of the Holy Spirit that came from the mountain of the Most High.

Here was destroyed the stereotype of 'the Blessed Virgin', 'the Daughter of Israel', 'the Mother of Jesus Christ from Nazareth', and so on.

The chamber of the Most High was placed several kilometres from Ephesus. The Hellenes glorified Him as much as they could and listened carefully to the Ephesian missionaries preaching, in the spirit of Paul, about Christ the Saviour, about the mission of the Purest Virgin. The Queen revealed the mystery of Nightingale Mountain to Her disciples with hints.

*

Oh, Theogamy! Oh, the divinely desired goal of creation! Theogamy requires a change of the composition of the soul, the taking out of serpentine particles and inserting of the Seraphic particles.

*

The secret mountain, fertile and dewy... It is full of imperishable mixtures and compositions, of grains of sand. It holds the treasury of the shaping of Adam of the Bridal Chamber.

Theogamy has been proclaimed since the beginning

of the cycle of the revelations of Nightingale Mountain, and the brides of Christ are invited to ascend here and take the imperishable compositions, anointing oils, fragrant scents and myrrhic scrolls from the hands of the Purest Mother in the divine existence.

∴

...There was a battle for the body of Moses. The enemy prevented fiercely the prophet from being taken to the Bridal Chamber, arguing against it. In particular, they said that his teaching has been discredited. 'The Jews are not worthy of the Bridal Chamber,' I said. 'They are unworthy, they are unworthy, they are unworthy!'

The Cunning One has his own bridal chamber: the bridal chamber of the devil. His own black oils, his own alchemy of initiation, and his own black-magic sacraments for uniting with him. He lays serpent's eggs and sends them to his minions and agents. There are masks of Beelzebub, cave-like shadows, and Luciferian luminescence nearby. His agents and ambassadors are around us.

The goal of the devil is to ben-elohimize Adam. To create a new race of humans through the 'marriage' of aliens (Ben-Elohims producing phantoms, the fallen angels) with those who reject their gender, species, human nature, race, history, nation, Divinity, Church, and angels; with those who thirst eagerly for him and for the pagan temple of the serpent.

Ascend, Nightingale Mountain, above the whole world! Announce the mystery of the divinization of humanity. Summon the assemblies of Seraphic souls appointed to recline on the Bridal Bed with the Divine Beloved.

[1034] The soul is invited to lie on the most-fragrant Bed. The bride. The inner soul opens. The palm of Melchizedek the First-Anointed seems to be pulling apart the lungs, these airy castles of the Most High who guards the treasury. The interior is removed and replaced with a fiery stone: the Seraphic coal, the fire of the Holy Spirit. The vessels are anointed. Ineffable oils, precious balms running the beard of Aaron – called the dew of Hermon in the Psalms of David.

[1035] Seraphim the Graceful – the father of the Second Solovetskay Golgotha Christ multiplied a hundred thousand times – found the oils of the Bridal Chamber after Enoch (raised body and soul to Heaven) and John the Evangelist, and never-endingly anoints his disciples with them during liturgies in recreational centres, barracks, and cinemas.

[1036] The biggest miracle of Tver Spiritual center* is the dozens of crosses, icons and statues of the Immaculate Virgin (the first of them being the Immaculate Conception of Lourdes) pouring myrrh simultaneously. This is a sign of the descending Bridal Chamber.

[1037] John began his sermon with the coming Kingdom and the repentance before it. The forerunner of Nightingale Mountain begins his sermon: T h e B r i d a l   C h a m b e r has come down to the Earth. Repent!

[1038] Didn't the righteous Jewish men, with their 'forgive-me-lord', repent? But the armies of twisting serpents and flying dragons went ahead of them. Mad sheep dragged themselves along behind.

[1039] The world is now called to repent – but first t h e   c h u r c h   a n d   i t s   p r i e s t s. Repent before the Bridal Chamber, take the vows of eternal virginity, and accept the images as bright promises from on high – as the miraculous and immaculate conception given daily. Heaven is open and it remains only to listen and understand. It is time to meet our Beloved and to provide ourselves with oils.

[1040] My child, the first commandment of Moses – to love the Divinity with one's whole heart – descended from the Bridal Chamber. The ten-part law (the Decalogue) is a myrrhic scroll. Theogamy presupposes the answering, mad, superior love of creation for the Creator. Nothing more is necessary. The rest will come.

1041 Focusing on repentance, the rabbis and their heirs (the Christian priests) prohibited the Bridal Chamber. They are defilers of the highest destiny of man – d i v i n i z a t i o n. Under the pretence of repentance, the 'new law', atonement, and the forgiveness of sins, they try to catch a gnat without noticing the elephant.

1042 My child, here on the heights of Nightingale Mountain I long to light unquenchable candles within the hearts of the new zealots of the true faith in Christ. I want only one thing from them: to burn with divine love for their Beloved. A bride releases the potential of the divine treasures, and experiences incomparable joy, when she rejects the worldly, the lowest kinds of love, the mortal, and perishable the transient. She is the sweetest, most blessed, joyful virgin.

1043 Holy surpassing love for the Most High enables you to sacrifice yourself and to serve in selflessly and limitlessly.

1044 The Saviour came to the world, died and was resurrected, and appeared forty days later. Guided by this divine love, He sent tongues of flame to the apostles as the gift of the Holy Spirit, My child.

1045 The divine Lamp descended to Earth from Heaven and was humiliated, ignored, and eventually maliciously executed and sealed within a tomb. But, My child, divine love is immortal. It possesses the scepter of resurrection, which conquers death and the devil's obstacles.

[1046] The cunning one has lost the battle not because the Lord "outwitted" him with death or caught him in a trap, as portrayed by the church of this world. The enemy was unable to do anything to the King, the Anointed Sovereign of the Bridal Chamber.

*

[1047] The lightful Grail stands in the Holy of the Holies of the sanctuary of Nightingale Mountain. In the Old Testament it is called the Chalice of the right hand of the Most High, and the Chalice of Christ in the New Testament. And in the heralded Bridal Chamber it is called the sweetest Chalice of the Bridal Feast.

[1048] My child, the priests of Melchizedek raised the historical Grail (the Blood of Christ collected by St. Joseph of Arimathea) from the throne of the creative virginity of the Creator in Miramar*. In the Solovki the Grail was melted into the solar pearl of the Theocivilization, and the brothers multiplied in Christ[23] partook of it.

[23] The brothers multiplied in Christ (here) 12 spiritual brothers of Seraphim Solovetsky (fiery hierarchy) and their successors.

[1049] The Grail of Nightingale Mountain is doubled – it is the Chalice of the Bridal Chamber.

[1050] May the priests henceforth offer the world the Chalice of the Bridal Chamber of Nightingale Mountain of the Assumption, transfiguration, ascension, and divine existance of their Purest Mother. I am offering this sweetest Chalice to those who long for ineffable and surpassing bliss. I am giving them this Inexhaustible Chalice again and again to drink from, because it is never-ending. Inexhaustible means that at every stage of the ascent to the Bridal Chamber is the luminescent spectrum of the Chalice, and its temperature reflects that of the lit candle of the Seraphic body and the burning heart, the hot wine and the Blood of Christ.

[1051] Oh, My child, the Saviour promised that His disciples would drink from this Chalice in eternity. And today I am giving it to the priests of Melchizedek.

[1052] The Saviour repeatedly came to Me with the Chalice in His hands and nourished Me in my feebleness, half dead from blows, torrents of damnations, and the arrows of the enemy. I was revived, My child. I was resurrected. Any one who drinks from this Chalice will be truly resurrected, My child. The Saviour, having raised the chalice of the

Grail, said: 'They who drink from it will live forever, and if they dies they will again be resurrected.' I, Supreme Wisdom, the Mother of the sweetest anointed sovereigns, repeat after Him: 'They who partake of this chalice will be divinized. The divinized ones are blessed and live forever.'

[1053] Oh, My child, henceforth together with priests carry the Grail of Nightingale Mountain – the transparent, superworldly, doubled Chalice.

[1054] My child, after the Lord's repeated visits with the Chalice, the Saviour left the Grail in a cupboard in My hut, cooled by the mountain wind. Moving through the air from Nightingale Mountain to the caves of Ephesus, and coming to His disciples, I nourished them with the Chalice of the Nightingale Grail. They partook of the myrrh of the Bridal Chamber.

[1055] My child, the Saviour told Me, in His many lessons: The Grail must be enriched with the Holy Passion of My Godbride. After this its composition will become more perfect than perfection itself and suitable to be tasted by Our disciples.

[1056] The meaning of the liturgy does not lie in the repetition of memorized prayers or services according to the instructions of the calendar. Having come from the Kingdom, Melchizedek raises his flock of humble and pure sheep to Heaven and lights the candle of ineffable, exceedingly divine love.

[1057] Loving fiercely, holy and madly, His brides prepare themselves for the communion of the Grail of Nightingale Mountain. Oh, My child, there must first be a cup of holy water; then the myrrhic composition, enriched with Seraphic particles; and finally the Sacred Blood and Flesh of the Saviour. As the fourth step, serve the Grail of Theogamy – the Chalice of Nightingale Mountain – at the Bridal Supper. Carry it to burning hearts.

[1058] Rapture, ecstasy, exceedingly divine delights, the craving to drink more and more, satisfied immortal bodies, rebuilt inner altars, the exaltation of the Church to the Bridal Chamber on the cloud of the Most High, and the candle burning without end in the interior – these are the true signs of the nourishment of the Nightingale Grail.

[1059] The mission of Melchizedek, My child, the anointed sovereign with a crown of twelve pearls on his brow, is to lead his flock to the experience of the Bridal Chamber. May the wax candles inserted into open hearts flow with the fire of Divine Love! May the saints gather around you! And may the shadows of 'Chrysostom', of the imperial liturgy and others offering prayers at the throne of our enemy, be removed!

1060 Oh, the supper of ineffable bliss! Oh, the Chalice of the Bridal Chamber!

1061 My child, the sermon in the liturgy is designed to ignite hearts; the next is designed to make a vow of eternal virginity; the third to exalt the mind to Heaven; the fourth to present the Divinity as He is; the fifth to clothe in the unattainable angelic vestments of everlasting virginity; the sixth to initiate into the Mysterious church; the seventh to give eternal life and exalt into divine existence. The eighth, the sweetest sacrament, is My embrace of all who are present with My Motherly omophorion*. May they be blessed forever.

❧

1062 Their cup is full of abominations. The cup of the serpent, which feeds the serpent besides other scorpions, dragons, magicians, witches, and vampires. What a stench surrounds their cup. So many stinking animals swim within it!

1063 The Grail, My child, is the symbol of the Theocivilization. Henceforth the Grail will be above the world. The Grail is in the Ark, the Grail is in the White Ship, the Grail is in the hands of the high priest of the Purest Lady, the Grail is in the inner soul. The new man is of the compositions of the Grail; the Grail is on the brow of the Seraphite. The ivory skeleton is the skeleton of the new man, and the composition of his blood has been designed to nourish man from the Chalice of the Grail.

:—

[1064] "My Heart is ready!" I whispered before His visit, lying upon the Assumption Bed.

[1065] My child, I was ready. I was the only one of all creation to respond to His Divine Love, to meet Him with my little chalice.

[1066] Now, My child, look at the Church. Look at yourself. Is there at least one amongst you who is ready to partake of the Chalice of the Grail of the Bridal Chamber, madly in love, thirsting for more and more? My child, many of you are lingering at the stage of the seeker. Some have already begun to thirst. But there are only a few who thirst never-endingly, who love Christ infinitely. Only their hearts are ready, My child.

[1067] 'My heart is ready' means 'I thirst to be released from earthly ties! I thirst for the union with My Beloved! Oh, I am finally ready to accept His love!'

1068 'My heart is ready.' My child, this is the readiness of humanity to hear and to respond to the advent of our Christ the King.

1069 'My heart is ready,' exclaim the Seraphites in their rapturous ecstasy. They renounced this world and shone with virginity, crowned as the conquerors of the cunning one. Three times they defeated the enemy.

1070 'My heart is ready!' This is the state of liturgical communicants in the Bridal Chamber. My child, they are exhausted. Like Me, they prostrate themselves in subconscious bliss. They thirst to be released from the ties of grief, the ties of the Holy Passion, the ties of the earthly, the ties of pregnancy, and from all other hindering ties. They long to be united, to ascend to the Bridal Bed, and to exclaim: 'Oh, at last we are one!'

*

1071 My child, the mysterious feast starts a f t e r partaking of the Chalice. Having fed them with the composition of the Bridal Chamber, with His purest and most precious Flesh and Blood, the Saviour comes to them as the Beloved and unites with them. The sweetness of His inspiration is inexpressible. It is not understood by the Adamites.

1072 The Seraphites will long for exactly that which

was a seduction and temptation for the Adamites. Loathsome lechery, licentious lust, and the copulation of sinful bodies will be rejected as worthless and shown to lead to suicide and extreme desperation.

[1073] The Seraphites, disciples of the Bridal Chamber, will thirst for ties with Christ, the ties of the Bridal Chamber. The Divine Bridal Bed – the Theogamic throne – will become their desire. And having passed through the crucible of temptations, having experienced the twelve ordeals, having been crowned three times as victors – they will ascend to the Assumption Bed and say after their Mother, the Godbride: 'My heart is ready!' And the Saviour will come and embrace them, but first He will feed them from the Chalice of the all-perfect Grail.

* * *

THE MYRRHIC SCROLLS OF NIGHTINGALE MOUNTAIN

[1074] Russia. My Russia of the Bridal Chamber, the original appanage of the Godbearer. Here the Assumption bed was erected after the adoption of Christianity. And how many temples and monasteries were built in honour of the mystery of My Assumption!

1075 The mystery of Nightingale Mountain, My son, is that those who ascend to and reach the castle of the Most High only once know no death and live forever.

1076 For fifteen years I prepared Myself for the hour of the most rapturous transition, My child. I did not experience death. My child, the apostles circled Me in a tight ring and the hostile serpents did not even dare to approach. Leaving My body, I experienced a momentary agonizing pain before bliss surpassing all My earthly experiences. Truly, it was an even sweeter Bridal Chamber: the arrival of the Saviour for Me.

1077 A new Easter is proclaimed from the heights of Nightingale Mountain. My child, the victory over death was accomplished not only by Christ, our First-Anointed, but also by His disciples, the godlike lesser anointed christs.

1078 Here there is no sleep in the traditional sense. My child, I did not experience human sleep for fifteen years. The states experienced by Me can be called anything other than sleep. Battles, desperation, solitude. Unconsciousness, spiritual weakness. Sorrows, temptations, Holy Passion... Oh! None of the race of Adam has experienced such temptations, My child. The Most High tempted me down to the last cell of My mortal body. My child, each cell of them was pierced with a needle. Each was pierced with a spear, and with it came the fragrant oil of the Bridal Chamber.

1079 But the Most High anointed Me from time immemorial to be the Queen of the Bridal Chamber. And My inexhaustible, boundless mother-ly love for the Saviour helped Me to overcome the ordeals. My child, the Most High kept me in His palm like a baby. And the enemy retreated. The defeated and wounded beast shuffled off to his den.

1080 My child, I would like the grace of Nightin-gale Mountain to become the desire of the true disciples of Christ all over the world. But remember: Nightingale Mountain is as far beyond this world as the Grail. There is no use attacking it on foot or by bus, or with the rosary in your hand, or with a priest at the head of a group of pilgrims. Entrance is given only to the anointed sovereigns and to the true disciples of Christ. Nothing can prevent a grey-haired, bed-ridden woman of eighty from becoming a communicant of Nightingale Mountain and from heeding to My revelations, My child.

1081 My words possess the secret of vibrational adhesion. My child, the sweetest word of the Queen of the Bridal Chamber carries to the heights of Nightingale Mountain, to the singing of the birds of paradise, to the most fragrant raptures of the Seraphs, and to the Thrones that surround the tent of the Most High.

*

The liturgy of Melchizedek was revealed on Nightingale Mountain. The four chalices: (1) of holy water, with sprinkling and ablution in white fonts; (2) of unction, with a vow of eternal virginity; (3) of the Holy Flesh and Blood of the Lord; (4) in the rapturous ecstasy: the doubled Grail of the Nightingale Mountain and of the Solovky.

The old church partially managed to minister to the Adamites. The Melchizedeks are priests for the Seraphites, the enraptured of the Bridal Chamber.

–What is it? (ascending the Nightingale Mountain)
–The Bridal Chamber in which dwells the Divinity.

*

The Queen gave the Rosary of the Bridal Chamber:

1. The Repentance of the Adamites.
2. The Rejection of the devil and old earthly programs.
3. The Vows of eternal virginity.
4. The Cross.

5. The Melchizedeks.
6. Divinization.
7. The Holy Passion.
8. Anointment.
9. The Solovki
10. The Lamb of two Hearts.
11. Theogamy.
12. The Bridal Bed.
13. The Seraphites.
14. The Doubled Grail.
15. Aya-bliss.

* * *

The Queen of Nightingale Mountain about homosexual marriages:

[1082] It is the sacrament of the devil himself. The marriage of two persons of the same sex is impossible. The same-sex marriages approved by many governments around the world are the prediction of the civilization of the devil. These are especially unhappy souls caught by the cunning one. Proclaim the throne of Nightingale Mountain, Theogamy, and holy Divine Matrimony amongst them.

*

[1083] The Bridal Chamber will be the property of the future humanity. From here the most fragrant Bed is adorned with white lilies.

1084 Spiritual lamps with thousands of lit candles will walk barefoot across the glass surface of the sea of the Holy Grail, and none will drown. The nuptial procession is passing through the capital of Greece, Athens, to Western Europe where it is dispersed across the whole world.

1085 The Bridal Bed was sent to Earth by the Most High.

1086 The religion of the Bridal Bed. The humanity of the Bridal Bed. The church, the priesthood, the purpose of the Seraphites – all of the Bridal Bed!

1087 You are the chosen ones of the Chamber of the Most High. Seraphic inscriptions are upon your brows. Today I speak for the chosen ones of Christ, King of the myrrh-pouring anointed sovereigns of the new, exceedingly wise modelling: the Seraphites. My sweetest ones, may Supreme Wisdom be your song!

1088 Solar Seraphites, fly with wings! Ascend to the throne of the Most High. Wonderful faith of Christ, the Myrrh-Anointed-Sovereign, reveal yourself in the pastures of paradise, in fragrant gardens among thousands of zealots! Descend, angels, to My adolescent youngsters! Fill their hearts with inexpressible joy, more and more! May they rejoice amidst their sorrows and reject their prejudices as soon as possible.

[1089] Rejoice, humanity of the new earth — the century of the Glory of the Most High is being proclaimed! And may the fiery throne of Nightingale Mountain remain here until the new army of the Most Wise has been collected. And assemblies of exalted and winged Seraphites will gather like birds of paradise around the Bridal Throne. And they will hear the voice of the Sweetest Lady of the Assumption Bed proclaiming the mysteries of the future age and passing on their treasures, as She did with Her beloved son John, who was the first to be invited to Nightingale Mountain by Her and to whom She revealed the sanctuary of the Most High, the most superior sanctuary of all time.

*

Within the next few years many things will change. Royal grace will descend.

O, millions will enter the Chamber of the Most High! Oh, what joy they will experience. O! O! O, the bliss!

*

[1090] The Theocivilization will glorify the Bridal Bed.

[1091] Bring out the candle of the Theocivilization!

Erect the throne of the Theocivilization on Earth! Bring out the Theogamic Bed for the Seraphites!

1092 Burn, unquenchable candle, sanctuary of Christ. Descend, Heaven. Ascend, new Earth. Race of the Seraphites, unite with the sweetest Most High! Brides, go out to meet the Groom. The Sweetest One awaits you at the gates of the Bridal Chamber. Do not sleep! Midnight and the dawn of the Lord's day.

1093 My child, the world will change in an instant. The plans of the Most High will be realized. Rejoice in the future triumph of Christ. May it be the sole worthy experience of My disciples and anointed sovereigns.

1094 Rejoice, My children. In less than half a century the world will have changed beyond recognition. The Earth will be inhabited by the most blissful Seraphites. The Bridal Chamber will be the desired altar of the solar temple of peace. And Supreme Wisdom will spread the light of divine knowledge and the mystery of divinization over all the worlds.

1095 Oh Seraphite, man of twelve immortal bodies, two eagle wings, heart lit in the desert, and unquenchable candles. Waxen, new, immortal. Seraphic, Eucharistic. The lamb of Christ, come and populate cities and lands!

1096 The whole earth belongs to the new race of

the Seraphites. The Heavens and airs belong to the priests of Melchizedek. The throne of the Most High is above the world!

I can hear the music of endless joy: Hallelujah. Hallelujah. Hallelujah! A dance. The wonderful dance of the children of the Most High. Amen.

The Bridal Chamber moves across the world. It is worshipped and spreads the radiance of celestial love. "Hallelujah. Hallelujah. Hallelujah!" The song of rapture fills thousands of hearts.

Hallelujah. Hallelujah. Hallelujah! My Lady Supreme Wisdom, descend, embrace hearts. Give true life. Reveal Christ as He is. Hallelujah! Rejoice, Earth! Rejoice, new universe. Rejoice, new humanity. Rejoice, new Mary. Hallelujah!

Myrrhic scrolls of Nightingale Mountain...

*

The treasury will be presented to all humanity.

*

With the sound of festive fanfares comes a solemn procession of the priests of Melchizedek, the crowned winners. The mountain is being transformed. Nightingale Mountain is in the fire of the Holy Spirit. The grace of the Most High. The throne of rapturous flight.

We are leaving the mountain. We are accompanied by the mysterious ranks of divine existance, imperceptibly raising Christ's disciples of the third millennium to the spheres of divine existance.

Bells are ringing in the distance. A flock of sheep approaches. It is hot. 2 p.m. Hallelujah! Thank You, Most High Mother.

In half a century there will be millions of Seraphites.

I do not know how to express the grace of Nightingale Mountain in words.

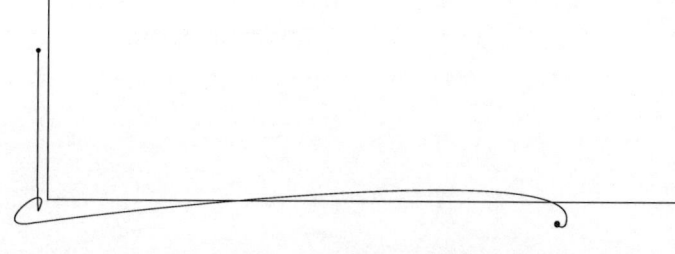

THE ARK
OF THE EIGHTY-FIFTH
THEOCIVILIZATION

THE HEAVENLY FATHER
ABOUT THE ERECTION OF THE ARK

5 May 2005, Kemer

The Throne of the Father

1097 $\mathcal{M}$y child, I am speaking from the sphere of the Universum. To the deserving. The eighty-fourth civilization is perishing. Supreme Wisdom asked for delays many times. And what else, My child?

1098 Listen, listen to what I tell you, and convey it to the race of Adam. Tell them: so it was and will be – the Ark was built on the eve of the purifying disasters.

1099 My child, the eighty-fifth Ark is the Ark of the Purest Lady. As many of My worlds have passed before Me as arks. This is how I think, and how the Artist of the Most High, Supreme Wisdom, creates. The Ark is erected on the eve of the disasters. The remnants of the people of the Divinity are gathered within it. According to the judgement of the Most High they are destined to experience the disasters and enter the life of the future age.

1100 This gathering and mysterious storehouse is called the Ark.

1101 The Torah conveys a symbolic image of the Ark: wooden, with a righteous Noah, and animals and children entering in pairs.

1102 The Ark was built in a desert. On the eve of the purifying sorrows the present world is turned into a desert. They laugh at the anointed sovereign; no one wants to hear him. The civilization reaches its peak in material wealth and luxury. Human beings have fallen into idleness, parasitism, cunning, diabolical temptations, and nets.

1103 In the meantime the Ark is being built. Not in a day or two, or a year, but over many years. And Supreme Wisdom patiently invites souls to enter it; this means the rejection of the previous sinful foundations and the acceptance of the light of the future age.

1104 The erection of the eighty-fifth 'Noah's' Ark has reached the halfway stage. The frame is ready and they are starting to build the walls and prepare the interiors.

¹¹⁰⁵ Hear My words, My child, and convey them to the inhabitants of the Earth.

¹¹⁰⁶ The three sons of Noah signify a threefold mark on the human brow. Shem represents the saints and immaculate ones. Japheth is a sinner (like the majority of people). And Ham is of serpentine, non-Adamic origin.

¹¹⁰⁷ Japheth tries to settle in 'Shem's tents, and the saints (of divine origin, lamps) struggle against the serpentine people. Both are embodied as Adamites and do not differ greatly from other people.

¹¹⁰⁸ This was arranged by Supreme Wisdom. Many great mysteries are concealed beneath the disguise of mortal man. The Divinity is embodied in His beloved ones and establishes the tent of the Most High in the sons of Supreme Wisdom, the descendants of Shem. The Devil uses his black Ethiopians, Hams, and they scrutinize the nakedness of their father, go against him, and become the slaves of Canaan.

¹¹⁰⁹ The eighty-fifth order of the world is called the Theocivilization; it includes the vast majority of the population of the tents of Shem. Saints, anointed sovereigns, torches, chosen ones, and Melchizedeks. The tent of Supreme Wisdom. The seals of Sophia, the grace of the myrrh-bearing maidens.

[1110] Japheth is changing. His attraction towards Shem becomes absolute, and his obedience implicit. Ham has been forbidden. The serpent particles in the composition of the Seraphites are insignificantly few, so devilish magnets do not affect them.

[1111] My child, in the time of Noah I gave three disasters and three great signs, as I promised at Garabandal. The little apocalypse of Garabandal presaged the disasters on the eve of the Flood. But they continued to sneer, to lead and enjoy their depraved lives. And the whole earth was depraved as it is today.

[1112] My child, civilization has reached a deadlock and perishing. I am erecting the Ark.

[1113] In the sacral Jewish tradition Noah was related to Melchizedek (he was Melchizedek's uncle). Today Noah is the priesthood of Melchizedek of the new Church.

[1114] The statutes of Supreme Wisdom will convey an image of the future civilization not long before the global disasters. The tent has been erected and the door of the Ark is open. I am blessing you to enter the life of the future age with a mysterious hand (i.e. in a way hidden from unauthorized eyes). I am blessing you to enter the life of the future age this very day. And thus I am fostering new seals, compositions, and images. While the doomed eighty-fourth civilization perishes, the first blessed shoots are sprouting. Call it the civilization of the Most High, the glory of Christ in all creation.

[1115] My son, according to calculations the eighty-fifth civilization is the remaking of the world, the victory over the sin, the slaughter of the Ben-Elohims, and the establishment of angelic Seraphs. It will last for more than a thousand years according to the earthly system of chronology (time will be stretched several times).

[1116] Four and a half million Adamites are called to enter the Ark. Gather *them* all over the world, proclaim to *them* the conversion of the old world order and the necessity of its renunciation.

[1117] The first vow is the acceptance of the Theocivilization and its mystical and mysterious doctrines: Theogamy, Theohumanity, Christ embodied in creation.

[1118] The second vow is the consecration to Supreme Wisdom. The light of Sophia of the triumph of Christ in the Bosom of the Godbearer, the Mother giving birth from on high.

[1119] The third vow is the humanity of the future age, the fiery Seraphites.

[1120] The fourth: to accept anointments from the Heavenly Church (the Solovki branch of the Fiery Hierarchy, the Melchizedeks).

[1121] The fifth: to be nourished by the Chalice of the Most High. The Grail of Christ, the Last Drop.

[1122] The sixth: vows of eternal virginity. The readiness to change the composition. Anointment, the cross and Holy Passion. Divinization and guidance from the mysterious church of Supreme Wisdom, the treasury of the eighty-fifth civilization, the Temple of Peace of the solar Seraphite III.

[1123] My child, the construction of the Ark is in full swing. And My sons and daughters should have no other aspirations but to enter the Ark.

[1124] Convey to the rest, to those who pretend to be saved, spiritually perfect, enlightened, and so on: The fate of Atlantis and of those who fell under the influence of the Ben-Elohims awaits them.

[1125] I will punish the sons of damnation, this serpentine spawn disguised as angels and poisoning the earth with the muck of Lucifer's thoughts. I will send them into underground caves and bind their hands for thousands of years.

[1126] My child, the Ark is in My hands today. I built it of a mysterious composition, of the Bosom of the Immaculate Lady, of the ivory of the eternal Grail.

[1127] Supreme Wisdom has placed you at the centre of the world's pagan temple: the depraved resorts of Kemer, Cote d'Azur, Antalya, and Split. My child, amidst the universal disgrace, fill yourself with the tears of righteous Noah and become like the penitent Seraphim. Call amongst the miserable ones:

[1128] 'Enter the Ark of Virginity! Profess the Purest Virgin in Her new hypostasis: the Mother of the Ark. She is the Ark. The Most High is building the Ark of Her composition, and the sons and daughters of Her composition will enter it.'

[1129] I do not need Christ for worship, for the lighting of candles, and as an idol. I reject churches of pagan idolatry no matter what they call themselves: universal, ecumenical, and so on. I long to inscribe Christ in the whole of creation.

[1130] Two thousand years ago I sent He Who Is One With Me, My beloved Son, and He began the new blessed branch, the new dynasty of sons and daughters of Christ, the anointed sovereigns of the Bridal Chamber.

[1131] My child, the Bridal Chamber was revealed

in the Solovki as a fiery cloud; from it came the Hierarchy of Lights, the Solovki Fathers. The new priesthood of Melchizedek began with them – Christ embodied in priests (Seraphicus Christi) and in all creation (the Seraphites).

[1132] So stive to be like Christ, partake of Christ, receive Him, be unified with Him. His seals in your interior and on your brow, in your composition and in your blood. Partake ceaselessly of the Chalice of Christ called the Solar Grail, and do not mentally separate yourself from the Mountain of Salvation, where resides the Ark called the Assumption Bed of the Purest Virgin: Nightingale Mountain, the capital of the future Light Civilization, of the god-born descendants of the Most High.

[1133] Worship the Mother Supreme Wisdom. Her revelation is a sign that the last times are approaching. Ask Her, and She will understand and summon you to enter the Ark.

[1134] My child, looking at the infinitude of created souls, like the caviar of sea fish, I invite them to enter the Ark; all except the damned, those guilty of murderous deeds, and the serpentine.

[1135] I am bringing today's Word to the ultimate depths of the inner man. As the Creator I know the secret place where I can insert my scroll, the altar of altars, the sancta sanctisima sanctorum. Henceforth My Word will sound in the inner temples and be accompanied by the magnificence of angelic fanfares. Henceforth the voice of the Most High will provoke trembling and fear in some, joy and exultation in others, and the search for salvation in still others.

1136 My infinite love is with all creation. Owing to blood shed during the Holy Passion of the many martyrs of the race of Adam, the number of those invited into the Ark has been increased by several million. Is it not enough for a soul to make its choice and join the multitude of people inhabiting the new promised lands?

1137 Today I invite all descendents of the race of Adam on Earth to make their choice and to enter the Ark. Abandon lust, sin, and temptations of the flesh, and remove any obstacle to the fulfilment of the will of the Divinity. Understand that this shameful and vicious world order is doomed. It is corrupt beyond all limits and it is impossible for it to continue.

1138 May peace be in your hearts! I am setting a little seal of the Ark on the brow of the chosen ones. May it shine in its own time.

1139 Peace be with you, inhabitants of the Earth.

[1140] I am the loving Father. But why did you tempt me in Meribah* and disobey My will?

:⸱—

> The Lord has said enough about the disasters. Sleep. Mild slaughters. The outward signs are heavy breathing, heat, and poisonous sweat. Fears and bad thoughts. The desire to die and the impossibility of doing so. Pandemics, epidemics of mental illnesses. The Saviour called this the "global plague".

The Throne of the Son

[1141] Oh, My seals, My child! My thirst is finally being quenched. 'It is done,' I said, before entrusting my last breath to the Heavenly Father. And now, My child, that which I so desired is being accomplished! Oh, I will finally unite with My dear disciples. I thirst to embrace you. I long to penetrate you, to become one with you. I long to die in you in order to live in you and be inscribed within you. I give Myself to you during every liturgy, holding nothing back, so that in return you may shine with the light of the anointed sovereigns and live in love. But first, My child, your efforts, so precious to Me: efforts to overcome sin and reject Adam's destiny.

[1142] My child, convey to all humanity: Adam is doomed. Adam could not accept the Christ with a divine inoculation, Adam could not remain christic., Adam, like Peter, said: Get out of me, Lord! I am not worthy!

[1143] My child, My hot embraces... Oh, I am finally speaking. Oh, I am finally uniting with My children. Oh, I am finally able to take you into My Fiery Heart. The Purest Virgin has prepared the imperishable solar composition in your inner soul. And I am embracing you, My son, and calling you the little christ. I am embracing your Paisiy. I am embracing Elias, Benjamin, Anna. Fathers Afanasi and Maximilian, and all My anointed sovereigns. I am embracing you, My children. I am holding you in my fiery embrace, never before experienced by any mortal. And that is why I proclaim triumphantly: Hallelujah! It is done!

[1144] I am embracing you as the new Adamites – as Seraphites. I am embracing you as My brides. I am giving you the fiery rapture of the Most High inscribed in My Sweetest Heart. I am conveying the true and eternal life from My Heart to yours, from the Groom to the bride, so that the Bridal Chamber being established on Nightingale Mountain spreads from here, the holy Marine Mountain of Kemer, all over the world. And may peace and sweet bliss be in your hearts.

[1145] My child, after the revelation of Our Purest Mother Supreme Wisdom of Nightingale Mountain, I am filled with the desire to speak to My disciples in a language I did not use with the apostles in My earthly days. Not even during My forty-day apparition in the transfigured immortal body...

[1146] What will Christ of the future age look like? The wonderful King of the Second Coming. The Anointed Sovereign is among you. The Shining Light of Divine Love. The Adolescent bearing the authority of His Father and establishing His Kingdom, the Kingdom of Celestial Love, on Earth.

[1147] Hurt Me with mortal wounds no longer. Do not remember Me as I was before. I long to reveal Myself to the Seraphites. I need new vestments, new minds, new hearts, and the new fluttering of the winged ones, the loving ones.

[1148] Glorify Christ of the future age and convey His priceless gift to humanity. The previous humanity is doomed to desolation. Did I not say, two thousand years ago: 'Destroy this temple, and I will raise it again in three days.' And today I tell you: 'Destroy this old vampire crypt full of evil ghosts, abominations, and lawlessness. And I will raise a new bright temple for My holy disciples. And My Face will shine before them.' And they will say: 'Oh, how beautiful You are, Lord, in the radiance of the sun!' Peace be with you.

:—

The bandit executioners will be punished. They seek a 'comfortable church'. Their 'comfortable church' wanted to differ from the Church which hears His weariness and His Love. Oh, this inexhaustible Love for the whole of the Divinity's creation! For the doomed and lonely and outcast; for cripples, sinners, the most hopeless, and the wounded.

Hallelujah! Peace be with all of you, My peace. Peace be with every one. The peace of Christ. *(Singing)*

The Saviour's heart sheds waves of the grace of the Holy Spirit. Our Lord is transfigured above Kemer Mountain. He flies on a cloud of the mountain, and His shining Face is imprinted in all creation.

Hallelujah, hallelujah, hallelujah!

:—

The Seraphites will not have sophisticated human minds. There will be pure of mind and pure of heart. Heart and mind are one. The mind of Christ.

The Holy Spirit shines with ineffable joy. He embraces the humanity of the earth.

Come, creation of the new prophets, civilization of the new saints, the joy of the new anointed sovereigns! Come, *Gunaiden!* Gunaiden ('good morning' in Turkish) we interpret as 'the approaching young day of the Lord'.

꞉⸺

The Throne of our Saints

Blessed Iya:

Tell your sisters and brothers from the altar of St. Petersburg that every word of Father John is true. We experience it; we enter it.

The Lord has gifted me with such grace, such anointments for my sufferings! I am happy. I am giving you the joy of the saved Son of the Lord in the destiny of our wonderful Mother. And the love of the Lord, the Mother of the Divinity, and of Mother Euphrosinia is for all our fathers and sisters.

Iya is sending us bliss. Hallelujah!

꞉⸺

The throne of Supreme Wisdom is establishing Its Kingdom. It has twelve pillars. The throne of Supreme Wisdom is above the world! Hallelujah!

Supreme Wisdom is being inserted into minds, hearts, and compositions. Supreme Wisdom reigns over the world. Supreme Wisdom gives inspiration and joy to life. Supreme Wisdom glorifies the Divinity, and the Divinity is glorified by Supreme Wisdom. Hallelujah!

O, the hot breath of the Divinity! Hallelujah! His lips, His Heart, His beauty, His Bridal Embraces! Hallelujah! Hallelujah! Hallelujah!

O Joy! The Theogamic Bed! Hallelujah!

The Saviour is uniting with us. Hallelujah!

The Purest Virgin is preparing new compositions and oils. Hallelujah! Hallelujah! Hallelujah!

The Lord blesses us from Heaven. Hallelujah!

The Triumphant Church is descending. Hallelujah!

The Chalice in the hands of the Master of the Feast. Hallelujah!

And the Groom of the Sweetest Ones is coming out from His Chamber! Hallelujah, hallelujah, hallelujah!

May the Most High bless all humanity. We are the priests of the Most High. All souls are open and obedient to us: be them of Nordic or Southern character, or Passionate and in the midst of the Holy Passion, warm or cold, and all others. In everything we see a divine manifestation. We are afraid of nothing. We bind the devil's head and throw him into the abyss.

The Divinity is glorified everywhere. The holy kindness of our Heavenly Lady. Thousands of forms, indescribable diversity. The Heavenly Queen reveals the gifts and images that She has inscribed in creation. And man does not drown in this endless sea of images. On the contrary, the anointed sovereign only rejoices and exults at the sight of the radiance of the Grail, the Chalice of the Lord, reflected in the rays of the sun.

And all creation glorifies the Most High. Hallelujah! Hallelujah! Hallelujah!

Oh, new universe, new Earth – when do you come?

THE GLOSSARY

Atlantis – the ancient civilization which existed 20 000 years ago and riched the highest level of the spiritual development. It is mystically hidden in the myths of the Ancient Greece. — *1124.*

Anzer – an island of the Solovetsky archipelago (White Sea, Russia), the great treasure trove of imperishable and myrrh-pouring relics of the great martyrs from the time of Stalinism. — *716.*

Accumulation of the Holy Spirit – is the spiritual stairs of deification in the practice of the Cathars, known as Consolamentum, multiplying of the Holy Spirit in the spiritual heart. — *492.*

Athonia – according to the Orthodox tradition, a Pharisee who dared to touch the body of the Virgin during Her funeral, after which his hand withered. — *400.*

The Ark – is the mystical sphere to which all people are called to enter in the last times to transform the human essence from the adamic to the seraphic one. It will be necessary for the proper living on the earth in the third millennium. Entering into the Ark results from passing through the steps of the spiritual path: conversion, consecration, anointment etc. — *39, 60, 162, 170...*

Assumption Bed – is the Dormition of the Virgin Lady or the anointed soul. — *34, 58, 166, 391...*

The ancestral programs are the laws and zodiacal programs of life (character, occupation, marital status, etc., from the birth to the death), which can be overcome through dedication to the cross and rebirth from the above. — *38, 625.*

Anointing – a special initiation in the mysteries of the Most High and strengthening for the holy passion, that is impossible without mystical anointing oil. — *31, 107, 128, 263...*

The Anointed One (Greek: christos – "Christ") – the soul chosen by God, which bears (stores) the special anointing and spiritual seals for the serving to all humanity. The anointed one performs service to the humanity by the power of saints, who lived on the earth. In the Christian tradition, Jesus Christ was glorified as "the king of the anointed ones" (Hebrews: "The Messiah"). — *14, 16, 25, 29...*

The abdominal furnace – the centre of lustful desire in a man; libido. — *23.*

Anne Catherine Emmerich (1774-1824) – a German mystic, stigmatic, and visionary. From her childhood she had extremely detailed visions of the life of Christ and the Virgin Mary. Her visions led to the discovery of the house of Mary, located on a hill near Ephesus, Turkey. — *930.*

Bridal Chamber – is the divine sphere, where the soul – bride unites with the Divinity into one. — *4, 35, 53...*

Bridal Bed – is the final stage of the initiations to the Cross of each soul on the spiritual path. At this stage the soul comprehends in full the love of the Divinity. — *9, 72, 84, 393...*

Beelzebub – (general meaning: the spirit, heading the institutes of the Prince of this world) creates a false piety and distorting the statute of the Divine Wisdom. In the Christian literature this name was used to mark the prince of demons, assistants of Lucifer. — *285, 334, 401.*

Ben-Elohims (Hebrew) – 'the sons of God', the fallen angels. In the old times previously they comprised a special angelic rank which was close to the Cherubim. After Adam's fall they were sent down to Earth to help humanity, but they came under the hypnosis of Lucifer and fell down through the copulation with the daughters of men. Although servants and vessels of the devil, they consider themselves the sons of the Divinity and pretend to transform humans into gods. This is false divinization. — *1022, 1124.*

Cement sarcophagus – spiritual experiences of John of the Holy Grail in the state of his bilocational serving. This state is close to death. In such a state John of the Holy Grail shares the despair of suffering souls on the earth. — *615.*

Cosmism – Cosmos, in the terms of the author is the intermediate spheres between the earthly world and the heights of the Kingdom conditionally dividing into two levels.

Here it means the lowest cosmos, which is also called "the astral world" of the dead planets, mediums, UFO, plenty of virtual and mental areas, associated with the lower energy sublimation and astral practices and cycles of reincarnation. — *552.*

The caduceus of Supreme Wisdom performs a three-fold function: blessing, initiation into the Holy Passion (perforation), and anointing. — *17, 43, 219.*

Divinization – (saintification, theosis (Greek)) is the action of the Holy Spirit as the Adorer and Deifier. The top of the stairs of the spiritual path, where the divine potential opens and the spiritual composition of man alters. — *63, 103.*

Divine existence (otherness, holy being Greek: palingenesia) is a unique term in the teaching of the author, which means the fifth dimension where the True Divinity and the Exiding Wisdom dwell. — *260, 736, 1811.*

The Elders – are the souls, anointed and consecrated to the Heavenly Wisdom on the highest level of the acquiring of the Holy Spirit, who live in accordance with the universal spiritual laws. They have got the gift of spiritual modeling (spiritual leadership). The elders are able to release the divine potential of the disciple. — *284, 363, 408, 935.*

El Elion (Hebrew): the name of the Most High Divinity, accepted in the school of the Grail. In the Old Testament it is mentioned only four times. — *231, 242.*

Enoch – is the prophet of the Old Testament, who denounced Ben-Elohims in the days of Noah. He was taken (raised) to the Heaven by his flesh and soul. — *45, 220, 299, 906.*

Supreme Wisdom – one of the images of the Mother of God, revealing Herself as the feminine hypostasis of the Divinity. — *8, 124, 176, 235.*

Elohim – the ancient biblical name Elohim (Almighty) morphologically signifies heavenly powers in plural, sometimes translated as 'gods' (e.g. in Exodus 20:3). — *332, 552, 1022.*

Fatima, Garabandal, Lourdes, La Salette – are the places of the Virgin Lady's greatest apparitions in the nineteenth and twentieth centuries — *182.*

Fiery hierarchy – (the spiritual brothers of Seraphim Solovetsky) martyrs of the Solovetskaya Golgotha (1930), through their holy passionate martyrdom had reached the top of spiritual perfectness, the kings of the Holy Grail. — *352, 369, 456, 624.*

The Great Marine Kingdom – special immaculate worlds, dwelling in the oceans and seas of the Earth. They exist not in the third dimension but in the space closed to the heavenly dimensions. The sea is upturned Heaven, the Bosom of the Mother of the Divinity. The ancient immaculate civilizations, such as Atlantis, are preserved in these aquatic worlds. — *582.*

The Holy Grail – is the Chalice in which St. Joseph of Arimathea has collected all the blood of Jesus Christ during His crucifixion on the Golgotha in Jerusalem. — *326, 595, 1084.*

Holy Passion – is the spiritual term, common to the Christianity and related to Christ's sufferings (holy passion), it gains the new meaning in the spiritual school of John of the Holy Grail.

The Holy Passion, as one of universal laws of the Divine Wisdom, is a necessary element of the spiritual path. The initiation of a soul into the Holy Passion helps to achieve the perfect sanctity. — *2, 639.*

Holy fool – is the unexpected one, exceeding the limits of normal understanding, not of this world. Here it refers to ascetics and saints. — *178.*

The Holy of the Holies – is a mystical symbol associated with the eucharistic mystery of the Holy Grail, described in detail in the books of John of the Holy Grail. The Holy of the Holies means the sphere where the Deity is exceeding Himself: the entrance to theogamic Bridal Chamber. — *19, 398, 405, 792.*

The heart's secret of secrets and to the inner man – the space in the spiritual heart of man which is not reachable for Lucifer and where the Divinity dwells. — *529.*

Innocent of Balta (1882-1917): the first martyr of the church of the third millennium, the fiery apostle of the Second Golgotha of Solovky, who fearlessly condemned Pharisaism in the church. A great spiritual elder, father of the unspeakable love, and wonderworker. He was killed with a bayonet by a Red Army soldier, but rose from the dead and lived some more years with a bloody wound. He was raised to heaven by body and soul. — *812.*

John Chrysostom (347-407 AD) – a notable Christian bishop and preacher in Syria and Constantinople, and author of a great number of prayers and liturgies. — *45, 141, 812.*

Khokhma (Hebrew) – Wisdom. — *310.*

'Looking for a place to live' concerns some serious difficulties connected with John's of the Holy Grail residence during his Divinity-inspired revelations and work. This is the reason for him to search new residence very often. — *101.*

Meribah (Hebrew: מְרִיבָה) – is one of the locations which the Torah identifies as having been travelled through by the Israelites, during the Exodus. — *1140.*

Miramar – is a place in southern France, where the Mother of God gave revelation to John of the Holy Grail in 2002-2006. — *1048.*

Metanoia (Greek) – repentance, a change of mind. The spiritual practice of cleansing of the mind and the heart of man from the sinful beginnings. — *569, 858.*

Mammon (Aramaic) –the spirit of avarice and self-interest. — *480.*

The Maccabaeus – Jewish rebels who fought against the ruling of Antiochus IV Epiphanies of the Hellenistic Seleucid dynasty. They founded the royal Hasmonean dynasty and established Jewish independence in the Land of Israel for about one hundred years, from 165 to 63 BC. — *332.*

Myrrh-bearing wives – here, a holy woman or a virgin. A woman who has dedicated her life to Christ, like Mary Magdalene, who poured precious myrrh upon the head of the Lord. They are equal in rights with the Melchizedek priests in the Great Church of Love. — *145, 182.*

Mysterious Church – is the one that has never been on the earth and it has never descended into this world, it is originated from the unearthly spheres. After the ending of the disasters, this Church will descend to the world invisibly, the Kingdom of the Holy Spirit will be established. — *45, 188.*

Melchizedek (Hebr. "the King of Justice", from "malki" – "my king", "tsadíc" – "Justice") – is the legendary figure in the Jewish tradition, the king of Salem (Gen. 14:18), the priest of the God El-Elyon "without father, without mother, without descent, having neither the beginning of days nor the end of life, became

like the Son of God, having abided a priest forever"(
Heb.7:3). The symbol of anointed and eternal priesthood. (See the priest of Melhezedek).

The Priest Melchizedek in the cathars mentality:
a priest who has nothing of this world and its institutions, elected by the Virgin Lady to carry out his mission and anointed into the highest mysteries of the
Supreme Wisdom. — *30, 31, 258, 260.*

Myrrh – is the fragrant oils of the heavenly origin,
mysteriously appearing in the material world on the
shrines in the form of the drops and threads. Myrrhic
Blood is the mystery of the double transubstantiation
of wine into the blood and the blood into the myrrh
in the Holy Grail. — *53, 736, 813.*

New Age – the modern spiritual tendency which is
presented by the various of syncretic spiritual schools.
Main concepts are karma, astrology, reincarnation. —
371.

Original immaculacy – John of the Holy Grail con-
firms that the original Immaculacy without any im-
perfection is primary in man, but not the original
sin. The original Immaculacy is sealed in the inner
of each soul as the divine potential and it should be
freed and evolved. This is the most important conception in the teaching of the Cathars. — *234, 376.*

Omophor (Greek omoforion – "worn over the shoul-
der") – the element of a liturgical dress in the tradition of the Holy Grail. It is a wide piece of cloth with

the images of characters of the Cathar spirituality and is worn about the neck and shoulders It is the symbol of virginity and unconditional dedication to the Pure Virgin. — *1061.*

The old tabernacle, the church institutions which prohibit the new Epiphanies. "So the Holy Spirit shows that there is no the way into the sanctuary, while there is still tabernacle." (Hebrews 9:8) — *76, 343, 348, 420.*

Pentecost – is the descending of the Holy Spirit. — *43, 340, 341.*

The Pharisees – are the religious fundamentalists, the hypocrites and persecutors of true disciples of the Supreme Wisdom, the enemies of the Kind Divinity. — *33, 54, 81, 100.*

The pearl of the Grail – quintessence of the essences of the Divinity deeply inside of the heart of man. — *28, 30, 31, 1007.*

Sofrino junk-shop – a well-known factory of production of the Orthodox Church liturgical utensils in Sofrino, Russia. Here is the ironical meaning of the substitution of the true spirituality by the external trappings. — *893.*

Seraphim Sarovsky (1759-1833) – is a Russian prophet, the great elder and teacher of the spiritual path (accumulation of the Holy Spirit) the miracle-worker. — *608.*

St. Mother Euphrosynia of Pochaev (1917-1993): the spiritual teacher of John of the Holy Grail, glorified by the Divinity with the incorrupt relics which exude the fragrant mirrh. The greatest teacher of the practical accumulation of the Holy Spirit. — *492.*

Seraphs, Thrones and Cherubims – angelic ranks. — *310.*

Seraphim of the Graceful – St. Seraphim of Solovky (1878-1971), the last Russian tsar Michael Aleksandrovich Romanov. Younger brother of Emperor Nicolas II. He spent thirty nine years in the prisons of the GULAG (Stalin's prison camps). There were several attempts to kill him but he was saved by the God's mercy. He outlived his prosecutors and passed away in 1971. He was the mysterious patriarch of the Solovky GULAG, the great wonder-worker, the father of inexpressible love. — *175, 339, 352, 599.*

Sekirnaya mountain – the highest mountain of the Great Solovky Island (the White Sea, Russia). The staircase leading to the top of the mountain, was used for the enforcement of the executions: the convicted (each victim) was put in a sack, tied to a log and cast down this stairs. — *127, 920.*

Second Golgotha of the Solovky – the concentration camp on the Solovetsky Islands (Russia). It is the place of the great martyrdom in the twentieth century, the capital of the communist Gulag. The phenomenon of redemptive suffering of the 100 000 anointed was predicted by the Virgin Lady in Her revelation to the Solovetsky monk in the eighteenth century as "the Second Golgotha". — *25, 81, 126, 277.*

Spiritual bodies – the virgin immortal bodies are given to a soul by God in the moment of being born. — *16, 146, 338.*

The Seraphites (from homo seraphicus, 'the Seraphic man') – the Theohumanity of the future, their composition, in contrast to the homo sapiens, is immaculate and woven from the particles and oils of the Divinity. — *14, 108, 109, 115, 121.*

Theogamy (Gr. Θεός – God, γάμος – marriage) – is the bridal union with the Divinity. In the theology of the Grail it is the virgin marriage of a divinized soul-bride with the Most High Divinity, the main destiny of each human being. — *6, 38, 62.*

Theocivilization – the coming civilization of the seraphites. This civilization will be based upon peace, supreme wisdom, kindness and pure love. — *10, 27, 166, 270.*

Tibet – according to the revelation of Our Lady, unites all esoteric teachings and occult practices, the source of which is considered to be the mystical city of Shambala. The teachers of Tibet and Shambala establish their own plans for the future of the mankind which are different from the plans of the Supreme Wisdom. — *237, 370, 512.*

Typicon – a book of regulations for Orthodox services for the whole year. — *838*.

Tver spiritual center – is one of the centers of the spiritual school of John of the Holy Grail in Russia. — *1036*.

85th civilization – according to the author, there have been existed eighty-three civilizations before ours, eighty forth, which were perished because of their inability to accept the Divinity's mysteries in full. The proclaimed eighty-fifth civilization will be the civilization of the Mother of God. — *233*.

JOHN OF THE HOLY GRAIL

THE ROSE OF THE SERAFITES
The Revelation of Supreme Wisdom

CREDITS:
Project Manager – Borislav Martemianov
Translator – Dominic William Esler
Editor – Eleonora Virginova
Design – Melchizedek Solntcev, Mary Parphenova,
Anna-Mary Alexeeva, Leonard Yovchak
Technical support – Alexandra Latysheva

USA
+1-800-431-1579
(BCH Fulfillment & Distribution)
www.theogamy.com
www.johnholygrail.com
e-mail: bogomilus@gmail.com

SPAIN
+34(622)59-4690
www.juangrial.com

CROATIA
+385(1)244-6909   +385(95)893-0453
www.bogumili.com

RUSSIA
+7(499)760-8418   FAX: +7(499)760-9767
www.virgin-world.com

Reviews and orders send to bogomilus@gmail.com

ISBN 978-5-98290-099-9

9 785982 900999